15.99

JAPAN AND THE NEW V

Japan and the New World Order

Global Investments, Trade and Finance

Rob Steven
Senior Lecturer in Political Science
University of New South Wales
Sydney, Australia

First published in Great Britain 1996 by
MACMILLAN PRESS LTD
Houndmills, Basingstoke, Hampshire RG21 6XS
and London
Companies and representatives
throughout the world

A catalogue record for this book is available
from the British Library.

ISBN 0–333–61005–9 hardcover
ISBN 0–333–61006–7 paperback

First published in the United States of America 1996 by
ST. MARTIN'S PRESS, INC.,
Scholarly and Reference Division,
175 Fifth Avenue,
New York, N.Y. 10010

ISBN 0–312–12966–1

Library of Congress Cataloging-in-Publication Data
Steven, Rob.
Japan and the new world order : global investments, trade and
finance / Rob Steven.
p.   cm.
Includes bibliographical references and index.
ISBN 0–312–12966–1 (cloth)
1. Japan—Foreign economic relations.   2. Investments, Japanese.
I. Title.
HF1601.S74   1996
337.52—dc20

95–33034
CIP

10   9   8   7   6   5   4   3   2   1
05   04   03   02   01   00   99   98   97   96

Printed in Great Britain by
Ipswich Book Co Ltd, Ipswich, Suffolk

Contents

List of Figures and Tables

FIGURES

TABLES

Preface

Since the focus of this study is on the most recent attempts by Japanese capital to 'export' the main problems it has had in production, marketing and finance, as well as the differences between doing so to advanced and to less developed countries, I have not had the space to include material and arguments which are not directly relevant. I have thus not covered ground that was included in my *Japan's New Imperialism* (Macmillan, 1990). However, the early 1990s – the main concern of this study – cannot really be understood without knowing something of what happened in the late 1980s, the period covered in the earlier work, which is thus useful background or additional reading on the topic. A book that purports to be about the whole world must necessarily be selective, and I have concentrated heavily on my main themes, even to the exclusion of certain matters, such as Japan's military participation in United Nations peace keeping operations, which do have some relevance to the topic.

Advanced capitalist powers like Japan can, under the new world order, displace their problems to the less developed world without the assistance of their own military power, even though they still at times require the collective might of all wielded through the United Nations. Instead they rely on the networks which link their productive, marketing and financial operations into an inter-connected and mutually-reinforcing system of power. Chapter 1 outlines how this new world order works in favour of the advanced countries, allowing underdevelopment and exploitation to continue through foreign investment, trade and international finance, especially when these three processes are combined with one another through the kind of networks possessed by Japanese capital. Chapter 2 analyses the uneven developments within Japan that have caused its stubborn tendencies towards recession since the mid-1970s and motivated its attempt to restore prosperity through increasing internationalisation. The huge drive to re-locate production in low-wage Asian countries to reduce costs or in high-wage advanced ones to be close to markets is examined through different windows in Chapters 3 and 4: the first looks at the emergence of Japanese capital's three main 'zone' strategies for North America, Europe and Asia; the second the industries concerned and the common interests of all the advanced countries in relation to the less developed countries. Chapter 5 shows how Japan's trade has served the same goals by connecting production in low-cost parts of the world with marketing in high-wage countries, a strategy which has resulted in growing conflict with other advanced powers. Chapter 6 argues that the common purposes which unite the advanced countries in their production strategies also bring them together in the world of finance and 'aid'. Finally, the Conclusion compares the patterns of underdevelopment in the Asian countries into which Japan's investment, trade and finance is increasingly being directed, with the smaller but no less devastating pockets of underdevelopment emerging in the advanced countries themselves, including Japan. The new world order functions in the interests of the rich, most but not all of whom live in the advanced countries.

ROB STEVEN

Acknowledgements

I have accumulated enormous debts over the years for the knowledge of Japan and Asia that informs this book. However, I am especially grateful to my good friend Katō Tetsurō for the help and stimulation he offered me during the years I researched and wrote it. Since its strongest feature in my view, in comparison with my previous books, is the coherence and strength of its central argument, I am heavily indebted to Vanessa Farrer, whose very sharp reading of what I thought was almost a final draft exposed the inadequacies and inconsistencies that sent me back again and again in attempts to work out the patterns that I think I finally discovered. Finally, I am indebted to the *Journal of Contemporary Asia* for permission to use material in Chapter 1 that was published in a shortened and earlier form by them in 1994.

ROB STEVEN

Abbreviations and Glossary of Japanese Terms

GENERAL

AFTA	ASEAN Tree Trade Area
APEC	Asia-Pacific Economic Cooperation Conference
DAC	Development Assistance Committee
ELG	Export-led growth
FDI	Foreign direct investment
GATT	General Agreement on Trade and Tariffs
IMF	International Monetary Fund
IPO	International Procurement Office
ISI	Import-substitution industrialisation
JETRO	Japan External Trade Organisation
JICA	Japan International Cooperation Agency
LDCs	Less developed countries
M&A	Mergers and acquisitions
MITI	Ministry of International Trade and Industry
NAFTA	North American Free Trade Area
NGO	Non-governmental organisation
ODA	Official Development Assistance
OECF	Overseas Economic Cooperation Fund
R&D	Research and Development
WTO	World Trade Organisation

COMPUTER/ELECTRONIC

ASIC	Apple specific integrated circuit
ATM	Asynchronous transfer mode
CATV	Cable Television
CD-I	Conversation compact disk
CD-ROM	Compact disk read-only memory
CMOS	Complementary metal oxide silicone
DCE	Distributed computing environments
DRAM	Dynamic random-access memory

EPROM	Erasable programmable read-only memory chip
FDD	Floppy-disk drive
FM	Flash memories
IC	Integrated circuit
LAN	Local area network
LSI	Large-scale integration
MOSS	Metal oxide silicone
MPEG	Motion picture expert group
MPU	Multi-processing unit
OEM	Original equipment manufacturing
PC	Personal computer
RISC	Reduced instruction set computer
S-VHS	Super-video high resolution
SRAM	Static random-access memory
VD	Video disk

NEWSPAPERS/MAGAZINES

TB	*Tokyo Business*
NW	*Nikkei Weekly*
FEER	*Far Eastern Economic Review*
NKS	*Nihon Keizai Shinbun*

GLOSSARY OF JAPANESE WORDS

endaka	High yen
endaka fukyō	High yen recession
karōshi	Death from overwork
Keidanren	Federation of Economic Organisations
keiretsu	Linked group of companies
keiretsuka	Incorporate into a keiretsu
keizai kyōryoku	Economic cooperation
kinyū keiretsu	Financial keiretsu
sōgō shōsha	General trading company
zaibatsu	Finance houses
zaiteku	Financial engineering

1 The Emerging New World Order

Japan's global investments, trade and financial dealings must be understood both in the context of the kind of world order that has been emerging over the past decade and in the context of the domestic forces within Japan that continue to make it necessary to participate in that order. This first chapter outlines the salient features of the global context, while the next chapter focuses on the domestic context.

The notion of a world order suggests that power relationships among the world's leading actors have achieved some degree of stability and predictability. It does not connote world peace, or even the absence of conflict. However, the ways the dominant relationships are constituted, who the main actors are and what the social forces are behind the stability are all areas of controversy and debate.

There are two broad streams of thought on how world orders are created and changed. The first and currently the most popular sees the 'world system' as a whole as the source of stability and change, not just in world orders, but also in developments within particular regions and countries. For example, to investigate Japan's relationship with the ASEAN region, on this view, requires first locating the roles of both in the world system and only then analysing their detailed interactions in the context of that whole. The second stream of thought believes the causal direction is the other way round: starting with nation states (in the non-Marxian versions) or 'social formations' based on 'modes of production' (in the Marxian versions), world orders are seen as the external consequences of what states and corporations do within their 'own' countries. And so the analysis begins with them, the parts, and ends with the whole.

There are no conclusive arguments or types of evidence which can resolve the differences between these competing perspectives. It is even possible that for different purposes each might be preferable to the other. I will be working within the second broad framework and leave the reader to judge the light it sheds on my analysis of Japan and the new world order. I also work loosely within the Marxian assumption that the moving force within a nation state or social formation is the mode of production, that is, capitalism and its developmental tendencies.

To see capitalist development as the dynamic force in history also implies definite theories on both what the main political relationships

1

within nation states are and on who the chief actors are. The key relationship between labour and capital requires brief explanation, because it circumscribes what the actors, that is, governments, corporations and mass movements, can do.

THE PROFIT SYSTEM: CAPITALISM

Capitalism is a system in which production takes place only to the extent that this is profitable. What is produced, which jobs are provided, at what wage levels and in which industries and sectors are all dependent on profitability. Governments too have to operate within the constraints of the profit system. For example, the only way to create secure jobs is to ensure that employers make sufficient profit out of hiring workers, and the only way to encourage the growth of a new industry is to help capital make money out of investing in it. Figure 1.1 broadly illustrates the functioning of the profit system.

Because money (M) is only invested if at the end more money (M') emerges, which is then re-invested, the appropriate point to break the circuit is at M. This emphasises the driving force behind the system. One could conceivably break it at C or C', but this would be appropriate only if the purpose of production, its driving force, was to produce useful things (C') by transforming some commodities (C, comprising means of production and wage labour) into others. Alternatively, one could highlight that when money is invested and wage labour is bought, workers are able to earn their livelihood. Defenders of the profit system often support particular ventures by emphasising the jobs that might be created, but since the creation of jobs is also only a by-product of money making, it would be just as misleading to break the circuit at this point. Money cannot be transformed into more money unless two *exchanges* take place.

Figure 1.1   The circuit of capital

M   ----------- C {MP + WL} P . . . . C'   ----------- M'
      exchange   time   exchange

M: money   C: commodities   MP: means of production
WL: wage labour   P: production   C':   new commodity
M': more money

Investing money involves buying commodities (C), which fall into two main categories: means of production (MP), comprising purchases from other businesses (such as machinery, fuels, materials and buildings) and wage labour (WL), that is, the required human skills and capacities which people have and which, in order to survive, they must sell on the market as commodities. One of the controversies in political economy is whether executive and managerial salaries should be seen as constituting very high wages for very high levels of skill and capacity, or whether they should be seen as a form of profit-distribution to persons whose social power enables them to create and monopolise a small number of high-paying jobs. Although a strong argument can be made for the latter view, it is not necessarily relevant here, since the jobs of all waged and salaried people depend on profitability, and the decisions of executives are not so much driven by their own greed as by the requirements of the profit system, that is, the necessity to accumulate in order to remain competitive.

During the production process (P) new commodities (C′) are made, and they are then exchanged for more money (M′) than was spent on means of production and wage labour because they include a surplus product. In non-Marxian economics this is referred to as a part of value-added, while Marxism calls it surplus value to emphasise that the immediate labourers have produced more than they are paid to live on. The important point is that capitalism requires the continual creation of a surplus product if it is to function at all, and that most wage and possibly even most salary earners contribute to the surplus product and are to that extent exploited.

If capitalism cannot function without exploitation and is in fact driven by the need continually to expand the degree and avenues of exploitation, what are the key political relationships and who are the chief political actors in such a system? The two questions are not the same, since grasping relationships involves very much more than identifying the concrete individuals or institutions that act them out.

The key relationship in a capitalist system is between capital and labour, but this operates as a very broad set of pressures and requires brief explanation. Capital can be seen as a situation constituted by a whole range of imperatives or tasks: to procure investment funds as cheaply as possible, to find the most promising avenues to invest them in, to utilise the most technically advanced and cheapest means of production appropriate to the ventures concerned, to locate and hire the most skilled, cooperative and least costly labourers (and managers), to ensure that the labour process is efficiently carried out and that the new commodities are of the highest possible quality, to ensure the sale of these commodities in the most favourable markets and then finally to re-invest as much of the profit as possible so that the ventures continue to remain competitive with rivals. This latter imperative, or function of capital, is of overriding importance, since the measure of profitability needed to remain in business is the level achieved by rivals, and threats to the survival of businesses always come from more efficient and more profitable competitors.

Labour can also be seen as a set of pressures which congregate around certain situations and which can be referred to as the corresponding tasks, or functions, of labour. These are to be as skilled and to work as long and as efficiently for no more reward than workers in rival firms, all so that the labour can contribute to the creation of the maximum surplus product. The situation faced by labour is thus one of exploitation, since capital must extract a surplus product to ensure its own survival and labour must surrender this surplus if it is to be purchased at all. The power that forces labour to surrender the surplus is that capital controls investment and therefore jobs, and the propertylessness which charac-terises the situation of labour makes it necessary to sell skills and capac-ities in order to earn a living. If the only way to secure a livelihood is to sell one's skills and capacities to capital, which buys them only if they can be exploited, then the situation of labour makes it impossible to escape exploitation.

It might appear that capital and labour do not have contradictory inter-ests, because capital must extract the maximum surplus from labour in order to remain competitive with rivals and so be able to pay labour the wages it needs to live on. Accumulation and growth are thus necessary conditions of the survival of both capital and labour. However, this harmony is only apparent because of the way the relationship between capital and labour is mediated through competition among capitals. Labour's livelihood is safe only so long as capital's profits are, but profits are always greatest where labour productivity and labour's exploitation is the greatest. And so the pressure that all capitals must put on labour to maximise exploitation comes from the more advanced and more efficient rivals who can extract the largest surpluses. The pressure to exploit to the greatest degree, which draws labour and capital into conflict, comes from the competition among capitals. This competition is not only the driving force that demands continual increases in the productivity of labour, it also creates the appearance that the fundamental relationships and conflicts within capitalist society are among capitals rather than between capital and labour. However, since surviving the competition with rivals depends on matching their capacity to exploit, it is clear that this competition is simply the motor of the more fundamental relationship, between the creator of the surplus product and its appropriator.

The institutions which express the relationship between labour and capital can vary enormously from one capitalist system to another. This is because the notions of labour and capital refer to situations and the pressures surrounding them rather than to particular wage earners, employers, or even their organisations, which are the most conspicuous actors in capitalist societies. It is possible in theory, and particularly in Japan it is in practice quite widespread, for labour unions to comprise salary earners who are relatively insulated from the situation of labour and who exist partly in the situation of capital, while the bulk of those who perform the function of labour remain unorganised, isolated from one another and do not appear on the stage as political actors.

The main actors representing capital also vary considerably across capitalist societies. Business and employers' organisations usually more unambiguously bring together those who perform the function of capital than do trade unions organise those performing the function of labour. However, the state is typically a much more contradictory player. A rich Marxist literature (Jessop, 1990; Clarke, 1991) has now more or less established that the state has 'a relative autonomy' from capital. This does not mean that the state in capitalist societies fails to represent the interests of capital, but that one cannot equate the two, since there are pressures and situations in capitalist societies other than the conflict between labour and capital which also constrain the behaviour of the state. And sometimes labour can be the predominant influence on the state, although there are usually quite narrow limits on the degree to which this occurs. Much less ambiguous in expressing the interests of capital is the multinational capitalist enterprise, which is often seen as vying with the state for the position of key player in world politics. The latter issue, especially the organisation of Japanese corporations into groups, is one to which we return in the next chapter. The task now is to provide a brief overview of how capitalism functions internationally.

INTERNATIONAL CAPITALISM

The term imperialism has become unfashionable in the context of such international political economic changes as the collapse of the Soviet empire, the growing conspicuousness of the United Nations as opposed to the United States in preserving international 'security' and the continued rapid economic development of the Asian region. By developing a theory of 'the new imperialism' which recognises these and other changes but which draws attention to the continuities with previous stages of imperialism, this chapter confronts the argument that the emerging new world order spells the end of all imperialisms.

Periodic Crises

Marxian analysis of international political economy begins with the forces within a society which require a move into the world beyond, forces which it sees as stemming from some or other 'crisis' or breakdown in the circuit of capital. Although there is a rich and complex literature on the malfunctioning of capitalism (Clarke, 1990), a simplified understanding can be obtained by looking at each of the points of typical breakdown in the circuit of capital, as revealed by Figure 1.2.

In the first place, sufficient money might not be available to take advantage of potentially profitable investment outlets, perhaps because of difficulties in the credit system, or perhaps because interest rates are too high for enough of this money to be productively invested. Mounting bad debts by borrowers can also lead banks to recall loans and cause acute shortages of funds, resulting in widespread bankruptcies. Whatever the specific causes, a credit crisis can reverberate throughout the system and cause extensive dislocations.

Second, what are commonly known as supply-side problems can appear, usually because the cost of the inputs (C), that is, means of production and wage labour, are too high in relation to those of rivals and therefore do not justify the investment. Apart from uncompetitive wage levels, common supply-side problems are that procurable technologies are no match for those of rivals, or that raw material prices have risen too highly. Unless more efficient technologies can be obtained, or cheaper supplies of raw materials can be found, capital accumulation will falter because of falling investment.

Figure 1.2   'Moments' of possible breakdown and types of capitalist crisis

$$M \text{---------- } C \{MP + WL\} \text{ } P \ldots \ldots C' \text{---------- } M'$$

Credit	Supply	Labour Process	Markets

M = Money invested

C = Commodities, comprising MP (means of production) and WL (wage labour)

P = Production process

C' = New commodity made in the production process

M' = More money than was initially invested

Third, the labour process might be the source of the bottleneck, perhaps because the organisation of work or the intensity of effort applied on the job makes the production process much less efficient than that of competitors. The Japanese employment system is often seen as giving capitalism in that country a distinctive source of extra profitability.

Finally, in spite of everything functioning smoothly up until the final production of the new commodity, there may not be an adequate market for it. This could occur for a large number of reasons commonly referred to as demand-side problems, and it can be just as devastating as any other interruption to the circuit. A typical scenario is that when wages are driven to the minimum in order to solve supply-side problems, the resulting fall in the purchasing power of workers exacerbates the demand-side problems of the consumer goods industries. The uneven development between Japan's enormous productive power in these industries, and the way pressures on Japanese wages have limited its consumption power, in fact constitutes the most stubborn problem Japanese capital has faced since the late 1970s and hence the outstanding driving force behind its international exploits as well as the uneven developments they have produced.

Displacement of Crisis

One of the first writers to attempt a systematic understanding of international capitalism was V. I. Lenin (Lenin, 1975), who saw moves towards internationalisation as attempts to solve problems like these by displacing them onto distant peoples. The most highly developed form of internationalisation in his time was trade, and the most advanced trading nation was Britain, which displaced the problem of insufficient domestic markets onto the colonies to which it exported its surplus of manufactures. The export of commodities was thus the first manifestation of the power of capitalist imperialism, which could thereby overcome problems of insufficient markets within Britain.

At the time of writing his *Imperialism: The Highest Stage of Capitalism*, Lenin had shifted his attention to foreign direct investment, which he saw as a response to supply-side problems which were choking off domestic investment. Although Lenin's actual arguments are not very convincing, his general line of reasoning remains useful. Foreign investment, in raw materials to secure cheap supplies and in manufacturing to secure cheap labour, is largely a response to a declining ability of the domestic environment to ensure profitability because of decreasing cost-effective supplies of these inputs.

The most important of all of Lenin's contributions lay in his theory of the source of the power of capital in the advanced countries that enabled it to displace its problems internationally. Not any capitalist enterprise could shift from a faltering domestic to a more exploitable world environment: only those in the advanced countries which were linked to what Lenin called 'finance capital' could do so. Since his own discussion of this concept is not adequate, it needs elaboration and refinement to be useful in a modern context. The power to displace problems internationally, to shift burdens from the domestic to the foreign, is the product of a distinctive *relationship* between *banking capital* and *industrial capital* that develops in the advanced countries, a relationship Lenin referred to as 'finance capital'. The power of the banks is strengthened by their relationship with the industrial corporations, whose power is in turn strengthened by their close ties to the banks. Each is more powerful because of its association with the other. Why is this?

The answer lies in the key role within any industry played by leading-edge technology in ensuring profitability in the face of competition from rivals. Far more important influences on the productivity of labour than the speed or intensity that capital can impose on the labour process, or even the skills that workers can be required to have, are the technologies with which capital can organise the entire production process. There are physical limits on how hard, fast or intensely people can work, and advantages over rivals through extra pressures on labour tend to diminish as soon as they are matched. But new technologies tend to provide enormous cost advantages without any apparent end and, as capitalism develops, the focus tends to shift to increasing labour productivity by this means rather than simply by coercion. In so far as coercion remains important, its role is to ensure the unobstructed introduction of new technology. The most profitable industrial corporations tend to be the ones that have developed the highest degree of technical know-how over long periods of high profitability, growth and accumulation. Advanced technology is thus as much a consequence of profitability, accumulation and growth as it is a cause of them.

Maintaining a technical lead over rivals therefore requires large investments and continuous growth, investments which are usually much greater than what can be financed simply by retained profits. One of the keys to the rapid technological development and power of Japan's giant car and electronics companies is that they managed to secure huge stable supplies of credit for their never-ending investments in new plant and equipment, mainly because the state served as guarantor of the loans they secured from the banks. Today, Japan's giant industrial corporations continue to have very intimate relationships with the nation's giant banks, which provide the credit they need to maintain the investments on which their cutting-edge technologies depend. Their power is thus enhanced by their relationships with the banks.

The reverse is equally true. Big banks must channel their lending to the most technically advanced and profitable borrowers, so that the risk of bad debts is minimised. Not too much credit can be allocated to small less-secure ventures, no matter how great their promise. In less developed countries, where the large banks arose out of merchant trade in the colonial period and remain heavily dependent on commerce, the risk of bad debts and banking crises is considerable because there are no core industrial companies to lend to whose profitability can be more or less guaranteed by their technical power. In the advanced countries, where 'finance capital' is the rule, the power of the large banks is enhanced by their relationship with profitable industrial corporations. The relationship of each with the other produces a qualitatively greater measure of power than each could achieve on its own. This power is sufficient to displace problems from one part of the world to another and constitutes the motive force behind the foreign investment, trade and lending which characterise capitalist imperialism.

The most obvious deficiency in Lenin's understanding of 'finance capital' is that he did not recognise the role of trading companies in international political economy or that the relationship on which capitalist imperialism rests is *triadic* rather than *dyadic*. Large institutions have developed round and specialise in each of the three key 'moments' in the circuit of capital: banks in providing money (M) for investment, industrial corporations in the actual production process (P) and trading companies in the marketing of the new products (C′). Just as the banks and industrial corporations need each other and are strengthened by their association, so do trading companies benefit from relations with the other two in ways which strengthen all three. Japanese trading companies provide one of the most advanced developments of these mutual relationships: their worldwide marketing networks help them sell products which are already more marketable because they were manufactured by the most technically-advanced companies which had easy access to the credit for the investments required to maintain their technical edge. Figure 1.3 illustrates the nature of this triadic relationship. The banks are happy to supply credit to industrial and trading companies, whose relationship with each other ensures efficient production and marketing and so secures the profitability of their loans. Each of the three plays a key part in the overall profitability of the circuit as a whole, but because the continued success of each also depends on the uninterrupted circulation of the whole, each serves and is served by its relationship with the others. Rather than call these relationships 'finance capital', it seems more appropriate to use the term *international capital* or even *imperialist capital*. The power stemming from the mutual relationships confers an ability to operate on the world stage, that is, to engage in capitalist imperialism.

To grasp the internationalisation of capitalism as a process of *imperialism*, it is important to see these three moments in the turnover of capital *in relation to* one another and as *serving* one another. Looked at in isolation, each can appear quite benign or even in a benevolent light. Foreign investment can present itself as a means of building new industries, providing jobs or transferring technology; trade can look like exchanging the surplus of one kind of product for different products; and foreign borrowing can masquerade as aid. But when the *links* between these are recognised by placing each in relation to the others in the context of the circuit as a whole, and when the power of the relationships among them cements their operations into an inter-connected system of power, then their overall function of surplus accumulation through international displacement of bottlenecks and crises becomes clearer. For example, when loans are provided through the Japanese banking system to Asian governments, the companies that usually win the contracts for the projects and then use related Japanese trading companies to import the necessary hardware, tend to have ties with the leading Japanese banks simply because this is one of the conditions on which their competitive power to win the contracts depends.

Figure 1.3   The triadic relationships constituting 'international capital'

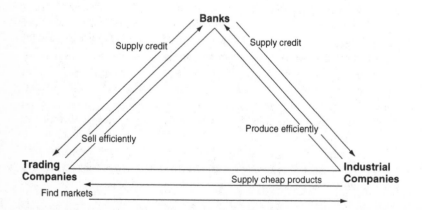

The imperialism of foreign investment, trade and lending do not, however, flow automatically from the internal triadic relationships among an advanced country's giant banks, industrial corporations and trading companies. Whether or not problems can be displaced internationally also depends on the power of capital in the recipient country, on whether or not capital there has been strengthened by similar triadic relationships.

In the following pages each of the three main forms of capital's internationalisation – foreign direct investment (FDI), international trade and overseas borrowing – is examined to show how it functions very differently when it takes place among advanced countries that possess the power of what has been called 'international capital', and when it takes place between these developed countries and less developed countries (LDCs) that lack the power of 'international capital'. Investment, trade and financial flows from the advanced countries to the less developed world are forms of displacing crisis from the former to the latter. However, when the movements are among the advanced countries, each with a power both to resist and to stimulate that of the others, the investments, trade and finance actually serve to strengthen the developed countries even further. These contrasting effects of capital's internationalisation on the different parts of the world have not received sufficient attention by critics of international capitalism, who tend to label FDI simply as bad, forgetting how it reinforces the power of the advanced countries when they engage with one another. The distinctiveness of labour migration into these countries from LDCs is normally grasped more fully (Miles, 1982), even though the close relationship between FDI and labour migration is not sufficiently explored.

IMPERIALISM OF FDI, TRADE AND DEBT

Foreign Direct Investment (FDI)

Because most of the world's foreign investment, in the manufacturing and non-manufacturing industries, moves from one advanced capitalist country to another rather than from them to less developed countries, it is often argued that FDI is not a form of imperialism. However, this argument fails to distinguish the very substantial differences that separate FDI in the advanced countries from that in the less developed countries. They amount to the difference between further strengthening the technical-industrial power in the recipient country and destroying that power. When American or Japanese companies invest in Europe, or when European and Japanese companies invest in the US, they do not simply bring with them vast technical capacities, but the environment in which their investment takes place allows them to appropriate some of the extensive technical power that exists in the country they enter. This is most obvious in joint ventures that involve technical tie-ups, which are heavily concentrated in the high-tech branches of the electronics industries, but it is no less important in its more subtle forms, for example, in the ability to appropriate some of the spin-offs of the widespread research and development (R&D) that goes on in the universities of the advanced countries. An advanced country is an ideal environment for technical transfers to occur, both ways, just as a less developed country is in most ways an environment that makes significant transfers almost impossible.

The reasons why the degrees of technology transfer are so very different in the two environments have to do with the nature of technology. Technology is not just the machinery, equipment or knowledge brought to a production process, but all of these simultaneously and more. It refers to the *manner* in which the production process is carried out and includes everything that affects the technique of production, including the structure and relationships within the work groups as well as the modes of communication on the job. New techniques are typically adaptations of certain aspects of older techniques, which is why high profitability and rapid growth are the real motor of technical change. Because a technology comprises so many aspects, the wide technical gaps between production in the advanced and less developed countries are difficult to bridge and technical transfers remain elusive. The reason is that the ability to use leading-edge ideas and practices depends on already being in possession of and employing ideas and practices which are close to that edge. So the kind of technical transfer from advanced to less developed countries that does occur is usually too little to bridge the gap.

Foreign direct investment from the advanced to the less developed world has as its typical outcome the destruction of existing forms of production and technology. The foreign manner of producing cannot be appropriated by the local people, because it is so very different from how they do things, but neither can they compete with it, because its long history of development under capitalist discipline (which requires the destruction of anything and everything less than the most efficient) give it a permanent competitive edge. Transporting Japanese machinery to South Korea or Thailand, for example, involves little real technology transfer, since the core of the technology lies in the *capacity to make* the appropriate machinery and constantly be able to improve on it, and not in finding workers with the skills to use it. Investment from one advanced country to another, however, opens up vast opportunities for mutual technical transfers, because the other side's techniques are not so very different from one's own and particular innovative practices can be taken on as-it-were one at a time.

The same reasoning explains why foreign investment in a less developed country usually destroys more jobs than it creates. Subsidiaries of multinational corporations are usually vastly more efficient than local enterprises, which do not survive the competition and whose more labour-intensive techniques usually mean many jobs are lost when they are driven to bankruptcy. Investment in an advanced country, on the other hand, can stimulate employment, because it does not typically drive local producers into oblivion but spurs them to greater efficiency and ensures their survival. Thus the increased competition from a powerful overseas producer stimulates efficiency in an advanced country, but in a less developed country it drives local production out of existence.

A related difference between FDI in advanced and in less developed countries lies in the degrees of forward and backward linkage that tend to occur. Not only does international capital normally bring with it into a less developed country most of the plant, equipment, sophisticated components and materials, but the purpose of the investment is frequently the procurement of a limited range of parts for export. Few linkages are with local producers, either backwards as sources of inputs, which tend to be imported by international capital, or forwards as markets, which are often external. This is because the level of technology in the less developed country allows only a limited range of industries to flourish. Profitable production of the goods linked to these industries can only take place in higher-tech environments, which are well within the reach of international capital but not that of local capital. Foreign investment in a less developed country thus stimulates very little wider economic activity.

An investor in another advanced country, where the latter's international capital cements the local credit, production and commercial systems into powerful mutually-supporting relationships, cannot similarly appropriate the bulk of the forward and backward linkages. High levels of local content tend to be the rule, and local markets are typically targeted, so that local economic activity is usually boosted rather than stifled by the foreign investment.

The overall result of FDI among the developed countries is to establish mutually-supporting and mutually-strengthening relationships among them, particularly in maintaining the most critical of all the advantages that preserve their leading position, namely, technology. These relationships ensure that foreign investment from any one advanced country commands the technical power of them all, so that their technical lead over capital in LDCs is widened. In a different way, therefore, foreign investment increases rather than narrows the divide between the developed and underdeveloped world. Within the former, it accelerates the advances of the already powerful, whereas when it moves to the latter it destroys the limited developments the less powerful might have achieved. The only alternative open to local capital in less developed countries is to ally itself with international capital in some way or another. Since the methods of doing so have varied from one stage of imperialism to the next, they are elaborated towards the end of this chapter, which examines the main stages in the history of capitalist imperialism. Rather, the relationship between FDI and labour migration must now be understood.

Except in cases where the local market is being specifically targeted, one of the main determinants of investment in the less developed world is whether or not the product or service can be transported back to the advanced country. In the construction and sex-related industries, whose outputs cannot easily be shipped back to the advanced countries but which require cheap labour from the less developed countries no less than do the manufacturing and raw-materials-related industries, the labour is encouraged to migrate to where it is needed.

Especially during the 1960s and 1970s, after it had become clear that decolonisation had not eliminated underdevelopment from the old colonial world and that the postwar boom in the advanced countries was showing increasing signs of collapse, migrant workers were widely recruited into the advanced countries as a reserve army of labour with which to lower costs and stem the tide of recession. It was not generally possible, without upsetting the political compromise on which the boom had rested, to create such a reserve from among the local populations, even though female labour did serve the purpose in a limited range of industries. And so the doors were opened to workers from the less developed world, from which continued poverty drove millions in search of better and more secure livelihoods (Miles, 1982). Although their legal status remained at best precarious in the countries where they settled, governments were happy to set aside legal niceties for the advantages of having found such an apparently easy solution to a problem they had only just begun to understand.

Migrant labour did not, however, greatly revive accumulation in the advanced world, and the racism towards migrants that had previously reinforced their vulnerability and ensured their compliance increasingly provoked reactions that threatened the political and social order. And so the 1970s saw moves to 'repatriate' migrants and an increasing shift of production sites to the less developed countries themselves, where not just labour but a whole range of costs could be minimised, such as of land, buildings, raw materials and energy. Henceforth migrant labour would be recruited much more selectively and largely by industries which could not be re-located, such as construction and prostitution. Whole buildings could not be imported from low-cost production sites, and the services of cheap sex workers, along with those of many others in the service industry, could only be provided in the advanced countries if the workers themselves were made to move (Gibson and Graham, 1986). Since Japan's reliance on foreign labour was minimal in the 1960s and 1970s, its use of migrant labour is a comparatively recent development of this latter kind that is limited to industries which cannot themselves move to the sources of cheap labour.

Labour migration and the ability to exploit it are directly related to the power of international capital. Significant migration is always from low- to high-wage countries, and the higher wages that capital can afford in the advanced countries reflect the greater productivity of labour there due to the greater technical power of international capital, just as the low wages in less developed countries reflect local capital's need to compensate for its technical backwardness by paying lower wages. Hence the migration of workers is a response to the unequal power possessed by capital in the advanced and less developed countries. And only international capital is in a firm position to exploit it, just as only international capital has the power to displace problems to distant shores through foreign investment. The phenomena of foreign investment and migrant labour are thus two sides of the same coin.

International Trade

Foreign trade is a much older and apparently more benign international activity, since it presents itself as bartering in order to secure products which cannot be produced locally. The market looks like a neutral mechanism which sets the fairest possible terms of exchange, from which both sides are assumed to benefit. Although Marxists recognise that the labour market is not a neutral arena, the market for other commodities is increasingly being accepted as a politically neutral space from which everyone can benefit, particularly when it embraces the whole world and when international trade gives access to otherwise unobtainable goods.

There are at least two ways in which world commodity markets are not politically neutral. First, they function in conjunction with labour markets to extend the most advanced forms and highest degrees of exploitation of labour to areas of lower labour productivity and exploitation. The need to survive competition from the imports and exports of more efficient rivals requires all capitals to emulate the world's most efficient methods of raising labour productivity. This competition among capitals which forces all to match the leading methods of exploiting labour takes place in the markets, whether domestic or international, in which the final outputs are sold. As far as the relationship between labour and capital is concerned, therefore, no market is politically neutral.

The other politically-charged aspect of the commodity market is the way capitals which cannot match the efficiency of rivals are driven into bankruptcy altogether. And when the free commodity market begins to embrace the whole world and the disappearing backward capitals are con-centrated in the less developed countries, a national dimension is imposed on the consequences of free commodity exchange. The advanced coun-tries whose capitals tend to survive are called 'rich in capital', while the less developed countries whose capitals do not are called 'rich in labour'. This ideological division of the world into capitalists and labourers is the starting point for the orthodox theory of trade as transactions which benefit both sides when they specialise in the industries of their 'comparative advantage'.

Comparative Advantage

The way the orthodox argument is put together makes trade beneficial for all participants regardless of *how efficiently* the traded goods are produced, so long as each side specialises in and exports the good it produces the *least inefficiently*. For example, even if both computers and wire-harnesses (electrical wiring systems for motor vehicles, a gruelling labour-intensive product to make) are produced more efficiently in Japan than in Thailand, because Thailand is less far behind in wire-harness production than it is in computer production, Thailand is said to have a comparative advantage in wire-harnesses, leaving Japan with a comparative advantage in computers. Each is supposed to gain from trade if it specialises in producing this good and imports the other. Readers who are familiar with details of this contro-versy might wish to skim though the next few pages.

The orthodox argument is best understood if expressed numerically, as in Figure 1.4, where it is assumed that in Japan 100 socially necessary hours are needed to make a computer and 140 to make a wire-harness, while in Thailand a computer requires 300 socially necessary hours and a wire-harness 200. Japan produces *both goods more efficiently* than Thailand, but its lead in computers is greater – making this the product of

Japan's comparative advantage – while Thailand's inefficiency is least in wire-harnesses, where its comparative advantage lies. The argument is not affected by the measure of productivity which is used, in this case the Marxian notion of 'socially necessary hours', that is, the production time of a firm with average technology and with workers of average skill who work at average speed, or more generally, production time under conditions of average efficiency for the industry.

What is crucial are the different domestic 'exchange ratios' *before trade*, that is, the different relative costs in Japan and Thailand of producing both products: Japan must forgo 1.4 computers in order to produce a wire-harness, while Thailand must forgo 1.5 wire-harnesses in order to produce a computer. The reasons for the relative efficiencies of the two countries in the two products lie in the lower cost of labour in Thailand, which cheapens labour-intensive goods like wire-harnesses more than it does high-tech products like computers. In Japan, capital's greater technical-industrial power cheapens high-tech products more than it does labour-intensive products.

Since the alleged gains from trade *depend entirely on the prices at which the goods are actually traded*, the way international prices are supposed to be formed must be examined. The comparative-advantage argument is essentially a monetarist one in which the money supply is the key variable in determining prices (Shaikh, 1979). It runs as follows. Japan's greater efficiency in both computer and wire-harness production would initially result in cheaper Japanese prices for both products corresponding to Japan's lower socially necessary production times. Thailand would then import both products, and money would flow from Thailand to Japan to

Figure 1.4   Comparative advantage and the gains from trade

	Japan	Thailand
Productivity (socially-necessary hours)		
Computers	100	300
Wire-harnesses	140	200
Domestic exchange ratios *before trade*		
of wire-harnesses for a computer	100/140 = 0.71	300/200 = **1.5**
of computers for a wire-harness	140/100 = **1.4**	200/300 = 0.67
Assumed trading prices (no transport costs):		
Computers (made in Japan)	150	150 (imported)
Wire-harnesses (made in Thailand)	150 (imported)	150
That is, exchange ratio *after trade*		
of wire-harnesses for a computer:	1.0	**1.0**
of computers for a wire-harness:	**1.0**	1.0

pay for them. The altered money supplies, or spending powers in the different countries, would inflate Japanese prices and deflate Thai prices. Because the initial price difference is greater in computers (100 in Japan versus 300 in Thailand) than in wire-harnesses (140 in Japan versus 200 in Thailand), the wire-harness price in Japan would be the first to exceed the Thai price. Japan's rising (from 140) and Thailand's falling (from 200) wire-harness prices do not have as far to move before they meet as do Japan's rising (from 100) and Thailand's falling (from 300) computer prices. In order to illustrate the orthodox argument as simply as possible, it was assumed in Figure 1.4 that 150 was the price at which Thailand got the edge on Japan in wire-harness production. At that point it would pay Thailand to specialise in producing this good and exporting it to Japan in exchange for computers. For the same reason it was assumed that computer prices in Japan had risen to 150 by the time Japan gave up on wire-harness production to specialise in computers. If computers and wire-harnesses do end up trading at these prices (for the sake of simplicity they are assumed to be the same prices), both parties would gain from specialising in the product of their comparative advantage and importing the other. Instead of having to forgo 1.4 computers to make a wire-harness, Japan would have to forgo only one computer to pay for an imported wire-harness. Thailand, on the other hand, could import a computer in exchange for only one wire-harness, whereas before trade it had to forgo 1.5 wire-harnesses to produce a computer. It is time to critique this argument.

The orthodox theory, that specialising in products of comparative advantage and trading to acquire others benefits both sides, rests or falls with the theory of the movement of international prices when Japan has an *absolute advantage* (that is, is more efficient than Thailand) in producing *both products*. The main weakness in monetarist price theory stems from its failure to distinguish the social class which gets the extra money from the sale in Thailand of Japanese-made computers and wire-harnesses. Only if the extra money from Japan's growing exports of computers and wire-harnesses ends up in the hands of Japanese workers, perhaps as a result of changes in Japan's taxation system, might one expect prices to move in the ways assumed by the comparative-advantage argument. Greater working-class spending power in pursuit of an unaltered quantity of goods would probably be inflationary. It all depends on the political power the different classes have in Japan to appropriate for themselves the benefits of Japan's enormous productive power. In practice, Japanese workers have been quite unable to win wages which even keep pace with the huge strides labour productivity has been making.

Absolute Advantage

It is the Japanese capitalists who export both goods who tend to get the extra money that flows back from Thailand, and they tend to re-invest it and thus further increase the efficiency and volume of both computer and wire-harness production in Japan, leading to a further *relative fall* rather than rise in Japanese prices. The resulting increased competitive pressure on Thai industry from Japanese exports will threaten to destroy it altogether, and, to cover its trade deficit, Thailand would have to export gold, natural resources or any other product in which it might have an *absolute advantage* over Japan, that is, a product it can make more efficiently than Japan. In practice, countries in this situation tend to incur mounting debt and be bled of their natural wealth. Apart from selling natural resources, the only way to reverse the situation would be to achieve an absolute advantage in an industry through some form of alliance with Japanese capital. For example, Japanese companies might invest in the Thai wire-harness industry and thereby *combine cheap Thai labour* with *advanced Japanese technology* to give Thailand such an absolute advantage in the industry. Whether or not both sides gained from trade in this new situation is a separate question, which is examined below. The point here is that trade is not generally regulated by the law of comparative advantage, but by the law of absolute advantage, because the power to export usually depends on being more competitive than rivals, not on specialising in what one is *least inefficient* at, even if it is one's best suit. The alleged benefits to both sides of trade in situations of comparative advantage thus tend to be illusory.

If trade results from absolute rather than comparative advantage, then the typical effect of exports from an advanced country is either to threaten the local industry with total ruin – which happens when there is a wide efficiency gap as in the case of exports to less developed countries – or to stimulate local industry to greater efficiency – which happens when this gap is not very wide as in the case of exports to other advanced countries. The different consequences of exports to the different types of countries are very similar to the effects of foreign investment. Exports are thus not just an alternative way to sell products for which the domestic market has no effective demand.

As far as exports are concerned, therefore, trade and foreign investment are two sides of the same coin which work together, particularly when they are institutionally linked via international capital's industrial and trading companies, to extend the power differences between capital in the advanced and capital in the less developed countries. The same

reinforcement of advantages and disadvantages occurs when we examine
the import side of trade.

Imports: Unequal Exchange

Since one country's exports are another country's imports, we must also
look at trade from the point of view of the buyers of the traded goods and
not just that of the local producers who compete with them. Although this
was the window opened by the theory of comparative advantage, the persistence of absolute advantage shifted attention to the local producers in
less developed countries whose very existence is threatened by imports.
And so, far from benefiting from trade, it was shown that less developed
countries are positively harmed by it. But might this harm not be more
than outweighed by the advantages to the purchasers of the traded goods?

The issue is not about getting the imported product cheaper from some
domestic producer, since the power to export reveals an absolute advantage over local producers. From the point of view of the purchaser, the
imported good is normally the best buy. Just as the labour-intensive manufactures which Japan imports from Southeast Asia are cheaper than what
any local producer can come up with, so too are the high-tech products
which Southeast Asia imports from Japan superior to anything local producers can manage. In this limited sense, both sides gain something from
the trade.

Rather, the issue in the debate over the benefits of trade is the exchange
ratio between the imported goods and those which must be exported in
order to pay for them. Once again, the problem concerns prices and the
broad forces which determine them internationally. In the discussion on
comparative advantage, it was shown that labour productivity is the key
influence on prices. The more cheaply a product can be made, the more
will businesses in competitive markets be forced to cut prices, and international markets are usually much more competitive than most domestic
ones because more of the world's leading producers are active in them.
The flow of money to the most competitive businesses allows them to
expand their operations, further increase their labour productivity and
further reduce their prices.

A second important influence on prices when both trading partners have
absolute advantages in the products they export is not discussed outside a
complex body of Marxist theory. The liberal notion of 'terms of trade',
which measures the movement of exchange ratios over time by plotting
changes in the relative prices of traded goods, expresses shifts in these
benefits. But because it is silent on the question whether any *particular*

exchange ratio at any point in time is *more beneficial* to either side, a brief digression to explain the Marxian notion of *unequal exchange* is necessary.

Marxism measures the benefits of any exchange in a capitalist system by means of *socially necessary hours,* or *value,* which was referred to above as the production time in a business with average technology and with workers of average skill who work at average speed (or simply a firm of average efficiency). In a capitalist society, businesses which lag technologically and which do not make the same demands on their workers as rival businesses sooner or later go bankrupt and disappear. Since it is *socially necessary* to keep up with rivals, one may assume that the value of a product is, as a rough approximation, the actual time taken to produce it. So long as the industry is competitive and inefficient firms do not survive, any existing firm in the industry more or less indicates what is socially necessary.

What is socially necessary in one country might not be so in another because not all governments protect their local producers to the same degree. Nevertheless, in the more competitive world markets in which trade is substantial and relatively free, and in which the power of imports to destroy inefficient local firms is backed by the free movement of foreign investment, the notion of world-wide socially necessary time, or *world value,* begins to have some meaning. It also raises the issue of unequal exchange, which refers to trade in products of the *same value* but at *different prices.*

Some Marxists (notably Emmanuel, 1972) have argued that the equilibrium prices of goods traded between the advanced and less developed countries normally involve unequal exchange in this sense. The argument is based on the orthodox Marxist theories of profit and price, or more fundamentally of surplus creation and surplus distribution. The surplus, which is created in the production place, comprises the difference between the *value* workers create and the *value* returned to them. This is then distributed in the market place via the price mechanism in various forms of profit, interest and rent. There are two main reasons why the surplus distributed to an industry, that is, the profit it receives, is usually very different from the surplus created in it. First, more surplus can be created in labour-intensive industries, because there is a greater potential difference between the socially necessary time its workers put in (the value they create) and the socially necessary time required to make what they buy with their wages (the value they get back). Second, more surplus is created in industries with low-paid workers because this also increases the difference between what they contribute and what is returned to them.

However, although not all industries create surplus at the same rate, the continued survival of all depends on an equal distribution of the *total* surplus in the form of equal rates of profit. This happens through the price mechanism. Industries whose rates of surplus creation are below average can raise prices until they receive average profits, while those with above-average rates of surplus creation must face falling prices until their profits are only average. The price changes result from the movement of capital from low- to high-profit industries and they only cease, and thus find their equilibrium levels, when profit rates in all industries are similar. What this in effect means is that prices are not equivalent to socially necessary production times. To raise profits to the average in below-average surplus-generating industries, prices must rise above socially necessary production time, whereas for profits to fall to the average in above-average surplus-generating industries, prices must fall below socially necessary production time. Equilibrium prices thus result in unequal exchanges between labour-intensive and capital-intensive products, as well as between products made by low-paid workers and products made by high-paid workers.

The common sense behind this notion of unequal exchange is apparent when it is applied to Thai–Japanese trade in computers and wire-harnesses resulting from absolute advantages, that is, when Japanese firms produce wire-harnesses in Thailand using the most advanced techniques in combination with cheap local labour. The large number of low-paid Thai workers create surplus at a rate that offers vast opportunities for profit-making, and capital moves from lower-profit situations in order to exploit them. The result is falling wire-harness prices, until the industry yields no more than average profits. In Japan, on the other hand, the capital-intensive computer industry faces pressure on profits from high wages, and capital will tend to leave the industry whenever prices fail to reach levels which maintain average profitability. When the two products are traded at prices which yield the same average rates of profit, the *exchange is unequal*. The prices of Thai exports are below the socially necessary time required to make wire-harnesses, while the prices of Japan's exports are above the socially necessary time needed to make computers. What Thailand loses as a result of trade are some of its resources, which in the absence of trade could be used to raise its own rate of accumulation. Japan alone benefits from this trade.

The criticisms of this argument which were made soon after it gained currency in the early 1970s were largely valid. It was pointed out that although working hours were long and wages were low in less developed countries, *surplus creation* was not in fact greater than in the advanced countries, because the level of technology used in less developed countries was very low. However, the massive foreign direct investment flows to the less developed world that characterised the 1980s and 1990s have meant that this is no longer the case. Today, there is good reason to believe that surplus creation is higher in the less developed than in the advanced countries, because long working hours and low wages now combine with advanced technology in the multinational corporations that dominate the production of traded goods in less developed countries. Unequal exchange is increasingly the rule rather than the exception.

Trade *among* the advanced countries is not unequal in the same sense, since the rates of surplus creation in the products exported are not very different. With very similar wage rates and degrees of labour-intensity, trading prices which yield average profits do not depart from *values* in ways which systematically transfer resources from one advanced country to another. However, the benefits to the advanced countries of unequal exchange with the less developed countries are substantial. They can also be more fully exploited because of the structure of international capital in the advanced countries. Trading companies work closely with their industrial and financial partners, typically through carefully targeted foreign investment projects, to ensure the most efficient production of, that is, the greatest possible surplus creation from, the goods which are traded. Enormous proportions of trade between the advanced and less developed countries simply comprise transactions that take place among the tentacles of international capital, and these transfer massive amounts of wealth from the poor to the rich through what is called trade between nations.

Unequal Exchange in Natural Resources

A different form of unequal exchange from the above occurs in trade in natural resources, which generally command prices above the socially necessary time needed to extract and transport them. Because natural resources cannot be manufactured, price hikes in situations of scarcity cannot be countered by immediate movements of capital into the industry. Natural resources are simply owned, and the power of ownership prevents the movement of capital to take advantage of high prices and profits. Marxists refer to it as their power to extract *rent*, which is a profit above the average that can be sustained because entry into the industry is restricted (Harvey, 1982). Not simply can prices above *value* be sustained – resulting in unequal exchange – but prices which allow permanent surplus profits.

Such rent-yielding natural resources offer an easy absolute advantage for capital that lacks the technical-industrial power to enter other industries. All that is required is ownership of the resources, although this is in practice not as simple as it sounds. Before World War Two, wars of colonisation and wars against rival colonial powers were necessary to acquire and sustain ownership of unexploited natural resources. Today the task is more complex, even if no less costly and therefore no less the monopoly of the already powerful. Because the costs and technologies involved in resource exploration and development are so substantial, de-colonisation in the postwar period has not transferred the power of owner-ship exclusively to the peoples who won their political independence. Both through its loans for and its direct investment in resource develop-ment, international capital retains a powerful lever with which to prise off shares of the rent which might have accrued to the owners of natural resources in less developed countries. The Japanese trading companies (*sōgō shōsha*), in addition to using these techniques through their associ-ations with banks and industrialists, also possess tremendous commercial power to force raw material prices to their lowest possible limits. The result is that the less developed countries, which are the main exporters of raw materials, lose much of the rent to the advanced countries, their main importers. Australia, which does not fit neatly into either category, has in recent years lost substantial revenues to Japanese importers in this way.

Trade in the products of nature among advanced countries, however, does not typically result in the loss of rent from the exporter to the importer. For example, even though close to a half of US exports to Japan comprise foodstuffs and raw materials, the development and sale of these rent-earning resources has remained firmly under the control of US capital, which thus benefits from the trade in raw materials with Japan. Again, the key basis of international capital's power is its technical-industrial base, which, when institutionally expressed through the triadic relationships of international capital, is exerted at each and every moment in the circuit of capital. In this case it can either prise rent from weaker capital in the less developed countries or it can resist attempts to cream off rent when confronting international capital of the same ilk.

In spite of having to share rent with international capital, less developed countries continue to rely on natural resources as the most secure source of an absolute advantage around which to structure their trade. In rare cases there may even be net benefits to them from the unequal exchange in this sector. However, while in the short and even the medium term, raw mater-ials might retain their cutting-edge, in the long term international capital can develop cheap synthetic substitutes which eat away at raw material prices or boost the often erratic fluctuations to which they have always been subject. For example, rising rents from oil in the 1970s spurred massive investments by international capital in alternative sources of energy, and as these came on stream towards the end of the decade, oil prices fluctuated wildly and wreaked havoc on some economies that relied heavily on high oil rents, such as Indonesia's. All less developed countries which rely on raw material exports experience these kinds of price fluctuations.

Nonetheless, rent remains an attractive source of easy profit making, and disputes over the ownership of natural resources remain the most consistent basis for war against the peoples of the less developed countries. The most recent example was the Gulf War, the real issue in which was Middle East oil rents.

In summary, trade with the advanced countries hurts the less developed countries in two distinct ways. First, it forces the latter to specialise in a narrow range of products in which they have absolute advantages, either because of their cheap labour or because of their stocks of raw materials, thus severing the forward and backward linkages needed to sustain the even development that gives international capital its distinctive strength. LDCs have to import so many inputs and export so much of their output that few opportunities remain to build local networks among the required range of *diverse* industries. Second, the absolute 'advantages' needed even to engage in trade, that is, low-cost labour and raw material supplies, result in exchanges that transfer massive amounts of wealth to the advanced countries.

The trading power wielded by international capital is a product of the three legs of the tripod that comprise it and the networks that connect them. On the export side, its marketing is enhanced by the technological-industrial dominance of the companies that make the products exported, a dominance which is in turn augmented by relationships between these companies and the leading banks. On the import side, the power to buy on the best possible terms is strengthened by links with the industrialists who invest in and develop the products concerned as well the banks which finance the developments. It is also boosted by the enormity of the purchases that large importers can make and the reliability of their reputations to keep up the demand. Because Japan's giant trading companies have regular distribution outlets in the networks of companies linked to them, contracts with them are very attractive. But they come at a price, lower prices.

Finance and Debt

Trade, whether on the import side to secure cheap supplies and to gain a share of raw material rents, or on the export side to maintain markets and keep rivals at bay, is more able to accomplish these goals for international capital when it is linked, not simply to foreign direct investment, but to the granting of credit. International capital's ability to lend money can appear as an almost miraculous power to create something out of nothing. However, although many financial institutions claim to possess it, most of them disappear into bankruptcy without ever understanding that the real power to grant credit does not lie with the bank itself. Rather, it lies in the production place of the bank's main borrowers, whose technical-industrial power ensures that the credit they receive is used to produce goods, not just to the value of what was borrowed, but including a surplus sufficient to cover the bank's interest and to return at least an average rate of profit to the borrowers. When banks grant credit in excess of the deposits they hold, they create 'fictitious capital', because the production processes they thereby set in motion consume resources which can only be paid for if in the future the ventures turn out to be profitable. If they fail, the loans cannot be repaid and the banks end up unable to meet all their obligations should their depositors withdraw their money. Repeated failure of ventures undertaken by a bank's borrowers will eventually lead its lenders to do just that, to withdraw their cash, and the bank will collapse. What keeps a bank sufficiently reliable to attract lenders is the profitability of its borrowers, and that in turn depends on the latter's technical-industrial power. Banks belonging to international capital do most of their lending to their own highly profitable industrial companies, which thus secure their 'magical' powers, not least to continue granting credit to these leading industrial companies.

Indirect Investment and Finance

However, the forms in which modern corporations and governments borrow money extend well beyond the normal bank loans discussed so far, from selling various kinds of bonds and shares to the most complicated financial 'products' found mainly in the capital markets of the advanced countries. When these transactions are conducted across national boundaries, they are known as indirect investments. There is a convention that buying over 10 per cent of shares in an overseas company is a foreign direct investment, while fewer than 10 per cent ownership constitutes a foreign indirect investment. Ownership levels above this cutting off point are supposed to secure some *qualitative* power to control the production process, in particular technology and management, whereas anything less is considered similar to bank loans which only secure *quantitative* amounts of money in return.

The difference between direct and indirect investment is similar to a related difference between the *surplus creating* productive industries, such as manufacturing and construction, and the unproductive 'auxiliary' industries, like commerce and finance, to which some of the surplus is also *distributed*. In productive industries profit comes from actually *making* goods, whereas in unproductive industries it comes from *servicing* the making of goods. Indirect investments are more like the unproductive industries, since both are more concerned with the *quantitative* distribution of surplus.

The way the surplus which is created by the productive industries is then apportioned to the unproductive industries, to indirect investors and to the productive industries themselves, is through the price mechanism. Wholesale prices of manufactured goods ensure that some of the surplus created by the manufacturers is distributed back to them. But these prices also typically include margins for the shares going to the financiers and the land owners in the form of interest and rent costs, while retail prices allocate shares to those who market the products. Direct investment in productive industries thus both creates surplus and secures a share of its distribution. And because all industries which either create surplus or which provide unproductive auxiliary services (such as marketing, money lending and renting land) can also have shares of it distributed to them, all the various wholesale and retail prices of goods and services reflect the distributional shares of the different capitalists.

What sets indirect investments apart from all direct investments, both productive and unproductive, is that they are purely concerned with the quantitative problem of surplus distribution. In this respect they are unlike direct investments in the unproductive industries, which also secure control over the provision of auxiliary services. Indirect investments are much more like simple money lending, which is only interested in its quantitative rate of return. What then constitutes this purely quantitative problem of surplus distribution?

All capitalists who invest money (whether directly or indirectly, or whether in productive or in unproductive industries) are involved in this quantitative distributive process through the prices charged for what is done or offered by the institution in which they invest. And these prices are ones which, through competition, result in each good or service receiving a share of the surplus which is proportional to the quantitative amount of money invested in its provision, no matter which particular qualitative form the investment took, be it production, marketing, money lending, licensing technology or renting out land. The function of competition is both to eliminate inefficient enterprises *within* any of these industries, and to generate prices which ensure that the same quantitative rates of return on the amounts invested are received by each of the various *types* of capitalist enterprise. The relative prices of the whole range of activities required to make a capitalist system work are determined by a competitive process which gives each the same profit *rates* relative to amounts invested. In the long term competition tends to give productive capitalists, land owners, bond holders, foreign exchange speculators, stock holders and so on the same broad quantitative rates of return on their money. When these rates of return are not equal, capitalists move from lower earning investments to higher earning ones, and the prices of the goods or services change in response to these shifts and help the profit rates converge.

Indirect investments have no concern whatsoever other than this quantitative distributional process, whereas direct investments have other important functions. The most important of these is that *they increase the total amount of surplus that is created for distribution* among the whole range of capitalist industries. From the point of view of any individual investor, it might not matter whether the investment is direct or indirect, productive or unproductive, so long as the rate of return is right. The individual might not see beyond the purely quantitative distributional side of the operation. But from the point of view of capitalists as a whole, any increase in the total surplus created means an increase in what is subsequently distributed to each.

We can now finally show how the enormous flows of finance in the form of indirect investments among the advanced countries constitute a way of appropriating wealth from the less developed countries, wealth which is created through direct investments. Productive direct investments in LDCs help create the surplus that is distributed among the whole range of capitalists within the advanced countries, through the prices 'competitively determined' for their various activities, from the high value-added plant and equipment they export world-wide, the cheap manufactures they produce in LDCs and import back, the mark-ups they add for retailing, the interest rates they charge on their global bank loans and the rates of return they expect on all their portfolios (indirect investments), wherever they are or whatever form they take. The reasons why financial flows among advanced countries function to appropriate distributional shares of surplus from the less developed countries require further explanation.

Indirect investments in general and direct investment in the finance industry have something in common which concerns the role of credit and the institutions which specialise in providing it, namely, the banks. However, indirect investments provide finance in fragmented amounts which are too small to constrain the power of the borrower in the ways that the large-scale credit provided by banks both constrains and empowers its recipients. Nevertheless, these small portfolio investments must be acquired through stockbrokers and financial managers, which today comprise some of the world's largest multinational corporations, such as Meryll Lynch, Morgan Stanley and Nomura Securities. Their power stems not simply from the skill and experience they have in finding suitable outlets for the monies provided by their clients, but also in the sheer bulk of the finance they control due to the great number and wealth of the clients they attract, largely but not exclusively from the rich North. Among their largest clients are the government superannuation funds of the leading advanced countries. Along with other giant corporations representing international capital, they have managed, especially in the last decade, to eliminate an extraordinarily wide range of the barriers that used to curtail their global operations. They can now either themselves directly transfer or indirectly cause to be transferred across oceans and vast tracts of land, amounts that dwarf the GNPs of most countries, including some advanced ones, in a matter of minutes simply through the computerised networks to which they have access. If indirect investment is purely concerned with quantitative distribution, then it was perhaps to be expected that the quantities involved would be of these magnitudes.

The tidal waves of finance which often flow between countries and continents have two main consequences on the global creation and distribution of surpluses. The first is through the way they have taken away from governments the power to control their money supplies and interest rates, and thus the last remaining tool of economic management left to them by the prevailing neo-classical economic orthodoxy. The formidable competitive power of the most successful fund managers has come to set worldwide norms on rates of return. In the absence of barriers to cross-border financial movements, anyone purely interested in the quantitative side of their investments, such as wealthy individuals within LDCs, will entrust their money to these overseas fund managers unless they can secure comparable rates from local borrowers. Thus the internationalisation of these high rates of return means that it becomes increasingly difficult to raise finance, either from local or from international sources, for projects that are not profitable enough to service their borrowing at international capital's rates. The results can be catastrophic for the LDCs concerned.

Second, the liberalisation of financial markets and their dominance by international capital and its fund managers means that less developed countries are required to pay the price, in the form of higher interest rates on their escalating debt, of even the slightest signs of downswing in economic conditions in the advanced countries. Recessions mean little to the very rich who, through 'fund management' can instantly alter the form and location of their investments and thus always get the same high levels of return. So even though most of the financial flows that surge from one advanced country to another and then back again do not even bypass the LDCs, the effects of these flows on the latter are similar to the effects of actual lending to them by international banks.

The LDCs' own banks emerged on the coat-tails of colonial trade in raw materials, but after de-colonisation they continued to target natural resources as the most reliable productive activity for their borrowers, because local capital in other industries was too weak and lending to them was too risky. And so an enormous opening was left for international capital to take over the credit market for the technically-advanced industrial projects which only it was capable of carrying out profitably.

What is therefore most significant about the continued growth of Third World debt are not the absolute amounts owing to foreigners, since the extensive use of credit is indicative of a flourishing capitalism, but the growing privatisation of that debt and the control this gives to international capital. The foreign banks have become the only ones with sufficient resources and reliability to finance the large industrial and infrastructural projects needed in the less developed world, but because international capital alone is capable of carrying out these projects profitably, foreign banks are increasingly reluctant to grant credit other than to the proven industrial corporations linked to them. Key investment decisions are thus being taken out of the hands of local people in the less developed countries, not to mention their governments, and put into those of international capital and its world-wide profit-making networks. The main issue is therefore neither the absolute amount nor even the rapid growth of LDC debt, but its privatisation, which points to its growing linkages with foreign investment and trade under the control of international capital.

Aid and Official Debt

In spite of the growing privatisation of Third World debt, large proportions of it still comprise government loans obtained under one or other form of bilateral or multilateral aid. The importance of these loans lies mainly in the way they substitute for the *direct* colonial rule through which international capital worked before de-colonisation. They do this not just when the loans are tied and secure immediate concessions from the recipient country, but also when they are given without any apparent strings. Nominally untied aid is often given by governments of advanced countries to create a favourable climate in less developed countries for the operation of multinational corporations. This lending is analogous to social welfare spending within the advanced countries themselves and has become necessary 'social expenses' (O'Connor, 1973) to secure the cooperation of the less developed countries. The Japanese government appropriately refers to it as expenditure on 'economic cooperation'. In the period of classical colonialism, as is explained below, winning cooperation from colonies was the the task of the local state which the imperialist power directly controlled. However, since de-colonisation and the loss of direct state power in LDCs, advanced countries have had to operate at a distance and win cooperation by means of financial and other incentives. Aid extends *the reach* of an advanced country's state power all the way to the less developed country.

Analysis of the different forms of aid can be built round categories commonly used to analyse state expenditure *within* advanced countries. The most general are what O'Connor (1973) called *social capital*, comprising *social investment* and *social consumption*, and *social expenses*. If these are adapted to the context of international aid, we get the following:

1. *Social capital aid* comprises all the various forms of aid which directly or indirectly contribute to profit making and from which international capital can thus itself benefit.

    a) *Social investment aid* refers to aid which is specifically for improving the infrastructure on which most profit-making depends but which is usually too costly for local capital or the local state, let alone any one local or even foreign firm, to undertake without receiving external credit. Examples include the construction of ports, roads, irrigation works, power generation and communications systems.

      One might give the term *private investment aid,* or *aid for private investments*, to aid for projects which are also too costly for local capital or the local state to undertake unaided, but which, instead of being infrastructural projects that benefit all capitals using the infrastructure, are narrower ones that really only benefit the investors themselves. These projects might simply involve the development for export of a resource, such as Indonesia's natural gas. What is distinctive about this *private investment aid* is that the projects are financed by means of government 'aid' but assume the form of private investments which contribute little to the infrastructure used by business in general.

    b)   *Social consumption aid* refers to aid which helps either to cheapen the cost of labour or to raise its efficiency, for example, aid for education, health and housing.

2.   *Social expenses aid* has no purpose other than to win cooperation from the local people and their government. If the function of *social capital aid* is to assist accumulation for international capital, then the function of *social expenses aid* is to win legitimacy from the local people and their state for its operations. While legitimacy is normally also served by *social consumption aid* on things like education and health, *social expenses aid* has no purpose or effect other than to secure legitimacy. Because of the peculiar role of military power in preserving legitimacy in less developed countries, its most typical form is military aid.

    Once again, the importance of aid is not apparent unless attention is drawn to the links between aid, trade and investment. Outside this context, aid projects tend to look like paternalistic acts of goodwill through which resources are redistributed from rich to poor. Within this context, it is unlikely that much aid falls into that category, because the power relationships behind the aid and the ones served by it actually discriminate the other way round: in favour of the rich and against the poor. The growing importance of aid to the functioning of international capital is thus best revealed through an historical analysis of the institutional forms through which international capital has operated since the late nineteenth century. The remainder of this chapter analyses these different institutional arrangements, which constitute different stages of imperialism, or different world orders.

PROBLEM OF LEGITIMATION: STAGES OF IMPERIALISM

Most of what has been said so far about international capital has focused on issues of economic growth, or capital accumulation, and these have not varied as greatly over time as have the issues of social control in the countries exploited by international capital, that is, the issues of legitimation. International capital's methods of securing compliance have varied so much from one historical period to the next that they can be seen as marking distinct historical 'stages', or what might be called 'world orders'. What has propelled the system from one stage to the next were the struggles which could only be contained by means of new mechanisms of social control. These struggles have occurred both within the advanced countries and the less developed countries.

Classical Imperialism: The Colonial State

The earliest form of institutionalised control over less developed countries by international capital was their direct colonisation. To ensure that the colony remained open, particularly to trade and investment, it was conquered by military means, and state power became the preserve of the government in the advanced country which had effected the conquest. Each imperialist power came to possess its own exclusive colonies: in Asia, the British had India, Malaya and Burma; the Dutch had the East Indies; the French had much of Indo-China; the Japanese had Manchuria; and the US had the Philippines. Because colonies were not shared, the only way they could be exploited was through their exclusive acquisition: by conquest in the case of areas not yet colonised, or, in the case of existing colonies, by waging war against their imperialist occupiers. Colonialism through *direct* state power translated economic rivalry among imperialists directly into political and military rivalry, so that what Lenin discerned as a distinct characteristic of imperialism, that is, inter-imperialist rivalry and war, was merely a feature of this particular *stage* of imperialism, or this particular 'world order'.

If direct colonialism reached its height in the late nineteenth and early twentieth centuries, the Second World War marked the beginning of its end. In Asia, the transformation was more abrupt, because Japan's war to expel the European powers from much of colonial Asia coincided with struggles for independence by increasingly well-organised national liberation movements. In a matter of months, this combination dismantled the European empires that had ruled more than 500 million people. After the war, the Japanese were in turn expelled by a similar combination of even more powerful Asian nationalist movements and the victorious imperialists in the war against Japan. But because by this time any form of direct colonial rule had become almost impossible, the European powers were unable to reclaim their former colonies. In Africa, de-colonisation was a much slower process, mainly because the many white settler colonies required much longer struggles for independence than were needed elsewhere, but also because in many parts of the continent the nationalist movements had been slower in getting off the ground. In Latin America, the United States maintained an exclusive preserve even without itself directly possessing state power, thus anticipating a development which would characterise the next 'world order', that is, a neo-colonial stage of imperialism legitimated by a local upper class kept in power by the US military.

Super-Imperialism: The US State

The explosion of nationalism among colonised peoples after World War Two seriously threatened the whole imperialist order together with all the privileges enjoyed by international capital, particularly because that nationalism often combined with uncompromising anti-capitalist ideologies and organisations. In some cases, such as China, the nationalist movement became indistinguishable from the communist movement, while in others, such as the Dutch East Indies, nationalist and communist organisations worked closely together. The imperialist powers increasingly recognised that their only hope of retaining a foothold in their former colonies lay in driving a wedge between nationalism and anti-capitalism, and then coming to some accommodation with nationalism. At the very least, such an accommodation meant accepting the loss of state power. So the imperialist governments lent their full weight to those factions within the independence movements which promised to work with them in the future. In most cases military force had to be used against the anti-capitalist nationalists in order to prevent them from participating too greatly in the exercise of state power. Since only the United States seemed to have an unlimited capacity to wield the necessary military force, there was a gradual but steady shift from reliance on the previous coloniser to reliance on the United States for the continued military support which the newly independent regimes required.

If it took the military aid of a super-power to create and preserve governments that cooperated with international capital, then it took the military aid of another super-power to offer the anti-capitalist nationalists a realistic hope of dislodging those governments. And for most of the period from just after the War until around the mid-1980s, the Soviet Union was willing to offer military assistance to political movements that worked for a more radical break with the past. So long as the populations of the former colonies remained divided into supporters and opponents of continued capitalist penetration by the advanced powers, and so long as the two super-powers were willing to offer military backing to their preferred side, domestic conflict within the ex-colonies threatened to spill over into full-fledged war between the super-powers. The result was that the world lived under the cloud of a possible nuclear holocaust for more than thirty years.

During this time, social divisions within the ex-colonies were in most cases intensified by old and new forms of economic involvement by the advanced countries. But from the latter's point of view, the postwar world order turned out better than expected, because the burden of legitimating their activities shifted almost entirely to the local upper classes and to the US which helped preserve their hold on state power. Now that the neo-colonial system the US pioneered in Latin America had been universalised and access to less developed countries was made free, economic rivalry amongst the advanced powers no longer translated into political and military rivalry. The characteristic form in which wars were to be fought over *neo-colonies* in this period was intervention by the super-powers in the civil wars within them, leaving all the other advanced countries free to go about their neo-colonial business. This meant that the less developed countries could be freely exploited by more than one advanced country at a time.

International capital's free access to most of the less developed world offered the latter a much greater potential for capitalist development than before. But because it was normally spearheaded by massive amounts of foreign investment, trade and aid, the development tended to intensify the inequalities inherited from the past, even if not always the absolute poverty. From the point of view of most of the populations, neo-colonial-ism was more of a continuation with, than a break from, their experience under classical colonialism. But the new system was much less predictable than the old, and in some cases, such as South Korea, the rising local capi-talist classes mustered such independence that full escape from neo-colo-nialism even seemed possible.

Period of Transition: Multi-Polar 'Ultra-Imperialism'

From around the mid-1980s, a number of developments came to a head and soon combined to jettison the world into an entirely new stage of imperialism. This 'new world order' would be characterised by both the appearance of greater independence for the less developed countries and by the reality of a growing inability to break out of the imperialist system. Their apparently enhanced independence derived from the end of super-power rivalry and its imposition onto their internal conflicts. But the replacement of this rivalry with an unprecedented *cooperation* among the advanced countries in maintaining the 'new world order' strengthened the system and increased international capital's power to exploit, not just workers within the less developed countries, but also those within the advanced countries themselves. The geography of this new imperialism, or new world order, defies the patterns of the past and follows even less than before the boundaries of nation and state. Four main developments lay behind the transformation.

The first resulted from the economic growth in the neo-colonies that had been spearheaded by the investment, trade and financial operations of international capital. The weakness of local capital, characterised by its technical backwardness, forced it to ally in one way or another with international capital. Where it had little to bargain with, the form of the alliance was an open invitation to foreign investors to do more or less as they pleased in the hope that some of the benefits might trickle down. Singapore, which inherited a commercial and trading centre that had been severed from the source of its wealth in the hinterland of Malaya, and whose ruling party had left the anti-imperialist nationalists well before independence, had to tolerate almost totally free access to foreign investment.

South Korea, which became independent in a blaze of anti-Japanese nationalism fuelled by a love-hate relationship with the US (on whose military aid its governments depended), was in a much stronger bargaining position. Initially, it even managed to break international capital's links between trade, aid and investment by virtually excluding foreign investment and using foreign aid to import technology, for use and development by local capital. One of its skilfully played bargaining cards resulted from the way super-power rivalry had led to the division of Korea. The US had to make concessions to South Korean nationalism – even to allow imported foreign technology to help build and protect a technical-industrial base that would support an increasingly powerful local capitalist class – because any weakening of South Korea's *bourgeois* nationalism might lead to a strengthening of North Korea's *proletarian* nationalism and threaten the postwar neo-colonial world order.

Between these more or less extreme cases many different bargains were struck; for example, in Indonesia the initially high rates of local participation required in foreign investment projects reflected the power of Indonesian nationalism and the natural resources, particularly oil, over which it was gaining control. In at least one respect, all the different bargains were similar: as capitalist development quickened, local capital gained a strength, and in some cases even an independence, unheard of in the days of classical colonialism. Support from this class became an indispensable requirement for the operations of international capital as well as for the existence of the local state. One sign of the transition was the growing recognition by the US that it did not have the freedom to choose the governments of its neo-colonies, but that it simply had to prop up those governments that were most firmly supported by local capital. Simply conspiring through the CIA to have unfriendly leaders removed or assassinated, as was typical in Africa and Latin America in the 1950s and

1960s, gave way in the 1970s to a policy of explicit backing for *any* anti-communist government supported by the local ruling class. Richard Nixon's switch to 'Vietnamise' (withdraw US troops and let the Vietnamese fight it out) a war the US had by that time lost was an early recognition of the first development that would help create a new world order. Increasingly, international capital would have to work through a local state whose existence rested substantially on support from local capital.

The second and related development was the exhaustion of the US capacity to provide the military backing needed by all the anti-communist governments that had come to depend on it. By the mid-1980s the external deficit of the US was reaching crisis proportions, and radical surgery was needed to reverse each of the main contributors to it, not least military expenditure abroad and military aid to foreign governments. In an attempt to move towards a 'user-pays' system of international security, the US put added pressure on those who benefited most to share the burden more equitably, that is, local capital in the less developed countries and international capital from the other advanced countries.

By the mid-1980s, together with some older powers, such as Great Britain and France, new ones like Japan and Germany had gathered vast world-wide interests and had some untapped capacity to pay for their security. This constituted the third development that transformed the old order: the emergence of a number of more or less equal advanced powers that derived similar benefits from the world the US had been protecting. What the latter needed, to share the burden of policing the world, became available.

The final ingredient in the transition to the new world order was the Soviet Union's gradual withdrawal of support from anti-capitalist governments and movements in the less developed world, and soon afterwards the total disintegration of Soviet communism. Super-power rivalry and its imposition onto domestic divisions within less developed countries came to an almost abrupt end. Suddenly enormous possibilities were opened up for a whole new institutional arrangement, either one in which international capital would operate much as before or one in which it would increasingly be called to account by the growing nationalism of peoples now freed from the yoke of super-power rivalry.

The uncertainty whether the new world order would assume the form of a new imperialism or of greater freedom and democracy was resolved by the Gulf War. The ferocity of the slaughter left little doubt that imperialism was alive and well. However, there were clear signs of a break with the past. Even though it dominated the anti-Iraq coalition, the US military

managed, to an unprecedented degree, to share the burden and to legitimate its actions under the guise of an United Nations operation.

NEW WORLD ORDER: NEW IMPERIALISM

What had changed and what continues to take form is the institutional
arrangement through which international capital must operate now that
both super-power rivalry and the near monopoly of the US military in
maintaining the world order are being phased out. However, the ensemble
of institutions through which the new imperialism functions has many
layers and lacks the specific geographical loci that characterised the institutions of classical imperialism or even neo-colonial imperialism. They
might be referred to as a *multi-layered, geographically-diffuse, institutional ensemble*, and they comprise a complex set of linkages amongst the
governments of the advanced and less developed countries, various
alliances between local capital and international capital usually in the form
of joint ventures in the less developed countries, and a set of international
institutions which are partly autonomous of the others but partly avenues
through which the others operate.

The international institutions tend to be functionally more specific than
the corporate and governmental networks that operate within both the less
developed and the advanced countries. For example, the function of
lending military support to regimes which cooperate with international
capital is shifting to the Security Council of the United Nations, which in
practice means an alliance of the major advanced powers. It is unlikely
that the US will in future allow its military to play as conspicuous a role as
it did in the Gulf War or in Somalia, which marked a transition from the
previous world order, in which the US both called and fired the shots, to a
new one in which all the advanced powers jointly wield and pay for the
military might that is, and always has been, needed to maintain an imperialist order.

Other international institutions include the World Trade Organisation,
which aims to procure the maximum openness of less developed countries
to both trade and investment from the advanced countries, and international financial institutions, such as the World Bank and the IMF, which
try to ensure that credit from the advanced countries is not used to protect
'uncompetitive' industries, but is channelled into the most productive
activities, that is, the ones normally dominated by international capital.
Although these international institutions tend to focus on particular tasks
required by international capital, they share the broad function of adding

legitimacy to the enforcement of rules which under previous world orders more manifestly served the interests, not just of the advanced countries, but of particular imperialist powers. International institutions can more convincingly present themselves as the legitimate guardians of the international community.

At the next level, the institutional networks linking states and corporations vary widely from one advanced power to another. At one end, those of the US still tend to rely heavily on military aid as the main cement binding them into a coherently functioning ensemble that serves the interests of US capital. This reflects the long history of the US military's role of ensuring the openness of the less developed countries to international capital in general and to American capital in particular. At the opposite end we find the wide variety of highly institutionalised linkages characteristic of the way Japanese capital secures and legitimates its interests in less developed countries, reflecting the fact that military power or even (visible) military aid has not been among the resources Japanese capital was able to use during the previous neo-colonial world order.

It is appropriate to characterise the new world order both as a stage in the development of imperialism and as a *new* imperialism. If the greater technical-industrial power of international capital, that serves and is served by its greater financial and commercial power, is the source of its superior capacity to exploit, then what is new are not just the complex institutional networks through which imperialism now functions, but their *geographical diffuseness*. The end of inter-imperialist rivalry and the emergence of new relationships that bind capital from different advanced countries together make it difficult to isolate American from Japanese, British, French or German imperialism. Part of the power wielded by each derives from its mutually-supportive relationships with the others, so that the specific locus of the power of imperialism shifts among the members of the group and if anywhere resides in the *relationships* that hold them together. The most vivid manifestation and precise geographical location of the new imperialism is in such institutions as the G7, the G5, and the Security Council of the United Nations.

The geographical diffuseness of the new imperialism is almost equally apparent at the receiving end, that is, its victims. In the past it was relatively easy to speak of imperialism against Vietnam, or of neo-colonies like Thailand and Brazil. What the new imperialism seems to effect, however, is a deepening of the class divisions within both the advanced and the less developed countries, producing a tendency towards the homogenisation of their class structures, including sizeable internal 'colonies' within the advanced countries and growing pockets of wealth within the less developed countries.

If one recognises that the moving force behind this tendency is the triadic set of relationships among the leading productive, financial and commercial capitals that constitute international capital, then the appropriate theoretical concept to use is *imperialism*. There are geographical and social spaces within the advanced countries which are excluded from these relationships, for example, the millions of minute family firms in Japan that function more as a reserve army of labour than a repository of technical-industrial power, the African American community in the US and the degenerating sectors of British manufacturing. On the other hand, pockets of technical-industrial power fused to commercial and financial power are appearing within the less developed countries, although the only really significant ones are in South Korea. Nonetheless, their emergence reveals that the new imperialism gains its strength by allying and forming mutually supportive relationships with whatever source of power it comes across. In South Korea, that power was an unusually resilient nationalism.

Because international capital also continues to function through specific corporate and national networks and institutions, the term imperialism and the tradition associated with its analysis remains appropriate. Alternative windows through which to examine the global political economy do not focus as explicitly on the specific relationships, both within and across specific countries, which are the real basis of power in the global political economy.

Mapping out the full range of networks used by Japanese capital to further its global strategies is an ongoing task which this study is unable to complete. My focus is rather to concentrate more on the networks which link Japan's foreign direct investment, trade and financial operations together in mutually reinforcing ways in order to highlight the different impacts they are able to make on other advanced countries and on less developed countries. This difference marks the essence of imperialist power in the new world order.

2 Domestic Crisis: Motor of Internationalisation

It was widely recognised at the time that the massive outpour of Japanese foreign direct investment in the late 1980s resulted directly from the 'high yen recession' (*endaka fukyō*) of 1986–87. The near doubling of the yen's value in 1986 confronted Japan's leading export industries with what was in effect a near doubling of their domestic costs. Their three-pronged response comprised an outflow of foreign investment into countries with lower costs or no other way to maintain access to increasingly protected markets, an attempt to restructure into industries which were less dependent on exports, and a widespread domestic cost-down campaign to minimise the need to raise overseas prices (Steven, 1990).

A very fundamental problem of uneven development within Japan, which had been building for over a decade, suddenly burst into prominence and drove Japanese capitalism into a frenzy of international activity in an attempt to displace the unevenness onto distant shores, especially in the United States and Asia. However, its lack of success in the former would subsequently steer it with even greater intensity towards Asia, in cooperation with rather than in opposition to the US. The new world order would open up vast opportunities for Japanese capital to use its considerable strength in diverse attempts to rid itself of a weakness which kept popping up in new forms each time it seemed to have been overcome once and for all. That weakness is the continued unevenness between Japan's immense productive power in the consumer goods industries and the limits some of the main sources of this power place on the capacity of its domestic market to absorb consumer goods.

UNIQUE POWER OF JAPANESE CAPITAL

The seriousness of *endaka*, however, or the degree to which it expressed problems structurally associated with some of the distinctive features of Japanese capitalism, received little attention. As a late developer, Japan from the beginning had relied heavily on its lower wages as the key to surviving competition with the West. Low-cost production, deriving from an array of measures which weakened the labour movement and kept wages down, became the hallmark of Japan's success story. What these measure had in common was the way they all functioned to create divisions and competition among workers (Steven, 1983, 1990).

Divisions between regular workers and temporaries, between those with long periods of uninterrupted service and those with frequently broken service, between workers in large 'parent' firms and those in small firms which do work under contract, between male workers and female workers, between those from the 'best' schools and universities and those who lost out in the competition, between upper and lower members of minutely graded but all-encompassing hierarchies which include everyone, all these divisions tend to overlap so that at both ends privileges and disadvantages tend to accumulate. A core work force comprising no more than a fifth of the total is not 'low-paid' by any measure, but the remainder are bedevilled with insecurities of pay and employment.

What capital gets from Japan's employment system is the most thoroughly flexible labour force in the world. Its hours are flexible not simply because fewer than the required number of workers can be recruited and any shortage met by the customary system of 'compulsory overtime', but also by shedding any of the many categories of temporary worker. In an uncharacteristic and rare study comparing levels of unemployment in Japan and the US according to the *same measures*, Japan's Economic Planning Agency found that joblessness in Japan in 1977, 1982 and 1986 was higher than in the US. For example, if people wanting work had been added to the registered unemployed, Japan's unemployment rate in 1986 would have been 16.9 per cent, compared to 11.2 per cent for the US (*Keizai kikakuchō*, 1988, p. 122).

Wages are downwardly flexible in Japan because up to a third of annual pay comes in twice-yearly bonuses, which management is free to reduce at will, and because higher-paid regular workers, whose wages depend partly on the length of their uninterrupted service, can so easily be replaced with lower-paid irregulars. And finally, tasks can be flexibly allocated, because payment is never for a specific job but always for a specific person, who can be freely moved about from task to task without interference (Katō and Steven, 1993). For persons to distinguish themselves and earn much-needed merit payments or promotions, there is frequently no alternative to working extra hard and extra long, and that means susceptibility to the 'Japanese disease' of *karōshi,* that is, death from over work (Katō, 1994).

The power that Japanese capital can bring to bear on labour to achieve such an employment system results considerably from the ways its own organisational structure functions systematically to disorganise workers. That same structure of power is also used to protect it from foreign competition, both inside and outside Japan, and to constitute it into an efficient international force with unusual imperialist capacity, especially under the new world order.

Stateless State: *Keiretsu* System

One acute observer has suggested that Japan has no government to speak of, but is ruled by what he calls 'the System' (Van Wolferen, 1989). This comprises a multi-layered network that connects the whole spectrum of business interests with one another and with the many levels of Japan's various ministries. The network operates more through functional institutional relationships, which add enormous power to Japanese capital vis-a-vis both labour and foreign capital, than through the personal ties, based on family or school, which often mediate them. For example, functional relationships that bring money, industrial and commercial capital together are maintained through the *keiretsu* system, in which groups of companies covering the whole spectrum of capitalist activity share directors, stockholdings, key lending institutions and sales outlets. They also create coordinating bodies to enable the group to function almost as a distinct and highly efficient economic system of its own.

Japan's *keiretsu* system epitomises the power of international capital described in the previous chapter because it consolidates mutually-supportive *relationships* between banking capital, technologically-advanced industrial capital and commercial capital. The country's leading banks always have reliable customers, its main manufacturers always have access to finance and markets and its trading companies (sōgō shōsha) always have superior products with which to conquer markets. The *keiretsu* system is thus a set of relationships that constitute and consolidate the distinctive power of Japanese capital. However, their relationships with politicians are as much an embarrassment to them – due to the frequency of political scandals in Japan – as avenues of access to the really important institutions of state, the ministries, especially the Ministry of Finance and MITI (Ministry of International Trade and Industry). Japan's bureaucracy blends on behalf of all *keiretsu* the appropriate mixtures of the cooperation they need in the face of foreign competition or resistance from labour, with the competition they thrive on at home and abroad. The big six *keiretsu* are Mitsubishi, Mitsui, Sanwa, Dai-ichi Kangyo, Fuyo and Sumitomo. Figures 2.1 to 2.6 show the main tentacles of these core groups, that is, the members of their coordinating bodies. Since so many of the names that have become household words all over the world appear within their ranks, it is useful to know as much as possible about the specific networks through which they operate. Their actual networks extend well beyond these core members to include hundreds and in some cases even thousands of companies which are integrated into them. But at the very centre of each, is one of Japan's top banks, which is why the big six are often also referred to as *kinyū* (financial) *keiretsu*.

Figure 2.1   Core (29 member 'Fuyokai') of Fuyo *keiretsu*: centred on Fuji Bank and prewar *zaibatsu*

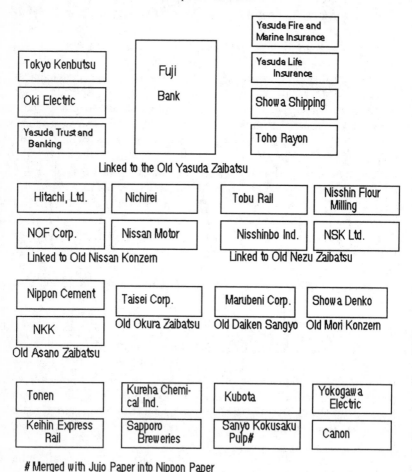

Merged with Jujo Paper into Nippon Paper

Source: Ōsono, 1992, p. 49

Although the Fuyo group is one of the three bank-centred *keiretsu* which emerged after World War Two, it is also the one which brought under a single umbrella companies from the largest number of different prewar *zaibatsu* (the predecessors of the modern *keiretsu*): Yasuda (Yasuda Bank became Fuji Bank), Asano, Nissan, Mori, Okura and Nezu. Its main coordinating body, the Fuyokai, comprises the presidents of 29 companies and has met since 1966. However, group cohesion is also

Figure 2.2   Core (44 member 'Sansuikai') of Sanwa *keiretsu*: centred on finance from Sanwa Bank

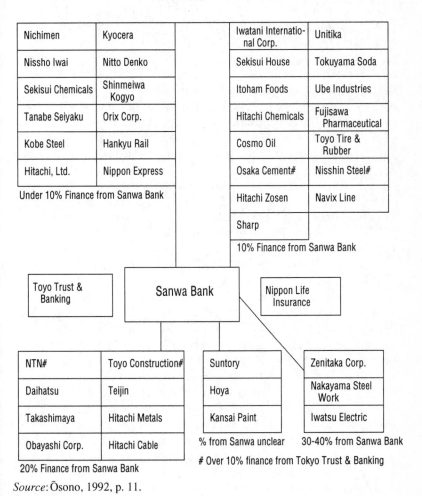

Source: Ōsono, 1992, p. 11.

maintained by means of cross shareholdings, interlocking directorships and reliance on Fuji Bank for finance and on Marubeni for marketing. With such giants as Nissan and Hitachi among its members, it also has a sound industrial base, even though both companies have a certain independence through having their own vertical *keiretsu* networks through which they procure their supplies (Ōsono, 1992, p. 8).

The Sanwa group has its base in the Kansai area, where its main bank arose in the 1930s out of mergers among a number of regional banks and where it soon attracted some of the country's leading textile companies. However, the recession soon forced it to shift into the heavy chemical industries and to link up with companies like Hitachi Zosen, Kobe Steel, Ube Industries and Maruzen Oil (now Cosmo Oil). Its presidential conferences began with the meeting of a 24-member Sansuikai in 1967, but it has been greatly strengthened in recent years through the addition of powerful independent companies like Kyocera, Suntory, Hoya and Nitto Denko. It is well served by leading *sōgō shōsha* (trading companies) in Nichimen, Nissho Iwai and Iwatani International, and it retains its edge in industries like heavy chemicals (with Sekisui, Ube and Hitachi), pharmaceuticals (Tanabe and Fujisawa) and iron and steel (Kobe and Nisshin). Sanwa has also attracted a number of Hitachi companies, although the anchor of that group, Hitachi Ltd., also has ties with the Fuyo and Dai-Ichi Kangyo *keiretsu* and is thus relatively autonomous of Sanwa. The group's leading bank has, however, lost ground to its regional competitors, Sumitomo Bank, Sakura Bank (merger between Taiyo Kobe and Mitsui in 1990) and Asahi Bank (merger between Kyowa and Saitama) (Ōsono, 1992, p. 10).

Japan's largest bank, Dai-Ichi Kangyo, was the outcome of a merger in 1971 which absorbed the country's oldest bank, Dai-Ichi. Although it was originally formed by the Furukawa (including Fujitsu and Furukawa Electric) and Kawasaki (including Kawasaki Steel and Kawasaki Kisen) groups, the DKB group has few historical ties among its 47 members. It is mainly kept together by the latter's reliance on their core bank for finance, but also by their use of the group's four *sōgō shōsha*, particularly Kanematsu and Itochu (the other two are Nissho Iwai and Kawasho). Itochu has the same prewar origins as Marubeni and served alongside it under Sumitomo Bank, but unlike Itochu, Marubeni joined the Fuyo group when the DKB merger took place. Cohesion among DKB members is also preserved by means of the usual interlocking directorships, cross shareholdings and meetings of core members employed by all *keiretsu*. On the production side, DKB has special strength in the steel industry (with Kawasaki and Kobe), in heavy industry (Kawasaki and Ishikawajima

Harima) and in electrical machinery (Fujitsu, Hitachi, Furukawa and Yaskawa). On every possible measure (group assets, employees, or turnover), the DKB is currently the largest of Japan's *keiretsu*.

Just as Marunouchi near Tokyo station could be called Mitsubishi's village, the area round the northern beach of Osaka's Yodoyabashi could

Figure 2.3   Core (47 member 'Sankinkai') of Dai-Ichi Kangyo *keiretsu*: Japan's newest and largest

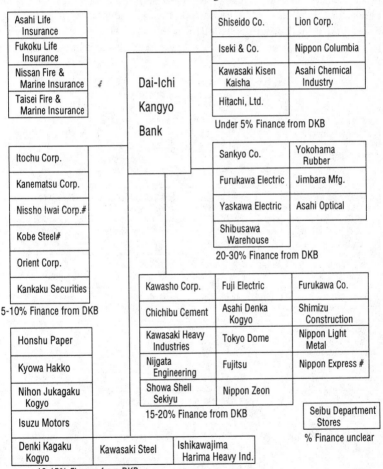

Source: Ōsono, 1992, p. 12–13.

be described as Sumitomo's village, since here we find the head offices of a number of the leading firms in the group's 20-member Hakusuikai, including the three leading 'houses' of Sumitomo Bank, Sumitomo Metal and Sumitomo Chemical, as well as Sumitomo Corporation, Sumitomo Trust & Banking, and Sumitomo Electric. Dating from the early Tokugawa period even before the rise of Mitsui, the group held its 300th year anniversary in 1990. Like Mitsui, its initial wealth was accumulated in commerce, but it then moved into copper, coal and other mining, metals, chemicals and fertilisers. Its focus has remained on raw materials, metals and chemicals, and it had no commercial section until after the war. Compared to Mitsui and Mitsubishi, it has been slow to modernise and has therefore lagged behind them, although its smaller 20-member

Figure 2.4   Core (20 member 'Hakusuikai') and quasi-members of 'United Sumitomo' keiretsu

Sumitomo Chemical	Sumitomo Bank	Sumitomo Metal Industries

Sumitomo Life Insurance	Sumitomo Corp.	Sumitomo Electric Industries	Sumitomo Realty & Dev.
Sumitomo Trust & Banking	Sumitomo Marine & Fire Insurance	Sumitomo Heavy Industries	Sumitomo Bakelite
Sumitomo Construction	NEC	Sumitomo Coal Mining	Sumitomo Cement
Sumitomo Forestry	Japan Sheet Glass	Sumitomo Warehouse	Sumitomo Metal Mining
Sumitomo Light Metal	20 Member Hakusuikai		

Quasi-Sumitomo

Asanuma Construction	Hanshin Electric Railway	Mazda Motor Corp.	JVC
Asahi Chemical Industry	Taisho Pharmaceutical	Sanyo Electric	Marudai Food
Asahi Breweries	Matsushita Electric Industrial		

Source: Ōsono, 1992, p. 15.

Hakusuikai comprises only those companies with direct links to Sumitomo, specifically in order to preserve a 'united Sumitomo'. However, some of Japan's industrial giants have also forged close ties with the group, such as Matsushita (which is a *keiretsu* in its own right), Toyo Kogyo (Mazda), and Asahi Breweries.

Figure 2.5   Core (26 member 'Nimokkai') and quasi-members of Mitsui *keiretsu*

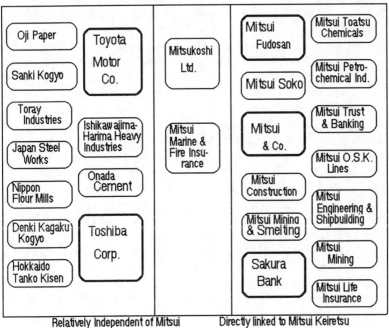

Relatively Independent of Mitsui   Directly linked to Mitsui Keiretsu

Nimokkai

Toyo Engineering	Tomen	General Sekiyu K.K.	Mitsui Norin
Mitsui Aluminium	Mitsui Home	Mitsui Liquid Gas	Mitsui Joho Kaihatsu
Mitsui Leasing & Development	Fujita Corp.	Kanebo	Jujo Paper#
Nihon Kogyo	Nippon Denso	Fuji Photo Film	Toa Gosei Kagaku Kogyo
Toshiba Machine	# merged with Sanyo Kokusaku Pulp into Nippon Paper		

Quasi-Mitsui Companies

Source: Ōsono, 1992, p. 17.

The 1990 merger of Taiyo Kobe and Mitsui to form Sakura Bank was the largest in Japan since the birth of DKB. Mitsui Bank had trailed behind its rivals in the other five financial *keiretsu*, and with lower levels of cross shareholding and of finance by the group's main bank, unity among members was inferior to that of Sumitomo or Mitsubishi. Moreover, since the group had over the years been plagued by a number of accidents and scandals involving leading members, it was hoped that the merger and dropping of the name of Mitsui could restore confidence to its main bank. Nevertheless, the 26-member Nimokkai includes many of Japan's top corporations, some of which, such as Mitsui Fudosan, Mitsui & Co. and Sakura Bank, retain direct links with the House of Mitsui, while others, such as Toyota Motor, Toshiba (both of which are also *keiretsu* in their own right), Onada Cement and Oji Paper, had been fully incorporated into the Mitsui *zaibatsu* in prewar years but have been strongly independent following their departure from and then re-entry into the group after the war.

Originating from the early Meiji period when the issue was to avoid colonisation through making the transition to modern capitalism, the Mitsubishi *keiretsu* has always had a policy of 'walking hand in hand with the nation'. It thus rose to strength in the pre-war period around heavy industry and military demand, and then in the post-war period became Japan's strongest group by concentrating on the heavy raw-materials processing and chemical industries, which the state had also equated with Japan's national interest. However, following the oil crisis of the 1970s, group members laid off vast numbers of workers and, following the rise of the yen in the 1980s, they restructured into new materials, biotechnology, information & communication, mechatronics, urban development and the industries related to aircraft, space and the military. Although comparatively late in internationalising, Mitsubishi has scored some spectacular overseas successes with the takeover of the Rockefeller group by Mitsubishi Estate, with the agreement between Mitsubishi Motors and Volvo, and with the cooperation between the Daimler-Benz group and four leading Mitsubishi companies: Mitsubishi Heavy Industries, Mitsubishi Electric, Mitsubishi Motors and Mitsubishi Corporation. Due to the real estate slump in the US, however, the takeover of the Rockefeller group has yet to yield dividends.

Apart from the horizontal associations which enable capital specialising in different 'moments' in the overall circuit (finance, production and marketing) to marshall one another's prowess, the *keiretsu* system also creates tight vertical relationships that bridge the institutional barriers assumed by technical divisions of labour, mainly in Japan's manufacturing industry. The *kanban* system, in which components are made by nominally inde-

Figure 2.6   Core (29 member 'Kinyokai') and related companies in
Mitsubishi *keiretsu*

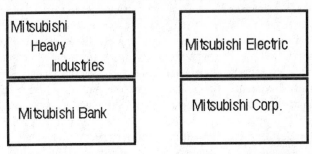

| Mitsubishi Heavy Industries | | Mitsubishi Electric | |
| Mitsubishi Bank | | Mitsubishi Corp. | |

Kirin Brewery	Asahi Glass	Mitsubishi Paper Mills	Meiji Life Insurance
Tokio Marine & Fire Insurance	Mitsubishi Trust & Banking	Mitsubishi Rayon	Mitsubishi Gas Chemical
Mitsubishi Oil	Mitsubishi Motors	Mitsubishi Steel Mfg.	Mitsubishi Materials
Mitsubishi Petrochemical	Mitsubishi Kakoki	Mitsubishi Kasei	Mitsubishi Plastics
Mitsubishi Shindo	Mitsubishi Cable	Mitsubishi Research Institute	Mitsubishi Estate
Mitsubishi Warehouse & Transport	Mitsubishi Construction	Mitsubishi Aluminium	Nippon Yusen K.K.
Nikon	**Kinyokai**		

Nihon Shintaku Ginko	Dai Nippon Toryo	Toyo Engineering Works	Mitsubishi Jimu Kikai
Mitsubishi Space Software	Mitsubishi New Catapillar	Mitsubishi Genshi Nenryo	Mitsubishi Genshi-ryoku Kogyo
DC Card	Mitsubishi Precision	Mitsubishi York	

Other Closely Related Companies

Source: Ōsono, 1992, p.19.

pendent 'child' companies and delivered to the 'parent' company just-in-time for assembly, represents a unique institutional division corresponding to technical divisions within an overall manufacturing process that in other countries are often brought under the same roof. Sub-contracting out the manufacture of components is a powerful weapon against labour, because it scatters workers into a wide range of separate and often minute work places and makes it impossible for them to communicate with one another. Communication is something only the representatives of capital can do, because the sub-contracting system requires regular and almost exclusive exchanges between producers and purchasers of components, exchanges which also frequently involve finance and technology. And because it is embedded with cultural expressions of benevolence from above to be matched by loyalty from below, the *kanban* system allows Japanese capital to *appropriate* for itself the enormous productive power of diverse cooperative communities and groups. In cases where a wide range of components are made through sub-contracts and re-sub-contracts right down to the minute family firm, the ingenuity and hard work of each family unit as well as its individual members can be harnessed in the service of capital. The nominal independence of the 'child' companies is denied by the reality of very high levels of dependence on the 'parent' companies for markets, finance and technology.

Although most large manufacturing companies work through vertical sub-contract relations like these, some networks assume such proportions that the term industrial *keiretsu*, or *konzern* as they were known in the prewar period, is entirely appropriate. For example, Toyota Motor Co., which itself employs over 75 000 workers in Japan and a further 35 000 in 24 other countries, has a total of some 40 000 local sub-contractors involved in the procurement of its parts, of which 25 are large corporations quoted on the stock exchange. Many of these latter have considerably internationalised their operations, for example, Toyoda Machine Works (which has almost 5000 employees in Japan and over 1000 overseas), Toyoda Gosei (with nearly 7000 in Japan and 2000 in Taiwan and North America making things like rubber parts), Toyoda Automatic Loom Works (with over 9000 in Japan and 1000 abroad engaged in a wide range of activities including vehicle assembly and the manufacture of textile machinery), Toyota Tsusho (a wholesale firm with about 2000 employees in Japan), Aisin Seiki (with 11 000 in Japan and 2000 overseas) and Japan's largest car parts maker, Nippon Denso, which has over 40 000 employees in Japan and nearly 11 000 in fifteen other countries (Shūkan Tōyō Keizai, 1993, pp. 509–12; Ōsono, 1992, pp. 20–1).

Many companies in the Toyota group are involved in activities other than motor vehicles; for example, even Toyota Motors itself engages so extensively in *zaiteku* (fund management) that it is sometimes referred to as 'Toyota Bank'. However, since the great majority are in what is broadly defined as a single industry, the links among members tend to be vertical rather than horizontal. And because vertical relationships involve all kinds of inequalities, the benefits are much less evenly distributed among member firms than they are in the horizontal *keiretsu*. Sub-contractors regularly face price squeezes, which involve substantial reductions during less prosperous times, and there is no question that the companies higher up in the hierarchy do the squeezing and those lower down the bleeding.

However, the real inequalities are in the conditions of the workers in the smaller companies, since, when all other costs and specifications are fixed from above, the main room for improving profitability is in the area of wages and conditions, which when all is considered are only about half those of workers in giant firms. Scattered across myriads of tiny institutions and with almost zero rates of unionisation, these workers are hard pressed to organise for any improvement. From capital's point of view, the main advantages of Toyota's famous *kanban* (just-in-time) delivery system lies in this almost total vulnerability of labour, which in the end pays for the storage costs of components that the parent company avoids, cancellation of contracts, cuts in contract prices and so on.

Although Toyota is the largest and most powerful of all the vertical *keiretsu*, even it still finds working through horizontal networks a sufficient advantage for it to remain within the financial *keiretsu* under whose umbrella it grew in pre-war days. Japan's largest car maker still benefits enormously from Mitsui's commercial and financial strength, especially the former, and so do Mitsui financial and commercial institutions from Toyota's productive power. Other vertical *keiretsu* operate in the same way. But not all of them share the Toyota group's heavy reliance on the regional proximity of key members to one another in and around Toyota city in western Japan's Aichi prefecture, where the big three core companies (Toyota Motor, Nippondenso and Aisin Seiki) function as a magnet of group cohesion.

Nissan, for example, does not have a similar regional base or giant parts maker of Nippon Denso proportions, but relies more on suppliers from all over Japan and even overseas. Cohesion among group members which are large enough to pick and choose, that is, the 19 quoted companies and many of the 191 members of Nissan's own Nishokai, is thus maintained much more through the parent company's ownership of controlling proportions of stock. For example, Nissan Motor owns 33 per cent of Calsonic (which has 5000 employees in Japan and 4000 in eight other countries producing 46 per cent of the company's output), 31 per cent of Kansei Corp. (3000 workers in Japan and half as many overseas), and 40 per cent of Nissan Diesel (5500 in Japan and a few hundred overseas).

Even though Nissan Motor, with its 53 000 workers in Japan and a further 45 000 abroad, towers over its suppliers and group members, group unity is inferior to that of Toyota. But just as Toyota benefits from its links with Mitsui, Nissan gains a lot from its membership in the Fuyo *keiretsu*, especially from Fuji Bank and Marubeni. The latter's trade networks have helped ease it into a large number of its key overseas ventures, which remain joint Nissan–Marubeni projects, for example, Nissan's 11 000 worker factory in Mexico (Shūkan Tōyō Keizai, 1994; Ōsono, 1992, pp. 22–23).

Similar pictures, each with its own idiosyncrasies, could be painted of a long list of leading industrial companies that have created their own vertical *keiretsu* which they have then brought into one, or in some cases such as Hitachi into more than one, of the large financial *keiretsu*. Hitachi Ltd, which has 81 000 employees in Japan and nearly 30 000 in sixteen other countries, also has 799 subsidiaries that it has constituted into an extremely powerful though relatively independent industrial *keiretsu*. Together with the parent company, the 'three houses' of Hitachi Metals (8 000 employees in Japan and half as many again abroad), Hitachi Cable (6500 in Japan and half as many overseas) and Hitachi Chemical (5500 in Japan and 2000 abroad) comprise the group's inner core and powerhouse. Other industrial *keiretsu* include Toshiba and Matsushita, which are of comparable stature to Hitachi; and NEC, Fujitsu, Nippon Steel, NKK, NTT and Mitsubishi Heavy Industries, which are not far behind. In the transport and service industry, the largest *keiretsu* are Tokyu, Seibu Tetsudo, Kintetsu and Hankyu, while in distribution we find Daiei, Sezon and Ito-Yokado (Ōsono, 1992, pp. 26–57).

Divide and Rule and Rule over the Divide

It is ironic how Japan's *keiretsu* system divides what is united under western capitalism and links together what is divided, the latter giving Japanese capital a peculiar strength and the former Japanese labour a special weakness. The various linkages – personal through presidential councils and 'old boy' networks, institutional through cross shareholdings and interlocking directorships and functional through reliance on member firms for finance and marketing – all help bind the *keiretsu* together into relatively autonomous economic systems. They enable group members to circumvent the need to use the *market* to achieve the exchanges that drive capital from one stage to the next through the circuit, from money capital into productive capital, into commodity capital and then back into money capital. To a qualitatively greater degree, US capitalism links these transformations via the market, its representatives arguing that the Japanese system undermines efficiency and fairness (as if the latter was a feature of capitalism).

The vertical *keiretsu*, through their institutional separation of so many more of the diverse technical tasks involved in modern manufacturing, allow Japanese capital to undermine the labour unity that US manufacturing encourages by bringing different technical tasks under one roof. Again the difference is one of degree, but the US expects Japan's greater institutional fragmentation of the manufacturing process to open up greater roles for the market to re-integrate it, whereas Japanese capitalism recognises markets more for what they are: opportunities for capital, to be adapted to capital's needs, rather than timeless expressions of human nature and of equal opportunity. Japan's horizontal *keiretsu,* on the other hand, build strong institutional bridges between all the different industries that must work in unison if the circuit of capital is to function smoothly, whereas in the US companies in different industries remain much more institutionally separate. Where bridges are built, as happens among members of American conglomerates, these usually tend to connect companies in broadly similar ranges of industries. The Japanese *keiretsu* derive much greater strength from the way group members in different industries pull together, something that makes sense both in terms of capital's requirements and of Japanese culture.

Even many traditional networks which continue to make Japanese society one of the most tightly-knit to survive into modern times have been harnessed by capital to ensure that the cohesion and cooperative power of the whole is transformed into the peculiar competitive edge of business. If looked at in this light, even the Japanese bureaucracy is only one institutional expression of Japanese society, one which is as enmeshed as any other in the capitalist relationships which have come to dominate that society. This seems to be what Van Wolferen captures in the phrase 'stateless state'. The Japanese 'system' of power functions both through bureaucratic and *keiretsu* networks, which operate horizontally to bring each industry into the service of all and all into the service of each, as well as vertically to ensure that not even the minutest pocket of productive capacity, energy or ingenuity is untapped. If the capacity to appropriate is the real essence of capital's power and of technological leadership, then Japanese technology does indeed lead the world. And it does so most cuttingly in industries which most fully combine the two types of *keiretsu* networks, that is, motor vehicles and electronics, which involve the most complex technical divisions of labour which can be broken down institutionally and then re-constituted in hierarchical sub-contracting relationships.

The power of Japanese capital is awesome. That much should be clear by now. However, this strength is also the fundamental source of a problem for which Japanese capital has hitherto seemed unable to find a permanent solution. Temporary detours round it have been found, both at home and abroad, but the problem has had a habit of somehow always returning to where it came from.

Too Strong for its Own Good

Super-efficient production, instantly effective cost-reduction, wage rises below increases in productivity and docile trade unions are all manifestations of the 'miraculous' power of Japanese capital. Yet capitalism requires markets for the goods it makes, and the absence of markets can be as undermining of the whole system as any failure in the production place. And when goods are produced that can only be bought with money from workers' pay packets, what appears to be the system's greatest source of strength, low wages, can turn into its greatest weakness. While on the production side low wages can help keep costs down, on the sales side they tend to reduce the capacity of buyers to clear the market. Low wages are thus good for producing cheaply, but they are bad for maintaining domestic sales.

For many years following the transition to capitalism in the late nineteenth century, Japanese capital relied on a low-cost accumulation model without having to face up to this problem, which was, partly through good fortune and partly by design, on the whole circumvented until quite recently. From the earliest years of the 1880s right up until the Second World War, this was done through varying combinations of two broad strategies. First, consumer goods like textiles, which launched Japan's industrial revolution and which exceeded what the domestic market could absorb, were exported. Second, consumer goods for which workers had to provide the market were increasingly replaced by producer goods purchased by Japanese capital. The state helped implement both strategies. It opened up overseas markets, sometimes by force just like other imperialist powers, and it assisted the restructuring into heavy industrial producer goods by subsidising them with surpluses earned in agriculture and light industry. Low wages did not undermine the marketability of Japan's cheaply produced output because Japanese workers were not targeted as its main buyers.

After World War Two, the emphasis shifted even further away from exporting consumer goods towards manufacturing heavy producer goods, such as iron and steel, chemicals and ships. These were in great demand due to the growing capital investments made by Japanese businesses in the period of rapid accumulation that began around the mid-1950s. Since investment comprised such a large proportion (over 20 per cent) of total demand, especially for the output of the fast growing heavy industries, high levels of uninterrupted growth were, by the end of the 1960s, hailed as the 'Japanese miracle'. Once again the low pay of Japanese workers did not greatly interfere with the process because those with more money than wage earners ensured that the required sales took place.

STRUCTURAL CRISIS: UNDERCONSUMPTION

The first signs of the trouble to come appeared with the 'oil shock' (sky-rocketing oil price) of October 1973, which hit Japan hard on the cost side because its industrial structure depended heavily on imported oil as well as on other imported raw materials, whose prices also rose substantially around that time. But it was the response to rising commodity prices which set Japanese capitalism on a collision course with itself. The key manoeuvre was to restructure out of the raw-material-processing heavy industries into the consumer goods branches of the machinery industries which were most receptive to new technology and the giant leap in labour productivity that was required to end the recession: motor vehicles and electric and electronic goods. Rising real wages before the recession of the 1970s had allowed these industries to mature on the basis of an expanding domestic market.

However, the sudden and prolonged stagnation of wages that Japanese capital forced onto workers, from the mid-1970s to this very day, increasingly drove the machinery industries into export markets in order to absorb the outputs of their growing productive power. Once again, the clash between the low-cost production of consumer goods and the preservation of viable markets had been avoided, this time by exporting the surplus to the advanced countries. Increasing exports of television sets and motor cars to the US and Europe, where high wages fed what seemed to be limitless markets, were the most visible forms of Japan's new industrial structure, and might.

Japan's first onslaught into world markets with cheap consumer goods ended in war: the rapid conquest in the 1920s and 1930s of the Asian and South American textile markets of western imperialist powers contributed substantially to the latter's growing antipathy towards their new rival. It was hardly surprising that Japan's second foray, this time with cars and TV sets into the domestic markets of its American and European

competitors, has met with almost equal hostility. However, since the entire
context in which the great powers act out their rivalries has changed, the
outcome is very unlikely to take a military form. Even full-scale trade
wars are unlikely to eventuate in today's world order, although limited
sanctions might from time to time be used to underline the fact that
advanced countries have to respect one another in ways that are unneces-
sary when they deal with LDCs. Since powers of more or less equal
stature cannot for long displace their problems onto one another, they tend
after a while to shift their attention to those less developed countries. This
is what the new imperialism is all about.

Endaka

Nonetheless, by 1985 the reaction in America and Europe against Japanese
exports was sufficient to force a near doubling of the value of the yen in
less than a year as a means of limiting their imports from Japan. Although
such currency revaluations are in effect formal recognitions of and rewards
for superior productive power – they allow greater volumes of imports to
be bought with given quantities of exports – they also make it harder to
export goods at the new exchange rate, because given amounts of a re-
valued yen translate into larger amounts of foreign currency. If yen prices
remain the same, prices in foreign currency increase by the amount of the
revaluation, which can be too much for some people to continue buying
Japanese goods. By undermining the export markets which were cultivated
to compensate for deficiencies at home, yen revaluations can therefore pre-
cipitate recessions on the demand side. In 1986–87 they sent the problem of
uneven development between Japan's production power and its consumption power back home in the form of a crisis of underconsumption.

Japan's wages were thus left simultaneously both too high and too low.
From the point of view of capital's costs, the rise of the yen made them
too high relative to wages elsewhere in the world, but from the point of
view of workers' spending power, both to clear the market of consumer
goods and to provide reasonable living standards, Japanese wages were
much too low. If anything, this situation has worsened since the late
1980s: Japanese prices in the second half of 1993 were as high as 1.72
times US prices (up from 1.52 times in 1991), so that real wages in Japan
were less than 60 per cent of US real wages (*NW*, 4 October, 1993, p. 2; 4
April 1994, p. 10).

Although the 'high yen recession' (*endaka fukyō*) took a heavy toll on
profits, wages and jobs in Japan's export industries, by the end of 1987
Japanese capital had launched an investment-led boom which persisted

solidly to the end of the decade. Not simply did domestic markets take the place of export markets, but the producer goods demanded by investment-hungry capitalists substituted for the consumer goods which workers could not afford. Having started from cost-cutting investments in plant and equipment in order to cut back prices forced up by the higher yen, the boom was soon fed by an optimistic belief that, because growing demand was internal rather than external, the structural causes of the recession had been thwarted. Amidst the euphoria of a thriving Japan alongside a languishing America and Europe, few noticed that the export industries, whose demand for investment goods (to reduce their costs) helped drive the boom, would as a result of these investments build up even greater productive capacity than before.

The new plant and equipment ushered in by the boom not only helped Japanese capital to produce cheaper goods than before, but also greater volumes of the same consumer goods which were struggling to find markets. Moreover, the added pressure on wages that accompanied the cost-down only served to reduce the capacity of the domestic market even further. The boomerang had come back. If the output of less efficient industries could not be adequately marketed in the early 1980s, either at home or abroad without provoking Japan's trading partners, then even narrower market limits would be bound to impose themselves on this larger productive power as it came on stream in the early 1990s. Japanese capital's almost knee-jerk response of accelerating its power to produce whenever it encounters a difficulty, thus once again came up against limits of its own creation.

By the end of 1990 the problem had unambiguously asserted itself and Japan entered its most serious recession ever. Since this is the context of the current phase of internationalisation, its main features require brief explanation: the basic obstacle of inadequate domestic markets for the consumer goods industries, the exacerbation of this due to layoffs and other attempts to cut costs once recession set in, the rapid rise and fall of land and other asset prices that inflamed the recessionary process, another leap in the value of the yen as Japan's trade balance with the US surged ahead once again and the linkages among all of these that made further internationalisation the most preferred counter-strategy for Japanese capital.

Bubble Economy

The inflation in land and other asset prices during the investment-led boom of the late 1980s resulted largely from the attempt to find safe investment outlets for Japan's enormous overseas surplus as well as for the large amounts of money made during the boom. Within Japan, much of this money poured into land, the stock exchange and the banking system, which in turn became more able to lend money for land and stocks. Externally, the money flowed into the full range of outlets: direct investment, bonds, stock markets, land and whatever speculative activity it could get hold of, including works of art and golf courses. In 1988 Tokyo residential land prices rose by almost 70 per cent and commercial land prices by more than 60 per cent. Although the rate of increase slowed thereafter, prices continued to rise well into 1991 (*NW*, 6 June 1993, p. 2; 28 March 1994, p. 3). Millionaires were born overnight, and people spoke of a 'new rich' (owners of assets) and a 'new poor' (the asset-less). Since the former spent much of their suddenly acquired wealth on further speculative investments, the rise in asset prices helped feed itself. On 29 December 1990 the Nikkei stock average index peaked at 38 915.87, having almost doubled from its level in early 1987, which was prior to the October crash (*NW*, 5 July 1993, p. S4). But before the term 'bubble economy' was applied to these happy days and their sudden demise, something had to interrupt the merry-go-round to expose it for what it was.

The pin that would burst the bubble was the old problem of Japan's productive capacity growing faster than its own market. The consumer goods industries were as reliant as ever on exports to Europe and America, but in attempts to turn the tide of recession both of these overseas markets were coming under increasing protection. The first omen was the sudden slowdown in the rise of household spending in Japan, from over three per cent in 1988 to a mere half a per cent in 1989, corresponding to an almost identical fall in the rise of salaried workers' disposable incomes. One of the staggering but almost unnoticed features of the big spending boom following the high yen recession is that it was confined to the middle and upper classes. The great mass of working class households barely kept pace with inflation, and the increase in consumer spending accompanying the boom resulted considerably from the inflated incomes of asset owners. So once asset prices peaked, so did the increase in their spending. And any reduction in domestic spending in a situation of limited overseas demand and rapidly expanding productive capacity had predictable consequences.

Worst Recession Ever

The downward path was almost a mirror image of the upward climb: faltering asset prices dealt a major blow to consumer spending, because they swept away the wealth that had boosted upper class consumption, which in turn had helped compensate for shortfalls in lower class consumption.

Japan was then left with its age-old predicament of having wage levels that were too low to absorb the output of its consumer goods industries. By the end of March 1992, 98–99 per cent of households had refrigerators and colour TV sets and 78.6 per cent had a passenger car. People either had no need to, or could not afford to, update their models (*NW*, 8 February 1993, p. 11). Once the bubble had been pricked, the slump was exacerbated by a *multiplier* that no amount of government spending could halt. Asset deflation was fed by and in turn fed the constant falls in both investment and consumer demand that dragged the country deeper and deeper into recession. The problem was compounded by the excessive investments that were made during the boom, especially by the export industries, which therefore had to reduce their productive capacity quite rapidly. Once they started to cut back on their plant and equipment and lay off workers, the shortfall in consumption was compounded even further.

On 18 August 1992 Japanese share prices plummeted to 14 390.41, their lowest level since March 1986 (*NW*, 5 July 1993, p. S4), and they have languished around the 20 000 mark ever since. Real estate prices followed the same pattern. By January 1993 average prices in Tokyo had fallen 30 per cent from their 1991 level, and in 1993 commercial land prices dropped by a further 18 per cent and residential land prices by 8 per cent. The slide has continued well into 1994 (*NW*, 28 March 1994, p. 3). This massive decline in asset prices intensified the recession in two main ways. First, the heavy bank lending that nourished the bubble economy translated into mounting bad debts after the bubble burst, and the resulting prolonged precariousness of the entire banking sector sustained the gloom surrounding asset prices in general and the stock exchange in particular (*FEER*, 23 April 1992, pp. 56–7). Second, since the asset price explosion was the main force behind the growth in domestic consumption during the boom, the collapse of these prices slashed the purchasing power of the asset holders who had spent so freely.

Rationalisations and Layoffs

The slump was thus not only fuelled by falling consumer demand, but also by cuts in equipment investment to compensate for the bullish capital investments of the late 1980s and to adjust to the shrinking market. In addition to mounting excess capacity and hence the decreasing productivity of plant and equipment, firms have been facing escalating depreciation charges. The ratio of the latter to recurring profits soared from just over 60 per cent in 1988 to just under 100 per cent in 1991. Although by fiscal 1992 labour costs were firmly under control and financial costs fell by

almost 16 per cent due to falling interest rates, depreciation costs continued to rise by 4.38 per cent (*FEER*, 28 January 1993, pp. 42 -3; *TB*,
January 1994, pp. 44–8). Capital spending has thus plunged by an average
of 6–9 per cent each year in 1992–94, with up to three times the average in
the manufacturing industry and even more in motor vehicles and electronics, the two engines of Japan's economy which seem unable to transcend
the limits on their domestic and overseas markets (*NW*, 7 June 1993, p. 2;
23 August 1993, p. 3; 10 January 1994, p. 3; 14 March 1994, p. 2).

In 1991–92, a rare phenomenon occurred in Japan when wages rose
above levels of productivity, but this was because productivity had stagnated due to the heavy fall in equipment investment that year. And so the
rise of the yen pulled Japan's price competitiveness in manufacturing (in
dollar terms) down in relation to that of the other advanced countries.
Table 2.1 shows how unit labour costs, which had risen much more mod-
estly than those in any other advanced country in the early 1980s, suddenly caught up (in yen) and then soared ahead (in dollars) because of the
rise of the yen.

Table 2.1   Changes (%) in advanced countries' price competitiveness, 1980–91

	US	Japan	Germany	UK	France	Italy
Labour Productivity						
1980–1985	2.7	4.0	2.8	5.6	3.7	5.1
1985–1990	3.1	5.2	1.7	4.3	3.5	2.8
1991	1.9	1.5	2.1	2.6	−0.2	3.3
Wage Increase						
1980–1985	6.0	4.3	5.4	9.3	12.4	16.5
1985–1990	3.8	4.7	4.9	7.8	4.1	7.0
1991	5.1	6.1	7.0	9.0	4.3	9.7
Unit Labour Costs (in own currency)						
1980–1985	3.1	0.3	2.6	3.5	8.3	10.9
1985–1990	0.7	−0.5	3.2	3.3	0.5	4.1
1991	3.2	4.5	5.0	6.2	4.6	6.2
Unit Labour Costs (in $)						
1980–1985	3.1	−0.8	−6.8	−8.0	−6.9	−5.5
1985–1990	0.7	10.0	16.3	10.2	11.1	14.2
1991	3.2	12.5	2.1	5.1	0.9	2.6

Source: Nihon bōeki shinkōkai, 1993b, p. 64.

The slump in consumer demand received an additional boost when businesses responded to their rising unit labour costs with large-scale layoffs and further cuts in investment. By November 1993, a Labour Ministry survey noted that capital's counter-recessionary measures had become much harsher than the ones taken during the high yen recession of the mid-1980s: a full 46 per cent of manufacturing firms (up six percentage points from the previous quarter) with over thirty workers were implementing 'employment adjustment measures' (mainly layoffs and overtime cuts), compared to 40 per cent during the worst quarter of the high yen recession. In the wholesale, retail and restaurant industries, the proportion was 36 per cent, compared to only 14 per cent in the mid-1980s. The Bank of Japan estimated that there were close to a million surplus workers at the end of 1992, while a MITI survey in November 1993 found that 68 per cent of firms considered themselves overstaffed (*NW*, 6 December 1993, p. 3; 13 December 1993, p. 8, *TB*, May 1993, pp. 10–11). In 1993 almost every day's news carried stories of job losses and rationalisations. In each of the first eight months that year, according to a Ministry of Labour survey, 49 000 workers were laid off (*NW*, 24 January 1994, pp. 1–2). In the first half of 1994, 140 000 jobs were lost in companies quoted on the stock exchange alone. Table 2.2 lists some of the larger rationalisations involving over 1000 workers that were announced in 1993–1994. Apart from the greater numbers involved than in the previous recession, for the first time ever sizeable contingents of white collar workers were involved.

The most widely used 'employment adjustment' measure was to reduce new hiring: 93 per cent of firms surveyed by *Nihon Keizai Shinbun* (Japan's largest business daily) in October 1993 hired fewer graduates from the class of 1994 than from the class of 1993, some by astonishing proportions, for example, Fujitsu by 75 per cent, Japan Travel Bureau by 54 per cent, Sony by 46 per cent and Mitsubishi Electric by 39 per cent (*NW*, 11 October 1993, p. 3). In addition to actual job losses, companies cut wages in ways which also affected job security. The most common were the use of compulsory holidays, such as Mazda's 'two-day layoffs' in mid-1994 (*NW*, 4 April 1994, p. 12), reductions in overtime and the increased use of contract workers, such as Toyota's use, for the first time ever in the car industry, of professional designers on a contract basis (*NW*, 28 March 1994, p. 13). Wages were also lowered by means for which the Japanese system is notorious. In fiscal 1993, winter bonuses were cut for the second straight year, while summer bonuses were cut for the first time since surveys began in 1975 (*NW*, 20 December 1993, p. 8). In the Spring 1994 wage negotiations, the lowest increase (average of 3 per cent) since the talks began in the mid-1950s was accepted (*NW*, 28 March 1994, p. 1).

Table 2.2   Some large-scale layoffs & employment adjustments reported in
1993–4

Company	Jobs Lost	Comments
NTT	33 000	Follows 97 000 cut since 1980
Fujitsu	6 000	Cut new hiring, by March 1995
Nissan	6 000	Close Zama plant (4 000) in 1995
Nippon Kokan	3 200	Reassign surplus to subsidiaries
Sumitomo Metal	4 300	By fiscal 1995
Nippon Steel	7 000	Within three years
Kawasaki Steel	2 900	Within three years
Kobe Steel	3 800	Double the original plan
Mitsui Trust & Banking	6 000	Reduce new hiring (1995)
JAL	2 800	Cut ground staff & flight attendants
Toshiba	10 000	3–5 years
Matsushita Electrical Ind.	2 000	Seconded to sales
Matsushita marketing companies	2 000	Transfer to affiliates
Takashimaya	1 500	Reduce new hiring
Kao	1 500	By 1998
Mazda	4 000	Close Ujina plant (3 000)
JVC	2 000	Follows 1 500 cut in late 1992
IBM Japan	3 000	'Voluntary' retirement
Oki Electric	2 000	Follows 1 500 cut in early 1993
Nomura	2 000	By 1997
Sanyo	3 000	By 1995
Toyota	2 300	Achieved in first half of 1994
Hitachi	2 200	Achieved in first half of 1994
Omron	1 500	Within three years

Source: *NW*, 1 March 1993, pp. 1, 8; 8 March 1993, pp. 1, 15; 15 March 1993,
pp. 8–9; 22 March 1993, pp. 1, 8; 5 July 1993, p. 8; 19 July 1993, p. 8; 2 August
1993, p. 11; 9 August 1993, p. 3; 2 September 1993, p. 12; 13 September 1993,
p. 10; 4 October 1993, p. 9; 11 October 1993, pp. 1, 8; 25 October 1993, p. 8; 1
November 1993, p. 1; 14 March 1994, p. 7; 5 September 1994, p. 10; *TB*, March
1993, pp. 44–5; May 1993, pp. 8–11; June 1993, pp. 32–7; January 1994, pp. 24–5

Starting wages for white collar workers also rose by the unprecedentedly
low rate of 2.2 per cent in 1993 and the even lower rate of 1.1 per cent in
1994 (*NW*, 6 September 1993, p. 2; 5 September 1994, p. 10). Another
first since surveys began in 1967 was the reduction in 1993 of total manufacturing employment in Japan (*NW*, 5 September 1994, p. 10). One of the
records established during the recession was the number of previous
records that were broken.

General Cost-down

The shake-up in Japanese industry extended well beyond the jobs and wages of workers, since all of Japan's traditional cost-down measures were widely mobilised. For example, sub-contractors were once again squeezed by parent companies. In 1993 Nissan cut contract prices by 5 per cent for 32 suppliers and by 3 per cent for another 50, Honda cut prices by 2 per cent for its 270 domestic suppliers, while Mazda implemented a 3 per cent across-the-board reduction (*NW,* 22 March 1993, p. 8; 18 October 1993, p. 8; 1 November 1993, p. 8). And women, once again, had to pay a higher price than men. For example, the vast majority of Japan's non-working population of 37.09 million in 1993 were females, of whom several million were in search of some kind of work but few of whom were included in the 1.67 million officially unemployed. Even among college graduates, the ratio of job offers to female job seekers fell from 1.58 in April 1991 to 0.93 two years later, while for males the decline was from 3.14 to 2.22. According to Recruit Company, which specialises in producing this sort of information, 20 000 female graduates failed to find a job in 1993 (*NW,* 28 June 1993, p. 10).

Another common response to the recession were decisions to slash loss-making operations. For example, Toshiba's sweeping rationalisation was expected to eliminate 38 out of its 100 product lines (*NW,* 12 April 1993, p. 8); Nissan has planned to cut its chassis models by 30 per cent (*NW,* 7 March 1994, p. 9); Hitachi has closed two VCR plants in Japan and is considering shifting all VCR production to Malaysia; NEC and Sansui have decided to abandon VCR production altogether; Kanebo decided to close three of its five domestic cotton spinning and weaving mills; Isuzu is to abandon car manufacturing; and JCV decided to pull out of hard disk production altogether (*NW,* 1 March 1993, pp. 1, 3; 14 June 1993, p. 8; 12 April 1993, p. 9).

Chronic Underconsumption and Falling Profits

All these and other cost-down measures which directly or indirectly affect working class jobs and incomes have hit back hard at the consumer goods industries. Cuts in overtime and summer bonuses alone were considered the main factor behind the one per cent fall in disposable income in the year to August 1993 (*NW,* 18 October 1993, p. 19). Declining incomes have also dealt a double punch due to continued increases in taxes: in 1992 the average annual wage of Japan's 49 million salaried workers increased by a mere 1.9 per cent, the lowest growth since 1958, whereas the proportion of income paid in tax increased to its highest level since 1957 (*NW*, 11 October 1993, p. 3). In many working class households savings or credit was even being used to sustain livelihoods, and as that becomes increasingly impossible further falls in consumption become necessary, with further recessionary consequences (*NW*, 8 March 1993, p. 15; *FEER*, 18 March 1993, pp. 36–7).

It is thus not surprising that corporate profitability has taken its most sustained battering ever, with four and probably five straight years of decline. Average pre-tax profits of all listed firms fell by 0.3 per cent in fiscal 1990, by 14.7 per cent in fiscal 1991, by 25.1 per cent in fiscal 1992, and by an estimated 20.2 per cent in fiscal 1993. Surveys of major firms have forecast a mixed picture for fiscal 1994, but with almost certain declines in the steel and chemical industries and for some automakers, such as Mazda. Japan's leading business daily, *Nihon Keizai Shinbun*, predicted an overall fall in profits of 0.9 per cent and a mere half a per cent growth in real GDP, compared to 0.2 per cent the previous year and 0.8 per cent in fiscal 1992. The consequence of such business pessimism is of course that is is harder to break out of the vicious circle of falling spending (*NW*, 21 June 1993, pp. 1, 23; 15 November 1993, pp. 1, 23; 10 January 1994, p. 3; 31 January 1994, pp. 1, 27; 7 March 1994, pp. 1, 27; 25 April 1994, p. 3).

Limits of State Intervention

The recession has proved as resistant to the interventions of successive Japanese governments as it has to Japanese capital's own measures. This is because the state is so closely tied to capital's interests that the only real solution, a redistribution of purchasing power to the classes which spend more on consumption, eludes the state just as thoroughly as it does individual businesses. One might have thought that the end of Liberal Democratic Party rule in mid-1993 and the formation of coalition governments more representative of labour and small business might have shifted the terrain on which problems were tackled. However, so thoroughly is Japan's state system structured round the promotion of capital accumulation that the flavour of politician in the Cabinet does not make much difference. Indeed, whether or not Japan has a Cabinet seems to contribute little to business confidence or strategy, as evidenced by capital's lack of concern during the protracted negotiations required to form the Hosokawa coalition following the splintering of the LDP, a period of 'helmlessness' that would have sent Wall Street into a dive but that could not even make the Tokyo Stock Exchange bat an eye-lid. Because parliamentarism in

Japan has more to do with legitimating the policies of state than with forming them, changes in the political make-up of the legitimating institutions have negligible effects on business strategy. Even the formation of the Murayama 'socialist' government in mid-1994 has had no noticeable effect on business confidence or strategy, perhaps because that government was kept in office by the very LDP which the socialists had opposed so vigorously for almost 40 years.

Besides, Shinseito (Renewal Party), the critical defector from the LDP and key power broker in the rise of the Hosokawa and the Hata governments (in August 1993 and April 1994 respectively), is the creation of the most powerful brokers of the old political establishment, tracing direct lines to the Tanaka and Takeshita factions of the LDP and having one Ozawa Ichiro, a man better known to Japan's underworld than its electorate, as its pivotal figure. Either way, Japan's state system is too remote from the interests of the great mass of Japanese to be able to press on capital the only real solution to Japan's worst recession ever, because that involves re-distributing income in favour of labour at the expense of capital. A substantial shift of income in favour of labour would substantially increase domestic demand for consumer goods, but it has never been seriously entertained, not even by the current Socialist-led government, simply because it would reduce capital's profits. So while Japanese capital has the institutional means to do almost anything it likes, it is caught between a rock and a hard place by its own inability to make meaningful concessions to labour.

In the crunch, however, both capital and the state have again and again favoured further cost reduction even at the expense of exacerbating the market shortfall. For example, the Hosokawa government was widely urged, not least by Japan's trading partners in Europe and America, to cut income taxes and put spending power into Japanese consumers' pockets, but all it contemplated was to substitute a rise in consumption tax for a cut in income tax (*NW*, 4 October 1993, p. 1). Again, the impact of Japan's growing public works programme continues to favour the needs of capital rather than labour, even since 1991 when the amounts spent by national and local governments leapt by almost 10 per cent to over ¥40 trillion. In 1993 the Ministry of Construction's share of central government projects was a mere three quarters of a percentage point below its 1965 level of 69.4 per cent. So while there has been a lot of recent talk about 'shifting Japan from a pro-producer to pro-consumer society' and public works towards 'non-civil-engineering projects' like 'hospitals, schools, research facilities and old people's homes,' analysis of actual budgetary allocations reveals very little real change. Even Japan's famous employment-adjustment grants are used not so much to keep workers in jobs as to help capital lay them off with minimal disruption. The government's main counter-cyclical weapon, regulation of the official discount (interest) rate, has always aimed at the investor rather than the consumer, and even the cut in this rate to a record low of 1.75 per cent in September 1993 failed to impact on corporate investment, for the simple reason that the main problem remains deficient consumer demand rather than the cost of money (*NW*, 22 March 1993, p. 4; 27 September 1993, pp. 1, 27; 1 November 1993, p. 3; 22 November 1993, p. 2; *FEER*, 25 February 1993, p. 55; 22 April 1993, p. 76;).

DEUS EX MACHINA: INTERNATIONALISATION

Since the main effect of the recessionary process was to multiply the already limited capacity of local spending to clear the output of Japan's consumer industries, and since investment and imports were also dragged into the doldrums to an almost unprecedented degree in post-war Japan, it was to be expected that producers would sooner or later step up their export drives, once again in the hope that this recurring problem could be exported. Table 2.3 shows that by 1991 exports had once again become the main engine of Japan's growth, which had become almost three times as dependent on exports that year as it was in 1985 when Japan's 'excessive exports' provoked a near doubling in the value of the yen.

The consequences of this leap in Japan's export dependence might have been anticipated: an increase in Japan's overseas surplus and another rise

Table 2.3   Dependence on domestic and foreign demand of Japan's GNP growth (%)

	1985	1986	1987	1988	1989	1990	1991	1992
GNP growth rate	5.2	2.6	4.3	6.2	4.8	4.8	4.1	1.5
Domestic demand growth rate	4.0	3.6	4.9	7.4	5.8	5.0	2.7	0.6
Dependence on domestic demand	77	138	114	119	121	104	66	40
Foreign demand growth rate	1.2	−1.0	−0.6	−1.2	−0.9	−0.2	1.4	0.9
Dependence on foreign demand	23	−38	−14	−19	−21	−4	34	60

Source: Nihon bōeki shinkōkai 1993b, p. 44.

in the value of the yen. At the very moment that the slump in domestic demand was beginning to bottom out, new limits were suddenly imposed on external markets by a 15 per cent appreciation of the yen in response to President Clinton's introduction in February 1993 of a new economic package to bolster the US economy against Japan's rising trade surplus. By mid-August the currency approached ¥100 to the dollar, and such signs of recovery as there might have been were swept away. Toyota projected a 66 per cent fall in its half-yearly profits to December, all on top of the debacle of fiscal 1992, the auto industry's worst performance in the post-war era (*NW*, 31 May 1993, p. 9; 16 August 1993, p. 1; 23 August 1993, pp. 1, 23; 22 November 1993, p. 9; 18 April 1994, p. 3).

The expedients open to Japanese capital when it faced the rise of the yen in the mid-1980s were of no avail. Whereas at that time, according to the Industrial Bank of Japan, 77 per cent of the yen's appreciation could be passed on in higher export prices, by the 1990s Japanese exports had to compete with a much wider range of high quality products and prices could no longer be raised with the same degree of impunity. Only 31 per cent of the profits lost from the yen's appreciation were being recovered by higher prices in 1993–94 (*NW*, 18 April 1994, p. 3). The second main strategy pursued in 1986–88 was 'brutal rationalisation' in order to reduce costs, one which by the 1990s was inflaming the basic cause of market saturation while achieving very little in cost reduction, because there was 'no more room left to squeeze production costs' (*TB*, January/February, 1993, pp. 38–9).

Further internationalisation, within the limits of what is affordable, has been seen as a panacea for almost all Japan's current problems. Indeed, it is being treated as the only way simultaneously to reduce costs of production, to find markets commensurate with Japan's productive power and to mitigate conflict with the United States and Europe. However, internationalisation is not a linear process that can be expanded or contracted as if on a continuum, since it involves at least three different processes – investment, trade and finance – each of which contains a number of aspects which do not necessarily work in the same direction. Internationalisation can just as easily magnify a difficulty by removing it from the domestic arena, which is more directly controllable, and then merely transform it into a different but equally intractable external problem, such as the unevenness between exports and imports. Whether or not such internationalisation can find real solutions to the uneven strengths of Japanese capitalism is the subject of the remaining chapters. The quest involves each of foreign direct investment, trade and finance, as well as the effects these have on one another.

3 Foreign Investment Zone Strategies

In terms of Figure 1.2 (p. 6 above), the main bottlenecks which foreign direct investment is intended to displace onto distant peoples are in the production process and in the supply of labour and the other inputs that go into production. It might seem strange then that Japan's strongest suit, its productive power, should require relocation, when the fundamental problems of Japanese capitalism have been on the demand side in the form of market deficiencies for consumer goods. However, we have seen how the attempt to resolve the market problem through export drives not only lifted the value of the yen and along with it production costs to levels that threatened Japan's traditional strength, but also provoked the growing protection of some export markets on which Japanese capital had come to depend. Foreign investment is therefore being driven by the need both to reduce production costs and to preserve or open up markets, but the combinations of these two motives vary, with the emphasis on cutting production costs in the less developed countries and on securing markets in the advanced countries. Production and marketing have thus become increasingly linked in Japanese capital's overseas operations.

Japan's FDI is increasingly being sent into the three regions of North America, Europe and Asia, in which some 85 per cent of the total is already located. In the peak year of 1989, 98 per cent of manufacturing investment went to these regions, and even in 1991, when the recession temporarily interrupted the flow, the proportion was 93 per cent (Shūkan tōyō keizai, 1993b, p. 10). The reasons for largely bypassing the rest of the world are simple as far as Japanese capital is concerned. Latin America is submerged in debt and the sole attraction in that region now lies in its tax havens, the Middle East remains torn by political and military conflict, Africa is stagnant and the old Soviet empire is still too riddled with uncertainty. This narrow regional focus reflects Japanese capital's recognition that the US and Europe are still the world's largest markets and sources of cutting-edge technology, but that Asia possesses the world's greatest production power as well as potential for market expansion. If production in Europe and America is the only sure way to *maintain* access to these increasingly protected markets and keep in touch with their production capabilities, then Japanese capital is happy to sacrifice some degree of

70

profit in order to do so (Shūkan tōyō keizai, 1993b, p. 11). Cost-cutting and market expansion can be achieved by producing in Asia.

Japanese capital gradually had to develop distinctive zone strategies to deal with the growing problems it came to face both within Japan and within each of the main regions into which these problems were being displaced. Its difficulties in the advanced countries centred on the market place, and included the tendency of both Europe and North America towards becoming trading 'blocks', the laying of anti-dumping charges against Japan, demands for higher levels of local content and calls for full reciprocity (equal trade and investment in both directions). Japanese capital's current strategy is to move away from treating the advanced countries simply as markets for its global output or as sources of particular technologies, and to shift planning and regional control to a regional headquarters, from which production, research and development, finance and marketing can all be organised and carried out in relation to one another within each of North America and Europe. Asia too, instead of serving simply as Japan's global production site, is to become a distinct zone in which production, marketing and finance are being integrated at the regional level. By 1998, according to the *Nikkei Weekly* (15 August 1994, p. 2), 'these offshore plants [in Asia] will be more self-sufficient, handling design, parts procurement, manufacturing and sales more-or-less on their own. Already at the end of 1991, of a sample of 25 major companies, 86 per cent either had or were planning to adopt such a three-zone strategy (Shūkan tōyō keizai, 1993a, p. 13).

Fully to understand each of the three main zone strategies, therefore, requires knowing something about the overseas marketing and financial strategies of Japanese capital as well. However, since these are the subjects of Chapters 5 and 6, it is not yet possible to say more about the different zone strategies beyond what is indicated by the patterns that emerge from Japan's foreign direct investments. Nevertheless, these are very revealing and reflect the basic importance of the 'moment' of production in a capitalist system.

In sharp contrast to the late 1980s, FDI in the 1990s is taking place in the midst of a recession characterised by asset deflation and acute problems of liquidity. The most striking effect of the difference has been the plunge in the absolute amounts of money involved, particularly in the unproductive industries and in the regions most closely associated with speculation, that is, finance and real estate in the US, where land prices have since slumped. Many of the speculative direct investments that took place during the 'bubble economy' years (1988–90) have either fallen away or shifted to the more appropriate institutional channels of fund managers, which are examined in Chapter 6. In the lean conditions of the current recession, FDI has become more exclusively a production strategy motivated by the need to cut costs and sell goods, rather than also a form of speculation.

The wave of FDI that is currently mounting and which is likely to peak some time in the late 1990s is thus very different from the wave resulting from the high yen recession of the 1980s. At that time production strategies were guided by both cost-cutting and market considerations, with the former sending companies into low-cost Asia and the latter into the high-wage advanced countries. This time there is to be an overall shift away from the advanced countries, with both considerations directing companies into Asia, especially ones with low wages but with such large populations that even small proportions of high earners translate into considerable market opportunities. The outstanding example is China.

Table 3.1 shows that during the years of the bubble economy the annual amounts invested overseas were in the order of the totals that had accumulated in the entire period up to 1980 or in the period 1981–85, and that the 1990s have been characterised by sharp falls. Nevertheless, even the trough year of 1992 was above the boom year of 1987, indicating that FDI in the 1990s has shifted to a new overall level.

Simple repetition of previous strategies to counter the rise of the yen are being recognised as insufficient, and companies are now planning specifically how to combine low-cost production with market potential, carefully linking these together in particular regions, and even countries, rather than attempting to do so on a global scale. The world is too big and too riddled with rivalries and limits on trade to allow production and market strategies to operate independently in the hope that trade can bring them together at the global level. That hope met with too little success following the previous wave of FDI associated with the high yen recession. Conscious re-structuring of production and market strategies by bringing them together in each region, it is now hoped, will harmonise these two activities and finally solve the problem which has eluded Japanese capital almost throughout its history. Clues to the directions of this restructuring are to be found in the changing geographical and industrial distributions of Japan's FDI.

GEOGRAPHICAL AND INDUSTRIAL DISTRIBUTION

The broad strategies being developed for each of the three main zones are actually adaptations of past strategies and are thus fairly accurately

Table 3.1   Japan's total accumulated FDI, fiscal years 1951–93

	Cases	$ million
1951–1975	13 005	15 943
1976	1 652	3 462
1977	1 761	2 806
1978	2 393	4 598
1979	2 694	4 995
1980	2 442	4 693
1951–1980	23 947	36 497
1981	2 563	8 931
1982	2 549	7 703
1983	2 754	8 145
1984	2 499	10 155
1985	2 613	12 217
1981–1985	12 978	47 151
1986	3 196	22 320
1987	4 584	33 364
1988	6 077	47 022
1989	6 589	67 540
1986–1989	20 446	170 246
1990	5 836	56 911
1991	4 564	41 584
1992	3 741	34 138
1993	3 488	36 025
1990–1993	17 629	168 658
Total (Rounded)	75 029	422 555

Source: Shūkan tōyō keizai, 1994b, p. 1, 290; Ōkurashō, 1994a.

reflected in the country and industrial distributions of Japan's total accumulated FDI. The advanced countries have specifically been selected for investment in the unproductive industries – commerce, finance, real estate and most services – or, in the case of manufacturing, for proximity to markets and leading-edge technology. The less developed countries have served either as tax havens, or as sites of low-cost manufacturing production and raw material procurement, although also for the size of their actual and potential markets.

Table 3.2 ranks the recipients of Japanese FDI in the advanced countries, in the tax havens and in the less developed countries by the *total accumulated amounts* in each at the end of March 1993 and by the industrial distribution of these amounts. Australia, Japan's third most preferred

Table 3.2 Main recipients of Japan's total* FDI as of March 1993 ($ million)

| | Manufacturing# | | | Sub-total | Pri/Min/Cons# | Commerce | Non-Manufacturing | | | | Grand |
	Sub-total	Materials	Machinery				Fin./Ins.	Services	Transport	Real Est	TOTAL
Advanced Countries											
United States	47 086	14 038	**22 812**	113 687	3 862	**20 407**	**21 960**	**27 112**	739	37 465	162 373
March 1994 grand total											177 098
United Kingdom	5 686	437	**4 555**	22 651	1 057	2 313	**11 990**	1 347	100	5 136	29 134
March 1994 grand total											31 661
Holland	3 629	733	2 448	12 587	82	2 815	**6 337**	1 470	90	2 374	16 222
March 1994 grand total											18 397
Canada	3 281	**2 007**	929	3 908	877	666	700	689	30	861	7 207
March 1994 grand total											7 769
Germany	2 025	757	1 071	4 105	28	**2 251**	1 085	293	29	360	6 573
March 1994 grand total											7 334
France	1 838	676	857	3 197	72	889	417	768	5	1 030	5 429
March 1994 grand total											5 974
Tax Havens											
Panama	3	–	1	18 727	216	886	2 290	922	**13 859**	92	18 739
March 1994 grand total											20 129
Cayman Islands	5	5	–	8 130	5	40	**7 380**	482	59	4	8 136
March 1994 grand total											8 977
Luxembourg	116	–	99	5 825	3	3	**5 599**	47	51	22	5 941
March 1994 grand total											5 985
Liberia	–	–	–	5 773	8	–	77	699	**4 127**	69	5 773
March 1994 grand total											6 275
Bahamas	–	–	–	3 695	4	1	**3 307**	30	276	6	3 695
March 1994 grand total											3 733

Table 3.2 Continued

| | Manufacturing# | | | Non-Manufacturing | | | | | | | Grand |
	Sub-total	Materials	Machinery	Sub-total	Pri/Min/Cons#	Commerce	Fin./Ins.	Services	Transport	Real Est	TOTAL
LDCs											
Indonesia	5 177	**3 430**	680	9 224	**7 384**	82	**1 017**	489	10	178	14 409
March 1994 grand total											15 222
Hong Kong	928	182	377	10 421	254	**2 977**	**2 900**	1 851	354	1 707	11 510
March 1994 grand total											12 748
Singapore	**3 251**	1 536	1 197	**4 465**	267	950	1 228	444	734	734	7 837
March 1994 grand total											8 481
Brazil	4 344	**2 491**	1 319	2 835	682	442	1 218	17	12	63	7 195
March 1994 grand total											7 614
Thailand	3 851	1 088	**1 908**	1 880	318	330	138	391	331	359	5 887
March 1994 grand total											6 465
China	1 675	293	**812**	2 632	131	85	25	**1 136**	51	187	4 472
March 1994 grand total											6 136
Malaysia	3 480	1 033	**1 773**	1 322	461	194	189	210	26	215	4 815
March 1994 grand total											5 615
South Korea	2 234	748	**1 058**	2 113	94	39	103	**1 813**	4	57	4 623
March 1994 grand total											4 868
Australia	2 478	996	1 350	18 152	**3 818**	1 815	1 883	2 735	40	**7 362**	20 763
March 1994 grand total											22 667

*Amounts listed by country and industry comprise the combined value of equity and loan capital, but not the minor items listed as 'branches' and 'real estate', whereas grand totals also include these latter amounts.

#In addition to machinery and materials, manufacturing sub-totals comprise textiles and 'other'. Machinery comprises general, electrical and transport machinery. Materials comprise foodstuffs.

d. Non-manufacturing sub-totals includes 'other'. Pri/Min/Cons refers to primary industries, mining and construction.

Source: Ōkurashō, 1993a, pp. 54–73; Ōkurashō 1994.

outlet in the world, does not fit neatly into any of the three categories: its wage structure corresponds to that of an advanced country, but its industrial structure is a mixture of ASEAN's reliance on mining and primary products, the medium-level technological capacity of the NICs and Hawaii's ability to attract investment in real estate and resorts. The figures in bold type in Table 3.2 highlight the degree to which investment in particular countries is concentrated in particular industries. For example, even in the tax havens, Japanese capital has favourites: Liberia and Panama for flag-of-convenience shipping, and the Cayman Islands, Luxembourg and the Bahamas for finance. Australia is targeted mainly for its minerals and real estate, Germany for its commercial potential, Indonesia for its resources, and the ASEAN countries and China for labour-intensive manufacturing.

The shift that has been taking place in the 1990s towards an even greater concentration than before on Asia for productive projects, particularly in the manufacturing industries, can be seen as a return to Japan's traditional focus on this region for its cost-effective investments in manufacturing and raw materials. Tighter financial circumstances have once again forced Japanese capital to pay more attention to the supply side, and Asia's cheap but highly productive labour is pulling in more Japanese companies, particularly smaller ones, than are the advanced countries whose distinctive contribution to productivity lies in technology. This was why productive investments in Asia continued to rise steadily even after the collapse of Japan's bubble economy.

In fact, most of the interest in Asia in the early 1990s was a *consequence* of the recession in Japan, because cost-cutting once again drove companies overseas. However, because this recession was triggered by market shortfalls, this time Asia received a lot of attention for its market potential as well. According to a survey by the Japan Machinery Exporters' Association in August 1994, manufacturing production by Japanese companies in Asia would have leapt by 41 per cent in the fiscal years 1992–94 to account for a quarter of the value of production within Japan, which was expected to shrink by 8 per cent (*NW*, 15 August 1994, p. 2). Table 3.3 shows how different profit rates in 1985–91 reflect these calculations. In most cases, especially in mining and manufacturing, the higher profits earned from production in Asia because of its lower costs just manage to offset the losses incurred in the advanced countries in order to secure markets, chiefly the US. Available data on results for fiscal 1992 suggested that the record net losses incurred in the US were more than offset by rising profits in Asia (*NW*, 15 April 1993, p. 3).

The degree to which the industrial and regional distributions of Japanese investment have actually changed as a result of the most recent

Table 3.3 Operating profit rates as a % of turnover, by region and industry, 1985–91

a) By year and region	1985	1986	1987	1988	1989	1990	1991
Total for overseas subsidiaries	1.3	1.4	2.2	2.9	1.8	1.8	0.4
Those in North America	−0.5	0.7	0.4	0.7	0.2	−0.9	−0.6
Those in Europe	1.7	1.2	2.0	2.3	2.3	3.2	0.0
Those in Asia	2.9	2.3	4.0	4.4	3.8	5.0	3.3
Total domestic companies	3.2	2.8	3.7	4.5	4.7	4.3	

b) By region & industry (1991)	N. America	Asia		Europe	Oceania	Total
		ASEAN	NICS			
Agriculture	8.4	0.4	−71.0	18.3	−8.9	−6.9
Mining	−2.6	36.9	0	−2.2	9.6	3.6
Construction	−2.4	4.5	2.8	6.0	−27.2	1.6
Manufacturing	−1.9	5.2	4.6	−0.6	0.3	0.9
Food	−1.9	−2.0	9.1	4.5	−2.1	0.2
Textiles	−6.7	12.0	3.5	10.2	1.8	6.3
Wood/Pulp	−20.7	1.7	−2.9	−50.3	4.3	−15.9
Chemicals	−1.0	6.0	4.4	1.5	−21.2	1.6
Iron & Steel	−6.3	5.7	3.3	−4.7	3.6	−1.1
Non-ferrous metals	−9.6	−3.9	3.5	−10.5	7.0	−1.5
General machinery	1.2	6.9	6.0	−4.6	7.5	0.8
Electrical machinery	0.0	3.2	3.8	−1.3	0.5	0.9
Transport machinery	−1.2	7.0	8.2	−0.2	−2.1	1.9
Precision machinery	−6.7	3.3	1.7	0.7	4.7	0.2
Petroleum/Coal	−7.6	1.3	−4.6	−6.0	3.9	−5.1
Other	−2.7	9.6	6.1	2.5	0.7	1.6
Commerce	0.2	1.8	1.3	0.7	0.4	0.6
Services	3.4	2.5	10.7	0.9	−11.9	2.0
Other	−21.9	5.2	8.0	−7.1	−17.8	−10.6

Source: Tsūshō sangyōshō sangyō seisakukyoku kokusai kigyōka, 1993a, p. 116; Nihon bōeki shinkōkai, 1993a, p. 76.

recession can be assessed from Table 3.4. For example, the shift away from overwhelming predominance in the advanced countries towards Asia in both manufacturing and the unproductive industries was clearly visible already in 1990, but it accelerated rapidly each year since then. One indicator of this shift is that while in 1986–89 manufacturing investment in Asia was 31 per cent of the amount that went into North America, in 1990

Table 3.4 Japan's FDI by industry and region, fiscal years 1981–93 ($ million)

	N. America	Latin A.	Europe	Asia	Oceania	Other*	Total*
1981–85							
Manufacturing	5 278	1 779	1 244	2 946	266	314	11 826
Agr./For./Fish./Min.	675	307	4	3 239	481	285	4 995
Other	10 942	7 364	4 951	3 312	965	1 790	29 321
1986–89							
Manufacturing	25 824	1 072	5 859	8 073	865	33	41 727
Agr./For./Fish./Min.	970	218	576	1 051	1 071	231	4 117
Other	54 540	19 925	26 525	11 445	7 704	1 924	122 063
1990–93							
Manufacturing	20 985	1 644	11 425	12 759	1 767	405	48 986
Agr./For./Fish./Min.	779	445	699	1 349	1 758	433	5 466
Other	53 924	10 964	25 603	11 443	8 270	2 110	112 310
1990: Manufacturing	6 793	649	4 593	3 068	383	0	15 486
Agr./For./Fish./Min.	246	66	152	286	784	5	1 540
Other	20 111	2 913	8 980	3 605	2 925	547	39 080
1991: Manufacturing	5 868	364	2 690	2 928	405	55	12 311
Agr./For./Fish./Min.	339	88	164	310	419	29	1 351
Other	12 581	2 885	6 232	2 581	2 452	728	27 458
1992: Manufacturing	4 177	267	2 101	3 104	247	161	10 057
Agr./For./Fish./Min.	121	192	119	445	245	379	1 500
Other	10 263	2 259	4 770	2 705	1 914	309	22 220

Table 3.4 Continued

	N. America	Latin A.	Europe	Asia	Oceania	Other*	Total*
1993: Manufacturing	4 147	364	2 041	3 659	732	189	11 132
Agr./For./Fish./Min.	73	99	264	308	310	20	1 075
Other	10 969	2 907	5 621	2 552	979	526	23 551
Total* Manufacturing	54 514	7 277	19 372	28 350	2 302	1 914	115 112
Agr./For./Fish./Min.	3 256	2 359	2 142	8 945	3 360	1 524	22 561
Other	125 384	40 203	59 717	28 030	12 294	6 764	277 732
TOTAL	184 868	49 917	83 673	47 519	18 098	11 798	422 555

*Amounts listed by region and industry comprise the combined value of equity and loan capital, but not the minor items listed under 'branches' and 'real estate', whereas totals also include these latter amounts. The other regions are Africa and the Middle East, both of which attract very little Japanese FDI, and the other industries are mainly the unproductive ones (commerce, finance, services and real estate), but also transport and construction.

Source: Ōkurashō, 1991a, pp. 54–61; 1993a, pp. 46–53; 1994, pp. 3–4.

the proportion was 45 per cent and in 1993 it was 88 per cent. So although it appeared that FDI as a whole had been falling in the early 1990s, the decline was mainly confined to the unproductive industries and to projects aimed at securing markets in the advanced countries. Most forms of cost-cutting investment, if anything, increased fairly steadily, especially in Asia, Oceania and Europe.

ZONE STRATEGIES

Zone strategies involve much more than simply changing industrial patterns of investment in the different parts of the world. Their essence is rather a conscious linking together of investment, that is, production, with marketing and finance as well as all the supporting activities associated with each of the three broad moments in the circuit of capital. In North America, most firms have been moving in this direction for some time. The organisation of local finance, production, sales and distribution has been based on the firm's regional head office, which is usually 100 per cent owned by the Japan head office and which then owns shares in the local subsidiaries (the 'grandchild companies' of the Japan head office). One of the next steps to be taken in North America is adding product development to the regional strategy, a phase which could considerably 'hollow out' functions of the Japan head office, which has hitherto jealously kept to itself all cutting-edge knowhow and design (Shūkan tōyō keizai, 1993a, p. 13). But apart from such *basic development*, which goes to the very heart of the company's existence, a more limited degree of product development can be transferred to each region without difficulty, because such *adaptational design* can be more attuned to local needs and tastes and so benefit greatly from reliance on local resources.

   It will not be easy to implement an identical organisational strategy in Europe, which has received the lowest level of internationalisation by Japanese capital among the three regions. Production bases are still largely inadequate, and sales networks also lag behind the powerful traditional distribution bases of local companies. Although they have bought up some local distributors, Japanese companies have had to rely largely on exports and their own *keiretsu*-linked distribution channels in Europe (Shūkan tōyō keizai, 1993b, p. 13). Japan has also been late in establishing local financial institutions, even though in order to participate in the Eurodollar market many firms established financial subsidiaries in London and Holland in the 1980s. Their assignment in Europe now is to link their financial with their production and commercial operations to form an integrated overall strategy comparable to what has been achieved in North America. One recent move in this direction was by Toyota, which set up distribution centres in both North America and Europe in 1993 to supply parts for maintenance and repair which had previously been distributed from Japan (*NW*, 1 March 1993, p. 9).

The same mission is driving Japanese companies into Asia, but with even greater obstacles in their way because the size and diversity of the region prevents it from forming a single block from which barriers against the movement of goods and services can be fully eliminated. Moreover, a unified strategy can be difficult to pursue in countries where nationalism is still potent, such as Indonesia, which has forced Japanese capital to set up large numbers of joint-venture companies compared to countries whose nationalist traditions have been broken, such as Singapore, where most subsidiaries are 100 per cent owned. However, this latter situation can be equally troublesome, since fully-owned companies often operate with little concern for anyone and simply export their products back to Japan through their own *keiretsu* networks. They rarely bother to work out how to become what are euphemistically called 'good corporate citizens'. This difficulty is one which has plagued Japanese capital throughout the history of its involvement in the region: how to legitimate its activities among the local communities. Within Japan this task of linking *keiretsu* together to pursue their mutual interests falls to Keidanren (the Federation of Economic Organisations) and the state, but outside the country the task is more difficult and the state's reach is more limited. Chapter 6 shows how 'aid' is used to extend that reach.

Japanese capital's Asia-zone strategy is thus still much more closely linked to the Japan head office than constituting a distinct system of finance, production and sales, either for the region as a whole or even for particular countries within it. The main future objective in Asia is therefore to organise production, marketing and finance of each product in relation to business cycles in Japan and in one or more Asian countries simultaneously. Figure 3.1 (slightly adapted from Shūkan tōyō keizai, 1993b, p. 14) summarises the three emerging zone strategies. The Asian zone is not simply separated from the others by its closer proximity to Japan, but by its status as the less developed region from which Japanese capital derives enormous wealth. So while increasingly independent strategies are being forged for each of the three zones, these will always be connected because of the very different benefits Japanese capital derives from each. In relations among the advanced countries, the benefits are more or less mutual, and the networks go both ways and bind the advanced countries into an increasingly unified system, which is held together by the zone networks.

However, in its relations with the Asian zone, the benefits do not flow equally in both directions, and Asia becomes dominated by Japanese networks as well as those of the other advanced countries which are able to muster a comparable presence in the region. As the previously-mentioned

Figure 3.1   Japanese capital's emerging zone strategies

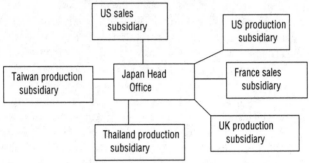

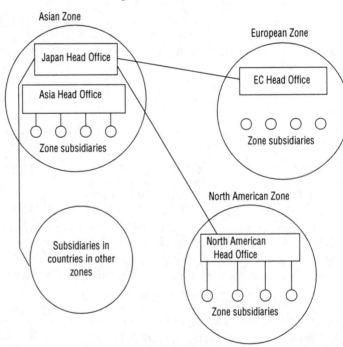

survey by the Japan Machinery Exporters' Association confirmed, 'companies generally regard the Asian manufacturing plants as supply bases for the US, Europe, Japan and Asia' (*NW,* 15 August 1994, p. 2).

ADVANCED COUNTRIES

Japan's investment in North America and Europe is driven by combinations of three broad strategic purposes. The first concerns markets, and it typically expresses itself in the large investments in the American auto industry in order to produce locally what became increasingly difficult to export because of growing protectionism within the United States. A similar situation arose in Europe and met with a similar response, which was quickened by the acceleration of the region towards fuller unity. Much investment in the electrical industry in both regions continues to be driven by the same quest for secure markets. However, related to these investments are a wide range of supporting ones, including component makers, raw material companies (especially in the metals and chemicals industries) and providers of financial and commercial services. Many of the market linkages which are catered for in Japan through the *keiretsu* system also serve Japanese capital abroad when the whole range of activities linked to the key products can themselves be transferred to proximate locations, as they increasingly are in the advanced countries, notably the US. However, many of these market-related investments in the US have come up against limits which have considerably slowed their growth. The US auto industry, partly because of competition from Japan, has reasserted itself and put a halt to the growing market shares of Japanese cars which characterised the 1980s.

The second broad purposes animating Japanese FDI in the advanced countries revolve around the ability to make large capital gains by taking advantage of one of the distinctive features of the advanced capitalist world, that is, its power to appropriate large proportions of the world's surplus and distribute them in the forms of high-priced assets, ranging from real estate to strategically-placed manufacturing companies. The FDI which was sent in by these kinds of speculative considerations reached its height during the boom of the late 1980s, and much of the money that had gone into them is now steered into more carefully planned money management, which is examined in Chapter 6.

The third driving force behind Japanese FDI in the developed countries is the need to keep in touch with the leading-edge technologies of rivals on which international capital's own survival increasingly depends. The 'strategic alliances' struck in the electrical industry, which are examined in detail in the next chapter, exemplify the importance of getting as close as possible to where the technological secrets of competitors are generated in order to appropriate them. These are the investments in the advanced countries which do not fluctuate very greatly and which continue to be fostered regardless of when or where recession might strike.

From the Rich to the Rich

Although there have been fluctuations, these three purposes have continued to send the bulk of the money invested abroad into the advanced countries. But Japan has not been alone in doing so, since all the developed countries are motivated by similar considerations: all the major waves of Japanese FDI, especially that of the late 1980s, coincided with movements from the entire advanced capitalist world which largely went into other parts of the advanced capitalist world. This most recent wave is merely a typical example.

In 1991 worldwide FDI fell by almost 20 per cent over the previous year's amount, the first such decline since 1982. The next year saw another similar decline, confirming that the boom of the 1980s had come to an end. Just as the two oil crises of the 1970s had interrupted the FDI booms of that decade, so did recession reverse the investment trend of the 1980s. Nevertheless, as Table 3.5 shows, the $242 billion injected in 1991–92 lifted the accumulated world total well over the $2000 billion level, of which nearly 85 per cent was accounted for by the top ten advanced capitalist countries alone. For three out of the previous four years, Japan had been the world's top foreign investor. Taiwan, the leading investor from the less developed world, has contributed only about 1 per cent of the world total.

But the advanced countries are not simply the leading sources of the world's FDI, they are also its main recipients. The US led the way throughout the 1980s, absorbing a full 36 per cent of the total in the peak year of 1989, but, following the slump in global FDI in 1991, the UK moved into first place, as revealed by Table 3.6. In all, the twenty leading advanced countries received over 80 per cent of worldwide FDI in the boom period of 1986–91. Among LDCs, there has been a shift from Latin America, which absorbed some 60 per cent of the total that went to LDCs in the 1970s, to Asia, which in the 1980s and 1990s came to receive roughly the same proportion of LDC-investment. But there has also been an overall move from the advanced to the less developed countries, as is normal in recession times when the pressure to reduce costs increases and the need to

Table 3.5 Main sources of recent world FDI flows (international payments, $ million)

	(1986)	1987	1988	1989	1990	1991	1992	Accumulated Total
World total	(93 767)	(139 629)	(171 567)	(216 767)	220 400	184 200	158 000	(2 200 000)#
Advanced	(91 843)	(137 047)	(165 473)	(206 846)	207 400	173 100	146 600	
US (1)	(18 690)	27 181	15 448	36 834	27 109	29 113	34 791	666 300
Japan	(14 480)	19 519	34 210	44 130	48 024	30 726	17 222	248 100
UK	(17 577)	31 286	37 123	35 193	18 728	15 593	16 533	229 300
Germany (2)	(10 506)	9 106	11 432	14 548	22 722	22 364	17 998	156 500
France	(5 403)	8 702	12 753	18 137	26 925	20 496	18 819	147 400
Holland	(4 228)	7 216	3 958	11 428	12 087	12 172	11 160	109 300
Canada	(3 863)	7 071	5 282	4 603	4 200	5 412	3 723	81 900
Switzerland	(1 460)	1 274	8 697	7 850	6 371	6 541	4 898	75 200
Italy	(2 694)	2 328	5 450	2 003	7 246	6 672	5 632	63 900
Sweden	(3 723)	4 520	7 228	9 738	14 055	6 747	1 363	60 000
Top 10	(82 624)	118 203	141 581	184 464	187 467	155 836	132 139	1 837 900
LDCs	(1 923)	(2 582)	(6 094)	(9 921)	13 000	11 100	11 100	n.a
Asia	(778)	(1 889)	(5 286)	(8 534)	11 400	9 500	10 400	n.a
South Korea	(110)	183	151	305	820	1 357	1 048	4 500
Taiwan	(n/a)	704	4 120	6 951	5 243	1 854	1 701	21 000
China	(450)	645	850	780	830	913	4 000	9 400

(1) Calculated on the basis of present value.
(2) Accumulated total as of 1991 at 1991 exchange rate.
#estimate of world total is made on basis of figures in the above sources.

Source: Nihon bōeki shinkōkai, 1994, p. 3; figures in brackets (1986 figures and some totals and sub-totals to 1989) come from Tsūshō sangyōshō seisakukyoku kokusai kigyōka, 1993, pp. 174–6 and are not entirely comparable because they are not revised in ways that Nihon bōeki shinkōkai, 1994 revised its figures. Nonetheless they are useful benchmarks.

preserve liquidity slashes the speculative investments which favour the advanced countries. In 1992 FDI in the latter fell by 21 per cent over the previous year, while it increased by almost the same percentage in the less developed countries. Capital's cost-cutting strategies were encouraged by a whole range of political-economic developments within the LDCs, although most of them resulted from concerted external pressures: structural adjustment programmes, economic liberalisation, deregulation and privatisation (Nihon bōeki shinkōkai, 1993a, pp. 4–5; 1994, p. 3).

Three features of global FDI in the 1980s served to bind the advanced capitalist countries even more closely to one another than before and therefore to affect their own international strategies. First, not just the advanced countries, but the three pivotal regions of Japan, the US and the ten leading EC countries dominated the scene, accounting for a full 90 per cent of the FDI carried out in 1991, a proportion far in excess of their 58 per cent share of world trade that year. Since they also remained its main recipients, foreign direct investment became the most important activity through which their fortunes were tied together: by 1988–90 investments from Europe, Japan and the US had soared to four times their 1979–81 level, whereas exports from these countries had risen only 1.9 times (Nihon bōeki shinkōkai, 1993a, p. 28). Second, the non-manufacturing investments which came vastly to exceed manufacturing investments were even more concentrated in the advanced countries and constituted a special bond amongst them, a theme developed further in Chapter 6. Finally, the proliferation of cross-border M&A activity among the firms of the three regions tied them into ever tighter inter-related networks (Nihon bōeki shinkōkai, 1993a, p. 6). Table 3.7 summarises the directions of the merry-go-round that circulates most worldwide FDI among the countries of the advanced capitalist world.

The common reasons for the fall in FDI from the three advanced capitalist regions in 1990–91 were their worsening profit situations, their falling bank balances and changes in the current and capital accounts of the three leading powers. Falling profits were first manifested in the US, but Japan and Europe soon followed: in each case a decline in equipment investment was closely followed by a decrease in FDI. Taking the industrialised countries as a whole, with the exception of 1975, in each year that the growth in domestic capital formation declined, namely 1974, 1975, 1980, 1981, 1982 and 1991, the growth in their overseas investment also fell. But by 1992 the US had emerged from recession and its foreign investment was once again on the increase, and even though Japan still languished, even it followed suit a year later. Falling profits thus functioned more as a signal to rationalise production at home and to

Table 3.6 Recipients of recent net flows of worldwide FDI (payments basis, $ million)

	1986	1987	1988	1989	1990	1991	1992	1985–91
Advanced	63 684	107 485	128 156	164 234	*159 199*	*114 300*	*90 200*	778 268
US	34 080	58 140	59 420	67 870	48 000	24 000	2 400	295 180
UK	7 309	14 106	18 263	28 165	32 576	21 104	–	126 255
France	3 256	5 140	8 487	10 313	13 223	15 235	–	58 249
Spain	3 451	4 571	7 021	8 428	13 841	10 502	–	49 782
Holland	3 514	2 891	5 037	8 206	11 461	4 123	–	36 606
Germany	722	1 490	875	10 626	8 388	6 591	–	31 414
Italy	–153	4 188	6 789	2 191	6 441	2 403	–	22 926
Canada	1 217	4 198	3 795	2 883	7 018	4 534	2 700	21 872
Japan	230	1 170	–520	–1 060	*1 760*	*1 370*	*2 700*	2 220
EC	–	–	–	–	*86 000*	*68 600*	*70 300*	
LDC	12 368	14 690	22 293	26 252	*29 800*	*41 500*	*49 700*	182 533
Africa	790	1 506	1 348	2 803	977	2 544	*n/a*	10 995
Asia	5 720	8 510	12 735	13 996	18 600	24 000	28 000	82 668
China	–	–	–	–	*3 500*	*4 400*	*11 200*	20 290
NICs	–	–	–	–	*5 900*	*6 000*	–	
ASEAN	–	–	–	6 600	7 500	–	–	
Middle East	2 471	134	1 672	1 710	2 627	*27 154*	–	38 095
Latin America	3 177	4 342	6 066	6 690	7 300	*12 000*	*13 000*	44 140
World	76 052	122 175	150 449	190 486	*200 434*	*170 240*	*139 900*	960 811

Source: The most recent figures, in italics, come from Nihon bōeki shinkōkai, 1994, p. 2. Other figures come from Tsūshō sangyōshō sangyō seisakukyoku kokusai kigyōka, 1993, pp. 174–6. They are not strictly comparable because of slight revisions made by the more recent source.

Table 3.7   Intra-regional FDI, 1980–91

	1980–82	1983–85	1986–88	1989–91	1989–91 1986–88%	1990 1991%
Japan → World	11 819	16 029	68 209	122 880	80.2	–36.0
US → World	29 193	31 444	67 603	92 475	36.8	–17.3
EC → World	63 781	59 461	170 220	247 639	45.5	–9.0
of which intra-EC	6 435	8 377	41 273	59 295	43.7	–2.1
3 Regions → World	104 793	106 934	306 032	462 994	51.3	–18.3
Intra 3-Regions						
Japan → US	4 318	6 970	36 583	62 035	69.6	–40.5
Japan → EC	1 439	2 907	12 135	28 747	136.9	–27.7
US → Japan	782	1 321	3 445	1 165	–66.2	–87.8
US → EC	16 798	15 074	27 063	40 937	51.3	49.6
EC → Japan	172	169	272	2 063	658.5	–43.0
EC → US	29 099	30 889	92 984	64 601	–30.5	–58.9
Intra-Regional Total	52 608	57 330	172 482	199 548	15.7	–32.2
Intra-Regional per cent	50.2	53.6	56.4	43.1	–	–

Source: Nihon bōeki shinkōkai, 1993a, p. 7.

reconstitute its relationship with foreign investment. Japan's response to changes in the trade cycle was thus unexceptional (Nihon bōeki shinkōkai, 1993a, p. 15).

Technology Tie-Ups

Especially in recession times, the cost-cutting motives for FDI tend to come to the fore and eventually to overshadow the pressures on liquidity resulting from shortages of credit and speculative monies. Among the advanced countries, such cost-cutting motives focus on the technological spinoffs which flow from the investments and which induce firms to conclude strategic alliances with one another (to be discussed in the next chapter). The most important technology which they tend to keep at home and which can only be accessed through FDI is product design and development. Hence FDI helps Japanese companies keep in touch with *basic developments* in Europe and North America in order to revitalise what they most require to retain their competitive edge. But as zone strategies take shape so does the need to *adapt* leading technologies to local conditions, which comprise combinations of social arrangements that affect industrial relations and organisation. For example, in Japan the *kanban* system is used to generate technological change for the parent companies of the vertical *keiretsu*, often through leaving it up to the 'child' companies to fathom out for themselves the best ways to improve productivity. But in the US and Europe, Japanese companies have to gear their technological development to the power they can expect to wield over their local component makers, and zone strategies have to involve more than merely enticing component makers from Japan into their service overseas. This is because a major problem in the advanced countries has been the independence of many of their local suppliers, which have resisted attempts to incorporate them into Japanese networks (*keiretsuka*). Hence, accompanying their attempt to link together local production, local marketing and local finance, they have tried to add local research and development, partly by increasing their research bases in the advanced countries. By the end of 1991, there were 70 overseas research and development bases, close to a quarter of which had been set up in the previous two years (seven in 1989, fourteen in 1990 and twelve in 1991). While some companies, such as Canon, undertake R&D all over the world, most focus on the US. Nissan, for example, is apparently trying to 'globalise R&D' by assembling the 'world's best brains' in its R&D base in Detroit (Nihon bōeki shinkōkai, 1993a, pp. 83–5).

The different zone strategies being developed by Japanese capital in this crucial area of technology are revealed in a major recent study by JETRO, which examined the technical tie-ups between Japanese and foreign companies that were concluded in the year to June 1992. Cooperation at the cutting-edge of technological progression, that is, in joint R&D and in computer-related industries, was found to occur almost exclusively among the advanced countries, whereas the great majority of agreements with Asian countries involved introducing new technology to the region and securing low-cost OEM supplies (original equipment manufacturing, in which a company puts its brand name to a product supplied by another company). These latter 'classical technical alliances', in which a more advanced country transfers technology to a less developed one, have been contrasted to what have been called the new 'strategic alliance' among MNCs from advanced countries (Burton and Saelens, 1994, p. 59). Table 3.8 presents the results of this study, although since some of the key correlations of the study could not be included in it, they will require further spelling out.

The most important feature of Japan's cooperation with the US is its focus on technology exchange, joint research and development, sales and business cooperation, and the microchip and computer industries. While

Table 3.8   Technology tie-ups in July 1991–June 1992, by region
(% & numbers)

Purpose	US	EC	Asia	Other	Cases
Introduce technology	24.7 (76)	32.1 (99)	31.8 (98)	11.4(35)	100(308)
Joint R&D	51.3 (78)	32.2 (49)	10.5 (16)	6.0 (9)	100(152)
OEM supplies	32.9 (28)	17.6 (15)	43.6 (37)	5.9 (5)	100 (85)
Sales cooperation	46.9 (22)	34.0 (16)	17.0 (8)	2.1 (1)	100 (47)
Business cooperation	47.7 (41)	25.6 (22)	18.6 (16)	8.1 (7)	100 (86)
Other forms of cooperation	34.4 (43)	28.8 (36)	32.0 (40)	4.8 (6)	100(125)
Total	35.9(288)	29.5(237)	26.8(215)	7.8(63)	100(803)
Industry					
Microchips	72.7 (32)	15.9 (7)	11.4 (5)	0.0 (0)	100 (44)
Computers	59.4 (60)	27.7 (28)	9.9 (10)	3.0 (3)	100(101)
Motor vehicles	15.8 (12)	31.6 (24)	30.3 (23)	22.3 (17)	100 (76)
Electrical machinery	21.4 (12)	39.3 (22)	28.6 (16)	10.7 (6)	100 (56)
Precision machinery	43.5 (10)	30.4 (7)	26.1 (6)	0.0 (0)	100 (23)
General Machinery	29.9 (40)	35.1 (47)	32.1 (43)	2.9 (4)	100(134)
Chemicals	46.3 (25)	29.6 (16)	18.5 (10)	5.6 (3)	100 (54)
Textiles	20.0 (7)	31.4 (11)	45.7 (16)	2.9 (1)	100 (35)
Sub-total	(198)	(162)	(129)	(34)	(523)
Other	(90)	(75)	(86)	(29)	(280)
Total	(288)	(237)	(215)	(63)	(803)

	Technology	Joint R&D	OEM supply	Sales	Business	Other
Microchips	9.1	43.2	22.7	–	18.2	–
Computers	21.8	31.7	15.8	10.9	13.9	–
Motor vehicles	65.8	10.5	–	–	–	–
Electrical machinery	44.6	33.9	10.7	–	10.7	–
Precision machinery	30.4	26.1	26.1	–	–	13.0
General machinery	59.7	14.2	9.7	–	9.7	–
Chemicals	38.9	20.4	–	11.1	–	14.8
Textiles	45.7	–	28.6	20.0	–	–

Source: Nihon bōeki shinkōkai, 1993a, pp. 90–1.

the same purpose dominates agreements with Europe, the industrial focus
is on general machinery and motor vehicles. Technology exchange, when
supplied by European to Japanese companies (59 cases) centres on general
machinery (21 cases, with seven in textiles and four in chemicals),

whereas when supplied by Japanese to European companies (37 cases) the focus is on the car industry (twelve cases, with seven in general machinery, four in electronics and four in computers). The main country from which Japan gets licensed technology in Europe is Germany (ten cases), while the main country to which it licenses technology is the UK (seven cases). Among the reasons for this pattern is that Japanese car companies have made the UK their production base in the region, and technology is often licensed to component makers. Out of the total of 237 agreements between Japan and Europe, Germany was involved in 57, the UK in 55 and France in 41, that is, the three European members of the advanced capitalist world's inner-inner circle, the G-5 (Nihon bōeki shinkōkai, 1993a, pp. 90–1).

The JETRO study revealed a very different but even more distinct pattern in Japan's technical agreements with Asia. Out of the 98 cases of technology licensing, 97 were ones in which Japanese companies supplied the technology for production in Asia. If these are added to the 37 cases of OEM supplies commissioned by Japanese companies from companies in Asia, the importance to Japanese capital of low-cost production in the region is apparent (63 per cent of all tie-ups in Asia fell into this category). Of the 97 licences supplied by Japanese companies to the region, three industries account for 62 per cent of the total: 29 in general machinery, nineteen in motor vehicles and twelve in electrical machinery. The industries comprising the 37 cases in which Japanese companies rely on OEM supplies from Asia are more diverse, with ten in textiles, five in general machinery, three in chemicals, three in microchips, three in electronics and two in computers. The weight of the NICs was found to be greater among the recipients of licences, while ASEAN, China and Vietnam received the main orders of OEM supplies (Nihon bōeki shinkōkai, 1993a, p. 92).

The question of technology control, development, transfer and access has been repeatedly singled out as the most important aspect which sets an advanced country apart from a less developed one. Although the ability to maintain technological supremacy once it has been obtained also rests on having the whole range of supporting activities, which broadly divide into marketing and financial services to back up what has been achieved in the production place, the most important overall supporting functions are ones which assist control, development and access to advanced technology. That, in the final analysis, is the main problem faced by the less developed world, and that problem in turn is the key to the patterns of Japan's FDI in Asia and its corresponding regional strategy.

LESS DEVELOPED COUNTRIES: ASIA ZONE

Among the less developed countries, the predominance of Asia as the most favoured target of recent worldwide FDI is unmistakable, with that region receiving more than the combined shares of Africa, the Middle East, Latin America and Eastern Europe. Asia has experienced three foreign investment waves in recent times: the first was in 1971–73, the second just before and after 1980, while the third and largest began in the latter half of the 1980s and has continued into the 1990s although at a slightly reduced pace. The source of that investment in the 1990s has moreover shifted more and more towards countries within rather than outside the region, notably Japan. Table 3.9 shows that its main recipients have also been changing from the NICs to ASEAN and more recently to China, Vietnam and South Asia.

The single most important reason for this ranking of the different parts of the region is that it reflects their relative actual and potential levels of labour productivity, which, once some basic infrastructure is in place, depends most heavily on their relative wages. The advanced countries can themselves bring in the most efficient plant and equipment in order to get the best of both worlds: high technology in combination with low wages. However, where the local infrastructure is inadequate, sufficiently reduced wages can still pay for the 'aid' needed to bring it up to required standards. Because of this importance of wages, capital in search of lower costs for its labour-intensive industries has had to re-locate from the higher waged NICs, not just to ASEAN countries, but from these to China, Vietnam and South Asia. Even ASEAN wages have been forced up in response to the recent foreign investment booms, especially in Thailand and Malaysia. China is currently the preferred alternative, not just because of the meagre payment of its workers (Table 3.10), but also because of its market potential, its political 'stability' and the enthusiastic welcome it gives to foreign investors. A survey by the Japan Export Import Bank in 1993 (Kaigai tōshi kenkyūjohō, January 1994, p. 26) revealed that 87 per cent of Japanese companies indicated a desire to invest in China some time in the future. Their reasons were to open up new markets (62 per cent), to secure cheap labour (47 per cent) and to re-export goods back to Japan (22 per cent). Many firms are already reaping the benefits without actually investing in China themselves, simply by 'consigning production [on an OEM basis] of low-end products to Hong Kong firms, which operate many low-cost plants in China' (*NW*, 3 May 1993, p. 9). Vietnam and India could be the next in line. Having obtained rights to oil field development in Vietnam in 1992 and recommenced yen loans around the

Table 3.9 Asian recipients of world FDI in 1986–92 ($ million, approval basis)

	1986	1987	1988	1989	1990	1991	1992
ASEAN	2 060.6	3 930.8	11 949.8	14 774.0	26 143.0	16 804.0	23 129.6
Philippines	78.2	166.6	451.5	804.2	961.3	782.9	629.8
Malaysia	203.4	297.7	767.5	1 255.5	2 302.5	2 254.8	2 185.1
Thailand	952.8	1 946.3	6 249.1	7 995.3	14 128.2	4 988.0	10 021.8
Indonesia	826.2	1 520.3	4 481.6	4 719.0	8 751.0	8 778.2	10 293.0
NICs	1 876.4	3 411.9	3 648.4	4 684.8	4 630.8	4 947.0	n.a.
South Korea	353.7	1 060.2	1 282.7	1 090.3	802.5	1 396.1	894.6
Taiwan	770.4	1 418.8	1 182.5	2 418.3	2 301.8	1 778.4	1 461.4
Hong Kong	205.4	245.3	359.3	342.8	302.8	348.0	n.a.
Singapore	546.8	687.6	823.8	833.4	1 223.7	1 424.6	1 710.9
China (promised)	2 834.0	3 709.0	5 297.0	5 600.0	6 596.0	11 977.0	58 123.5
(executed)	1 874.0	2 314.0	3 193.0	3 393.0	3 487.0	4 366.0	10 723.1
Vietnam	n.a.	n.a.	362.8	537.7	600.0	1 220.6	1 905.0
Sri Lanka	21.9	36.6	65.4	69.4	65.5	211.7	602.7
India	84.4	83.1	172.3	195.2	73.3	234.9	1 499.9
Pakistan	158.8	6.3	-62.7	27.8	71.8	n.a.	n.a.
Bangladesh	31.7	56.9	57.7	14.1	53.0	15.9	n.a.

Source: Nihon bōeki shinkōkai, 1993b, p. 26.

same time, Japan is expected to increase its investment, even though as late as 1993 it was still only in seventh place among foreign investors. Developments could be more rapid in India following the recent relaxation of that country's foreign investment laws: Japanese FDI soared almost ninefold in 1992 to $122 million, although the following year it dropped back to a mere $35 million (Nihon bōeki shinkōkai, 1993a, p. 180; Ōkurashō, 1994a).

Japan's main interest in the region is in surplus creation by means of cheap Asian labour, in the extraction of raw materials which are not available in Japan and more recently in expanding markets for Japanese goods. Cheap labour is the pre-eminent common enticement throughout the region, which continues to provide more of Japan's overseas workers than North America and Europe combined in spite of the latter's rapid growth since the mid-1980s, as revealed by Table 3.11. The shift towards Asia and ASEAN within the region is again particularly evident, as is the move away from the minor regions and even from the US. Other features of Japan's FDI have also been noted before, but are more pronounced when indicated by the numbers of workers involved, who are after all the source of the value *created* overseas: these are the focus on Asia for surplus creation, chiefly in manufacturing and in electrical machinery, as well as

Table 3.10   Annual manufacturing wages, by country, 1988–91/2

| | ¥1,000 | | | Index (US = 100) | |
	1988	1991	1992	1988	1991
US	322.8	389.8	–	100	100
Japan	354.5	404.0	409.8	110	108
Singapore	85.2	138.9	–	26	37
Hong Kong	92.7	145.0	–	29	39
Taiwan	91.7	148.4	163.9	28	40
South Korea	81.6	147.0	150.1	25	39
Mexico	62.5	108.7	–	19	29
South Africa	84.2	109.3	–	26	29
Malaysia	36.4	–		11	–
Thailand	22.4	29.6	30.0	6.9	7.9
Philippines	21.8	22.2	24.1	6.7	5.9
Indonesia	10.1	–	–	3.1	–
China	6.1	6.1	6.4	1.9	1.6
Pakistan	9.7	–	–	3.0	–

Source: Rōdō daijin kanbō kokusai rōdōka, 1994, p. 266.

Table 3.11 Workers in Japan's overseas subsidiaries, by industry, region and fiscal years

	North A.	Latin. A.	Asia	ASEAN	NICs	Europe	Oceania	Total
1984	156 959	131 103	488 074	268 243	–	73 091	39 057	925 754
1987*	261 518	134 735	587 026	220 588	326 953	119 344	46 269	1 168 349
1990	466 804	115 070	676 010	333 892	288 046	218 359	51 038	1 549 669
1991	444 289	105 519	744 520	394 330	277 459	250 608	56 368	1 620 829
Agr./For./Fish.	2 405	2 232	11 123	10 116	65	70	2 137	19 631
Mining	641	1 514	310	246	0	145	4 311	12 688
Construction	1 459	1 089	10 602	7 656	2 098	772	15	14 100
Mfg.	292 638	90 583	656 392	352 981	237 552	177 777	33 197	1 261 012
Commerce	120 390	6 413	38 617	13 807	24 211	62 684	9 737	238 975
Industrial breakdown (%):								
Manufacturing	65.9	85.8	88.2	89.5	85.6	70.9	58.9	1 261 012
Textiles	0.2	13.2	9.8	11.1	7.4	1.1	0.3	92 020
Chemicals	5.9	6.5	4.3	4.2	4.5	4.6	1.0	78 262
General M.	5.8	5.0	2.4	1.3	3.9	6.1	2.8	65 687
Electrical M.	15.3	21.6	36.7	35.8	41.1	26.3	4.2	435 796
Transport M.	13.4	28.9	15.1	17.7	9.7	14.8	28.2	257 264
Commerce	27.1	6.9	5.2	3.5	8.7	25.0	17.3	238 975
Services	2.7	0.7	1.5	1.2	2.8	1.4	8.2	37 588
Other	4.3	6.6	5.1	5.8	2.9	2.7	12.0	83 254
Total	100.0	100.0	100.0	100.0	100.0	100.0	100.0	1 620 829

*Since 1987, the data include 'grandchild' companies and Singapore is no longer included in ASEAN.

Source: Tsūshō sangyōshō sangyō seisakukyoku kokusai kigyōka, 1993a, pp. 126, 149–50.

the concentration on the advanced countries for marketing-related investments.

Up until around the mid-1980s, Japanese capital had organised a clear division of labour between the NICs and the ASEAN countries, the main role of the former being low-cost manufacturing production, that of the latter supplying cheap raw materials. However, a number of developments came to a head in the mid-1980s to make ASEAN take over as Japan's (and that of many advanced countries) main site of low-cost production, not just in Asia, but world-wide. The growing export strengths of the NICs resulted in rises in their exchange rates and wage levels, and Japan's own currency hikes suddenly quite radically altered the relative wage costs in Japan, the NICs and ASEAN. The importance of the NICs in manufacturing shifted to products requiring intermediate technology, such as VCRs and colour TVs, even though manufacturing as a whole declined in importance, notably in Singapore and Hong Kong. The former increasingly attracted investments in commerce and distribution, while the latter has been functioning as a gateway to China, also mainly in the distribution industry. Table 3.12 shows how FDI in the two 'manufacturing' NICs, South Korea and Taiwan, has been falling in line with the recession, while that in the more 'unproductive' NICs has held its own.

In contrast to the development in the NICs, Table 3.13 shows the amounts invested in each of the main ASEAN countries in 1989–92 by the two leading advanced countries and by all four Asian NICs. The revival of FDI in the region in 1992 following the slump in 1990–91 confirms its continued attractiveness, especially to Japanese and American firms and especially in comparison with their investment in the

Table 3.12　Japan's FDI in Asian NICs, fiscal years 1988–93

	S. Korea $US mil	Hong Kong HK$ mil	Singapore S$ mil	Taiwan US$ mil
1988	483	1 662	747	372
1989	606	1 898	1 902	494
1990	284	1 785	840	446
1991	260	925	613	405
1992	225	735	670	292
1993	245	1 238	644	292
1951–93	4 868	12 748	8 481	3 719

Source: Shūkan tōyō keizai, 1988–1994b, Ōkurashō, 1994a.

Table 3.13   FDI in main ASEAN countries, 1989–92 ($ million)

		Malaysia	Thailand	Indonesia	Philippines	Total
Japan	1989	393	3 524	769	157	4 843
	1990	658	2 754	2 241	306	5 911
	1991	531	1 760	929	210	3 430
	1992	308	1 967	1 503	72	3 850
US	1989	47	549	348	111	1 056
	1990	69	1 091	153	59	1 372
	1991	166	1 130	276	87	1 659
	1992	223	1 233	923	62	2 441
NICs	1989	543	2 011	1 197	322	4 075
	1990	1 001	2 696	2 598	384	6 679
	1991	1 015	1 583	1 981	68	4 647
	1992	345	939	2 646	65	3 995
World Total	1989	1 255	7 996	4 719	804	14 774
	1990	2 367	8 029	8 750	961	20 863
	1991	2 255	4 987	8 778	783	16 863
	1992	2 298	10 021	10 313	286	22 708

Source: Nihon bōeki shinkōkai, 1993a, p. 179, 1994, p. 167.

Asian NICs. Investment from the advanced countries in Asia is primarily propelled by cost-reducing strategies, and so the shift from the NICs to ASEAN and other even lower-wage countries is most marked in their case. Investment in Asia from other Asian countries shows little change in its geographical location, since it has always come mainly from the NICs and gone mainly into the less developed ASEAN countries. Liberalisation of investment regulations in China and Vietnam has simply meant that these low wage countries have been added to those from the ASEAN region.

If one looks purely at the total value of recent investment in Asia, the most rapidly increasing sources have been the complex networks of capital belonging to ethnic Chinese within the region which link Hong Kong, Taiwan and Singapore to China, on the one hand, and to ASEAN, on the other. Of the $32 billion invested in China and $81 in ASEAN in 1985–92, the shares of the three ethnic Chinese NICs were 69 per cent and 25 per cent respectively. Japan's shares were only 11 per cent and 21 per cent, while those of the US were 9 per cent in each (Nihon bōeki shinkōkai, 1994, p. 14). If South Korea is included, the combined shares of the four NICs in Malaysia soared from 24 per cent in 1986 to 49 per cent in 1990, 16 per cent to 62 per cent in Thailand (mainly because of a $6.1 billion investment from Hong Kong in Thailand's fast railway), 11 per cent to 30 per cent in Indonesia and from 10 per cent to 40 per cent in the Philippines. Japan's shares averaged around a third of the total in each of these countries, having fallen to that level in Thailand but risen to it in the Philippines. However, the NICs share of investment in ASEAN countries as a whole slumped back from 49 per cent in 1990 to 28 per cent in 1991, leaving Japan once again as the undisputed leader (Watanabe 1992, p. 136–41; Nihon bōeki shinkōkai, 1993a, p. 20).

However, with very few limited exceptions, the capital of ethnic Chinese in the region either concentrates on the unproductive industries associated with its historical origins in colonial trade, or where it does have some sort of industrial base, this derives predominantly from its links with industrial capital in some advanced country. Japanese and US capital, on the other hand, concentrate on the productive industries in which their leading-edge technological power is institutionalised and reproduced through the (inter-linked) multinational corporations that spearhead their investments. While the Chinese networks are held together through *personal* ties cemented by mutual ownership of stock, the networks of international capital are based on *functional* relationships between institutionalised industrial, financial and commercial seats of power. Although the latter are also cemented together by things like cross-share-holdings and personal ties, their *power* is not limited to the strength of these linkages, as it is in the case of the Chinese networks. Rather, it rests on technological leadership and functional connections among independently powerful industrial, financial and commercial institutions.

Japan's FDI thus differs widely from NICs' FDI, most significantly in the technological levels of the industries targeted: NICs' investment is concentrated in services and light manufacturing, particularly textiles and footwear – the NICs supplied 88 per cent of FDI in the Indonesian textile industry in 1985–90 – while Japanese investment favours raw materials and machinery, chiefly electrical and transport machinery (Watanabe 1992, p. 136–41). Second, Japanese investment embraces a wide range of connected activities, such as the procurement of components as well as their assembly into sophisticated products like VCRs and colour TVs, whereas NICs' investment is not supported by such *functional* networks, but focuses on *particular* labour-intensive *branches* of industries. Often these are even brought into the service of Japanese networks, as is common for Taiwanese firms which produce components for Japanese electronic companies in Malaysia. The only pattern which compares to the Japanese one involves South Korean electronic giants like Samsung, but their nexuses are qualitatively smaller and less frequently used outside the country (Sekiguchi, 1992, p. 171; Kohama, 1992b, pp. 240–2;).

Currently, the most prominent recipient of worldwide FDI in Asia is China, whose radical liberalisation policies (including the liberalisation measures relating to FDI in April 1990) have attracted colossal investments from overseas Chinese in particular, but also from international capital generally. By 1991 the 'freeze' following the Tien-An-Men massacre had begun to thaw, and foreign investment that year topped its peak level of 1989, only to increase fivefold in 1992 and show every sign of maintaining the pace in 1993. Table 3.14 shows the amounts on a promised basis in the period 1989–March 1993.

Clearly, Japan is the most consistent of all the advanced countries to invest in Asia, although in most cases it is closely followed by the US with which it cooperates closely in order to preserve their joint technological leadership. Japan's zone strategy focuses overwhelmingly on low-cost production in the labour-intensive branches of the manufacturing industry, and it increasingly involves a deliberate division of labour among different groups of countries according to their capacities to operate the various levels of Japanese technology and according to their different wage levels. However, some countries, such as China and Vietnam, are in addition to their cheap labour forces also important for their potential markets and, like the ASEAN countries, for their raw material supplies.

In comparison to the advanced capitalist countries, Japan's FDI is still modest in terms of the ratio of overseas production it has brought about (an average of about 6.4 per cent, compared to more than three times that for the US) and in terms of its relation to GNP. Even before World War

Table 3.14   FDI in China, by country of origin and year
($ million, promised basis)

	1989	1990	1991	1992	Jan–Mar. 1993
Hong Kong	3 160	3 833	7 215	40 044	15 881
Taiwan	431	890	1 389	5 543	2 130
Singapore	111	103	155	997	413
US	641	358	548	3 121	1 209
Japan	439	457	812	2 173	459
Other	818	955	1 858	6 246	5 201
TOTAL	5 600	6 596	11 977	58 124	25 293

Source: Nihon bōeki shinkōkai, 1993b, p. 27; 1994a, p. 227.

Two, when Japan was carving out its empire in classical fashion by means of military conquest, FDI played only a very minor role. The reasons for this lateness lay in the way sections of Japan's own domestic work force provided the kind of low-cost labour which other powers found in their colonies. If Japan almost succeeded in making the transition from feudalism to modern capitalism without either becoming a colony or acquiring colonies, this was because it had its own internal quasi-colonial labour force with which to achieve the same end. After the war, this same low-cost labour force enabled Japanese capital to accomplish a 'miraculous' transformation of the country without any reliance on what Europe, North America and Australia all used as an alternative to the colonial labour to which their access had been cut off following de-colonisation: labour migration.

LABOUR MIGRATION: WORKERS FROM ASIA ZONE

Japan's use of migrant labour has lagged behind that of the West, for the same reason that FDI lagged. There was no need to bring migrants into the country during the boom of the 1950s and 60s because Japan's own labour force contained segments who were as cheap as any who could be imported but who were subjected to far more effective discipline by Japan's hierarchical tradition of social control than could be imposed on outsiders. And during the 1970s, when the other advanced powers began to count the cost of the racism they used to make migrants substitute for the loss of their colonies, Japan was able to use a new expedient to avoid having to face the same problem. The foreign investment boom that began in the late 1960s provided widespread access to even cheaper labourers and without any of the responsibilities that resulted from importing them. By the time the limits on Japan's internal colonies began to assert themselves, a process that began with the wage rises of the 1960s and early 1970s and culminated in the rise of the yen a decade later, the obvious solution was to move production to alternative labour supplies rather than vice versa.

But there were some jobs and some industries which were extremely difficult to re-locate. Buildings required in Japan had to be built at home, and the same applied to many services. These two industries were ones in which Japan's own domestic 'colonial' labourers had by this time congregated, with Burakumin (the 'village' people of ancient times who had been set aside as an 'untouchable' caste) and Japanese of Korean ancestry in the building industry and women in the service industry. But even Japan's 'invisible races' (De Vos and Wagatsuma, 1966) were increasingly unable to meet the demand for the full range of non-exportable 3-D jobs (3-K in Japanese) requiring colonial labour, the dirty (*kitanai*), dangerous (*kiken*) and difficult (*kitsui*) tasks that remained within the country. They are most heavily concentrated in the construction and sex industries, the strongholds of the *yakuza* (gangsters).

The rise of the yen was the main catalyst which pulled in streams of Asian migrants, most of them illegally, into these kinds of jobs: the men into the construction industry and into the small manufacturers which were hardest hit by the rising yen, the women into the sex and fast food industries. Japan's inexperience in confronting racism meant the government could turn a blind eye to the whole process, preferring to let the *yakuza* organise the operation, including the discipline needed to ensure total compliance. If this involved kidnapping, murder, confiscation of passports and robbery, not to mention the 'normal' problems faced by migrant labourers stemming from poverty and discrimination by employers, landlords, schools and social services, then the official response would be denial.

However, by the end of the 1980s the problem had reached such proportions, both in terms of the numbers of illegal migrants and the abuse they received, that even the government finally recognised the need for some 'basic plan for immigration control', which is what the 1989 amendment to the Immigration Control Act sought to achieve. The purpose of the Basic Plan was to legalise as much of the labour migration as possible in order to control it, by widening the categories of legitimate entry so that *unskilled* workers could somehow be authorised to work. However, although 'people of Japanese ancestry' (145 000 in 1992, plus as many spouses of Japanese), 'entertainers' (84 000), 'trainees' (43 600) and various 'students' (about 100 000) have come to constitute a significant group of migrants who can one way or another find their way into legal 3-D jobs, about another 300 000 'temporary visitors' are also estimated to be bucking the system with the tacit blessing of the authorities, who continue to prosecute overstayers working illegally in a show of concern to keep Japan Japanese and the *yakuza* brokers, who feed most voraciously on them, in check. One study found that nearly 80 per cent of all prosecuted 'overstayers' were brought into Japan by these 'brokers', who are still the main 'regulators' of the total of about 800 000 unskilled migrant labourers at the disposal of Japanese capital (Hōmushō nyūkoku kanrikyoku, 1994; Umetani, 1993, pp. 94, 134; Komai, 1994; Iyotani, 1994).

In 1992 there was an 89 per cent leap in the number of prosecutions to 67 824, of whom 93 per cent were overstayers (almost 90 per cent on temporary visitor's visas) and 92 per cent were working illegally (Hōmushō nyūkoku kanrikyoku, 1993). The jobs they were found to have been doing were predictable: 39 per cent were construction workers (accounting for half the men), 25 per cent were in production process jobs (many in the metals, chemicals and fast food industries) and 8 per cent were hostesses (accounting for half the women, if one adds those who owned up to being 'prostitutes'). If their countries of origin are any guide to where the as yet undetected mass of illegal migrants hail from, then the latter would break down into Malaysian (23 per cent, of whom almost 80 per cent were men), Iranian (22 per cent, almost all men), Korean (also 22 per cent, with 80 per cent male), Thai (12 per cent, of whom two-thirds were women, probably 'entertainers'), Filipino (6 per cent, almost 60 per cent female, also probably 'entertainers'), Chinese (5 per cent, evenly distributed) and Pakistani (2 per cent, almost all men) (*Ibid,* p. 2). The actual countries from which Japan's illegal migrants have come fall somewhere between this distribution of the persons who were prosecuted and the distribution of those migrants who were found to be working legally: in 1993, 85 per cent of Asian 'entertainers' were from the Philippines, with Korea, China, Taiwan and Thailand providing most of the remainder. Among trainees, almost 90 per cent of whom were Asian, 45 per cent were from China, 12 per cent from Thailand, 10 per cent from each of South Korea and Indonesia, 8 per cent from the Philippines and 6 per cent from Malaysia (Hōmushō nyūkoku kanrikyoku, 1994, Table 6). One study estimated that almost 20 per cent of the 300 000 illegal migrant workers in Japan in May 1993 came from Thailand, with another 10 to 13 per cent from each of Iran, Malaysia, South Korea, the Philippines and China, and a further 2 to 3 per cent from each of Bangladesh, Pakistan, Taiwan and Myanmar (Kuwahara, 1993, p. 149). Among these migrant communities, unemployment averaged 15 per cent in 1993, with some 20 per cent among the Iranian population (Komai, 1994, p. 128).

Since some illegal migrants are known to have been paid wages as low as ¥100 an hour, which is not much more than they would get in their own countries, the Basic Plan had to meet some very high expectations among employers. The government's answers to these included 'trainees' and various categories of 'students', who just like illegal migrants could work without being 'authorised to work'. Studies by the Pacific Asia Resource Centre have found that few 'trainees' do much more than the most unskilled jobs, most receive little training, and the fiction that they are not working excludes them from protection, in terms of wages and hours, by the Labour Standards Act (Hatade, 1992).

If looked at from other points of view than Japanese capital's need for a colonial labour force, the restricted access to legal work in Japan is one of the many 'imbalances' (Lincoln, 1993) which characterise Japan's relations with the outside world. Japanese travel abroad in three times the numbers that foreigners enter Japan (it was twice in 1985), and from all accounts they find legal jobs with at least three times the ease that foreigners do in Japan. Western imperialism, with its longer history and greater intensity, has provoked more widespread racism as well as anti-racist struggle, from which it now benefits in comparison to Japan, where anti-racist political activity is still in its infancy.

FDI IN JAPAN: CAPITAL FROM THE ADVANCED COUNTRIES

If Japan imports workers from the same countries into which it re-locates its labour-intensive foreign investments, then it imports capital from the same countries into which its capital-intensive investments have been primarily directed. Although the entry of foreign capital into Japan was until comparatively recently heavily restricted by law, this was for different reasons from the regime imposed on foreign labour and was designed to protect local capital from western competition. In spite of the gradual removal of these restrictions that began in the 1960s and that is yet to be completed, the entry of FDI into Japan has never remotely reached the proportions of Japanese FDI abroad. The annual amounts were less than one billion dollars right until 1987, and from that year to 1990 they remained no more than around two or three billion each year, partly because the rising yen and the inflation of asset prices that accompanied it made foreigners very nervous. It seemed that foreign investment finally began to take off in 1991, when the total amount leapt to $4.4 billion from $2.8 billion the previous year, but the mounting recession brought a small decline the following year and in 1993 a further sharp drop to some three billion. Moreover, the ratio of Japan's FDI to FDI in Japan has remained astronomically high, still averaging 15.47:1 at the end of 1991. It was 14.99 for the US; 24.18 for the UK; and 10.81 for Europe as a whole (Nihon bōeki shinkōkai, 1993a, pp. 521–4). Even though the bubble economy had forced foreign firms to sharpen their strategies in Japan, with some such as Bosch and Apple succeeding remarkably well (*Ibid*, pp. 101 ff.), FDI is still largely something that leaves rather than enters Japan. The persistence and enormity of the imbalance is all the more puzzling in the context of the new world order of increasing inter-connections among the advanced countries. The Japanese network system, on which the distinctive power of Japanese capital abroad depends, has given to capitalism at home its own idiosyncrasies, and problems. No matter how much the government might desire or 'declare' the openness of this system to foreign participation, its distinctiveness makes it a very hard one for newcomers to operate in successfully, no matter how great their technological might. The apparently endless conflict over US and European access to government contracts is one of the costs the system has had to tolerate in relation to the other advanced countries. Like the question of access of goods to the Japanese market, it seems neither to explode into full-scale conflict nor show any sign of resolution. The more-or-less equal power of the advanced countries tends to produce stalemates on issues of fundamental difference, which soon give way to the more important areas in which they can, and must if they wish to retain their power over less developed countries, cooperate.

Table 3.15 shows that North American, European and 'Japanese' FDI (i.e. foreign firms already in Japan) accounted for 86 per cent of the total as of March 1994. Most of this was in the machinery and chemical industries, which Table 3.16 shows accounts for the bulk of FDI in Japanese manufacturing. Apart from Hong Kong, the remainder comes from Singapore, Taiwan and China and is concentrated in commerce, services and light manufacturing, such as textiles and components for electrical

Table 3.15   FDI (reported) in Japan, by origin of foreign company, fiscal years

Country/Region	1989 $mil	1990 $mil	1991 $mil	1992 $mil	1993 $mil	1951–93 $mil	per cent
North America	1 667	806	2 098	1 424	1 079	13 504	45.1
US	1 642	664	1 334	1 337	930	12 174	40.7
Canada	35	142	764	87	150	1 330	4.4
Europe	625	1 361	1 348	1 450	1 026	8 823	29.5
Holland	248	734	323	207	283	2 277	7.6
Switzerland	87	142	176	513	149	1 995	6.7
UK	81	54	431	254	67	1 403	4.7
Germany	144	259	172	125	110	1 357	4.5
France	25	74	51	167	79	598	2.0
Other	40	98	195	184	339	1 193	4.0
Hong Kong	63	62	60	37	31	644	2.2
Japan*	198	231	639	334	344	3 399	11.4
Other	297	317	193	839	597	3 563	11.9
TOTAL	2 860	2 778	4 339	4 084	3 078	29 933	100.0

*Foreign companies in Japan.

Source: Nihon bōeki shinkōkai, 1993a, p. 524; Ōkurashō, 1994a.

Table 3.16   FDI (reported) in Japan, by industry and year, 1989–93

Industry	1989 $mil	1990 $mil	1991 $mil	1992 $mil	1993 $mil	1951–93 $mil	per cent
Manufacturing	1 172	1 570	1 896	1 609	1 564	16 839	56.3
Machinery	808	806	439	653	672	7 940	**26.5***
Chemicals	203	438	902	710	459	5 230	**17.5**
Petroleum	8	30	173	46	50	991	3.3
Metals	40	151	79	40	150	917	3.1
Foodstuffs	17	29	124	9	87	533	1.8
Glass, ceramics	6	6	5	73	44	249	0.8
Rubber/leather goods	29	1	56	–	4	156	0.5
Spinning	0	18	9	5	6	89	0.3
Other	61	92	109	73	92	735	2.5
Non-Manufacturing	1 688	1 208	2 444	2 476	1 514	13 094	43.7
Commerce/trade	544	730	783	1 194	879	5 800	**19.4**
Services	138	263	545	823	207	2 636	**8.8**
Finance/insurance	180	109	890	147	34	1 752	5.9
Real estate	647	24	69	230	90	1 208	4.0
Communications	23	21	99	48	27	323	1.1
Transport	47	12	26	19	43	227	0.8
Construction	9	9	23	0	1	114	0.4
Other	100	40	8	14	233	1 034	3.5
TOTAL	2 860	2 778	4 339	4 084	3 078	29 933	100.0

*Bold type highlights significant amounts.

Source: Nihon bōeki shinkōkai, 1993a, p. 524; Ōkurashō, 1994a.

companies. In fiscal 1993 Singapore and Taiwan provided a full 13 per cent of all FDI in Japan. According to a MITI survey at the end of fiscal 1991, 70 per cent of Asian firms in Japan were in commerce, with a further 6 per cent in services, 5 per cent in electrical machinery and 3.4 per cent in textiles. The contrast with the advanced countries is greatest when the proportions of employees are compared: 81 per cent of employees in US firms and 64 per cent in European firms in March 1992 were in manufacturing, while 67 per cent of employees in Asian firms were in commerce (Tsūshō sangyōshō sangyō seisakukyoku kokusai kigyōka,1993b, pp. 22, 42; Ōkurashō, 1994a).

The most powerful foreign companies in Japan are actually joint ventures involving giant American or European companies, such as Fuji-Xerox (between Fuji Photo Film and Britain's Xerox) and Tonen (between a number of companies in the Fuyo *keiretsu* and America's Mobil and Exon). But the main other success stories have also required tie-ups with leading Japanese firms, for example, Apple, which has close to 10 per cent of Japan's personal computer market (it is only behind NEC with over half the market and Fujitsu, with which it runs neck and neck), has over 2 000 dealers in Japan, including Minolta, Fuji-Xerox and Canon (*NW*, 26 April 1993, pp. 1, 8). According to a recent study (Kojima, 1992, p. 19), the main purposes of European and American companies in Japan are similar to those of Japanese companies in their countries of origin: to expand their sales in the Japanese market (41 per cent), which is the main attraction for automakers, to establish themselves in the Asian region (21 per cent), which is most important in finance, information and resorts, and finally to take advantage of Japanese technology (12 per cent), which has pulled in most chemical, pharmaceutical and electrical firms.

In addition to their links with Japanese firms, foreign companies in Japan operate through their own networks much in the way that Japanese firms abroad do. For example, in the chemical and electrical industries, the advanced countries import about a third of their supplies, about half through the channels of the investing companies (Tsūshō sangyōshō sangyō seisakukyoku kokusai kigyōka,1993b, p. 109). However, among Asian firms in the electrical industry, less than 8 per cent of supplies are imported, since without their own comparable networks they tend to get their supplies from the local Japanese companies for which they typically make components. In commerce, however, just over half their supplies tend to be imported, of which over three-quarters come via the investing company. As far as their markets are concerned, manufacturing companies from the advanced countries export very little, only about a tenth, whereas Asian companies export from a third (in the electrical industry) to a half (in textiles) their output, almost all of it back to Asia. Again the distinctiveness of the regions of the advanced capitalist world compared to Asia takes the same forms we have repeatedly encountered. If there are networks in Asia which link investment and trade, then these are confined to the labour-intensive industries which have been allocated to the Asian countries concerned. Otherwise the networks are almost entirely commercial and involve the marketing of goods procured in Japan (*Ibid*, pp. 212–15).

CONCLUSION

If all the features of Japanese foreign direct investment are looked at in relation to one another in the advanced and the less developed countries, the nature of the emerging zone strategies can be more precisely mapped out. In the advanced countries, Japanese FDI functions to consolidate and inter-link the fortunes of the two sides, each strengthening and stimulating the other to achieve even greater competitive power, which becomes Japanese capital's overall zone strategy. However, because there are few sources of countervailing power in the less developed countries to interact in mutually supportive ways with Japanese capital, the latter operates in Asia much more in accordance with its own requirements, making its strategy in the Asia zone largely into one of *appropriation*.

In the advanced countries of Europe and North America, where most of the money from Japan is invested, the bulk of it goes into those sectors that distribute surpluses which are created elsewhere, especially in the less developed world. Money that does flow into the productive industries is there either to keep a hold on the local market or on local technology, which these days is developing most prolifically in the information and communications-equipment related industries. Entry and survival in these industries requires such monumental costs that even the leading MNCs from the advanced countries cannot cope without forming strategic alliances with one another, thereby ensuring that they alone, in alliance with one another, have the capacity to withstand the competition. Far from being ruined by the power of rivals, capital in the advanced countries is stimulated by foreign investment, which serves as a source of innovation and continual rejuvenation.

The technological linkages that consolidate the power of international capital in the production place are also served by numerous forward and backward linkages involving both parties in the market place: components for the manufacturing industries can be acquired with almost equal ease from local as from Japanese suppliers, and even when they cannot, in the long run the competition serves to strengthen the productive power of local producers and to stimulate markets for them. If, as is revealed in Chapter 5, in some cases Japanese capital brings in especially low-cost components from its Asia zone, the effects are no different from the similar import policies of the local American or European companies, even though they can at times be more telling. This is because although US firms in particular are constantly having to compete with low-cost imports from their own subsidiaries in Asia, when the imports come from Japanese subsidiaries they enter via the networks of a powerful rival rather than their own networks.

Similarly, few destructive effects result from the destinations chosen to market the products of Japanese subsidiaries in the advanced countries. If they are sold locally the same stimulation is given to the domestic industry, whereas if they are exported this has little impact on the overall structures of production and trade. The only anticipated development associated with Japanese FDI and its zone strategy in the advanced countries which has not yet materialised is its reciprocity. The more or less equal investment by European and American capital in one another's domestic environment cement their relationship into the increasingly full-fledged mutuality that characterises the current world order, an integration which Japanese capital will only fully achieve when it can host as much FDI at home as it sends abroad.

In the less developed zone of Asia, Japan's investments are in the mining, labour-intensive manufacturing and raw-material related industries for the predominant purpose of *surplus creation*, which is greatest when low wages can be combined with advanced technology. Japanese capital achieves this most fully in the electrical industry, whose largely female labour force is in some cases, such as South Korea, paid only half the male rate, and its presence either destroys local competitors or forces them into some or other unequal alliance with it, either as component makers or as 'local receptacles' (Yoshihara, 1988) to legitimate its presence. In either case, the only kind of technical transfer that tends to occur is the capacity to perform a limited range of tasks (Morris-Suzuki, 1992), whose sole use is to the Japanese companies which commission them. Because the result is the undoing of the forward and backward linkages among local producers (through which they used to buy and sell to one another) and because plant and equipment as well as sophisticated components come from Japan, the overall technological effect is the destruction rather than the enhancement of local knowhow. In this kind of situation where Japanese capital has *appropriated* and integrated into its own networks the productive power of local capital, it ceases to make the same difference whether the final products are sold in the domestic market or exported. Although the latter severs the linkages among local business to a greater degree, since Japanese capital often already dominates the *productive* networks, its sales strategies simply tend to reinforce what has already been achieved. The new emphasis on production for local markets in Asia then merely allows the same Japanese goods to conquer the markets which had previously been attacked by means of exports from Japan. Since investment and trade are thus intimately linked, the fuller implications of Japan's zone strategies as well as the degrees to which they can be combined into an overall global strategy need to await analysis of Japan's trade. Before that is possible a more detailed examination of how Japanese capital operates in the different zones in a few key industries must be looked at through the window of foreign investment as well.

4 Foreign Investment Industrial Strategies

In comparison to the almost blind 'rush' into Asia in the late 1980s, a combination of conscious and unconscious motives has driven Japanese businesses to become increasingly selective in making their foreign direct investments (FDI) in the 1990s. What separates the flood of money that went into overseas ventures in the late 1980s from the current trends is that Japanese investors have moved away from the indiscriminate projects that at times accompanied the bubble economy to ones with a much more proven capacity to solve particular difficulties for them. We have seen how these are falling into increasingly distinct geographical and industrial patterns, each associated with some or other persistent problem within Japan, and each contributing to the development of distinct zone strategies.

Up until the late 1980s Japanese capital tended to see its foreign investment in terms of *global* opportunities to solve the problems that most stubbornly resisted domestic solutions. At first the strategies for doing so emerged piecemeal within each industry, which sought out the geographical locations that seemed best suited to its peculiar difficulties. Because of *keiretsu* and other linkages among a number of industries, these strategies were not entirely uncoordinated with one another and resulted in some powerful overall trends. And so by the end of the 1980s this global approach began to give way to a more consciously-planned three-zone strategy, which would have been put into effect by the state in the pre-war world order, or guided by military considerations had Japan been in the seat of the US after the war. As it happened, the framework of the three-zone strategy was built by the *keiretsu* network system, which laid a firm foundation for the links that would be more deliberately forged within each main region between production, marketing and finance as well as between component manufacture and assembly. Regions that could not develop towards this higher level of integration were gradually phased out.

The purpose of this chapter is to look at the new zone strategies through the windows of the main industries in which Japanese FDI has been concentrated, because this allows us to trace the function of each zone in relation to the others and of particular countries within zones. The contrast between the cooperative and mutually-strengthening relationships among the advanced capitalist zones, on the one hand, and the exploitative relationships between them and the Asia zone, on the other, stands out strongly in this light. The new 'zonal division of labour' that serves Japan's new imperialism in its pivotal industries – electrical machinery, motor vehicles and their main 'backup services' – is thus the theme of this chapter. Although securing supplies of key raw materials remains an important motive for investment in Asia, this issue is reserved for discussion in the next chapter.

In a comprehensive study on the production plans of major firms in response to the high yen in 1993, JETRO found that a full 60 per cent had strategies that in one way or another involved expanding overseas production, with less than one per cent intending to cut overseas production. The following were the questions from which only the main strategy could be selected:

1. Rely on domestic production for the domestic market and foreign production for the overseas market (25.5 per cent)
2. Expand overseas production (22.9 per cent)
3. Cut domestic production and expand overseas production (10.5 per cent)
4. Cut overseas production and expand domestic production (0.5 per cent)
5. Expand domestic production (40.5 per cent)

The fifth strategy – chosen mainly by companies in the food, pharmaceuticals and iron and steel industries – is associated with Japan's previously-dominant industrial structure of raw-material processing that had already over the past twenty years been rationalised both at home and abroad (Steven, 1990). To a lesser extent the same applies to the other strategy which involves domestic production, the first, which was selected mainly by firms in the chemical, rubber, textiles and transport-machinery (notably ship-building) industries. However, textile and clothing firms, the basis of Japan's prewar industrial structure, were most fully associated with the third strategy of shifting production overseas *from* Japan. The second strategy of simply expanding overseas production was the favourite among companies in Japan's cutting-edge industries, which build their strength at home and then move abroad for particular purposes, especially electrical machinery and components (Nihon bōeki shinkōkai, 1993b, p. 86).

JETRO also surveyed the degree to which the rise of the yen made new foreign investments necessary. Out of 857 responding firms, 40 per cent said that it did, while only half that proportion said it did not. The industries in which the inducement was the greatest were textiles and clothing, rubber products, non-ferrous metals and machinery, especially precision machinery. But the most outstanding revelation of the study was the very strong focus on countries with large *potential* markets. JETRO found that a full 35 per cent of its surveyed firms considered China to be the most attractive country in the world, a proportion three and a half times the next favourites (US and Europe with about 10 per cent each). Indonesia and Malaysia were selected by around 8 per cent, Thailand 7 per cent, with the NICs from 2 to 4 per cent. China's role is obviously pivotal to Japanese capital's Asia-zone strategy. Classified by type of investment, expansion of productive capacity stood out with 54 per cent, followed by expansion of markets with 30 per cent (Nihon bōeki shinkōkai, 1993b, p. 87).

Another view of the various pressures to internationalise production are the differences in existing overseas production ratios of the main branches of machinery. While the proportion of Japan's total production that is produced overseas was only 6.4 per cent in 1990 (compared to 3.2 per cent in 1982 and the US's 21 per cent), among the companies that had shifted abroad it was highest in general machinery (39 per cent in 1990), electrical machinery (22 per cent), and transport machinery (19 per cent) (Chūshō kigyōchō, 1994 p. 67; 1993 Tsūshō sangyōshō sangyō seisakukyoku kokusai kigyōka, pp. 20–21). Surveys conducted by the Small and Medium Enterprise Agency suggest that these ratios are all likely to increase substantially in the 1990s: of the companies with overseas subsidiaries, the proportion whose overseas production is more than 30 per cent of total production was expected to increase from 12 per cent to 19 per cent by around 1997, as revealed by Table 4.1. However, the table does not show variations among industries. It is thus time to examine what has actually been happening in the main industries concerned: electrical machinery, motor vehicles and 'unproductive' services.

Table 4.1   Shares of overseas production of parent firms (per cent of companies)

| | Overseas Production as Share of Total Production | | | | | | |
	0–5	*5–10*	*10–20*	*20–30*	*30–40*	*40–50*	*Over 50*
5 years ago	65.2	17.4	8.7	6.5	———	2.2	———
Now	34.7	24.5	24.5	4.1	8.2	2.0	2.0
5 years hence	16.5	20.8	29.2	14.6	6.3	6.3	6.3

Source: Nihon bōeki shinkōkai, 1993a, p. 87.

ELECTRICAL MACHINERY

More specific regional strategies as well as recent changes in them can be seen by breaking down the broad industrial categories examined in Chapter 3 and concentrating on developments since the mid-1980s. In some cases, there have been conscious decisions *not* to internationalise a particular activity. For example, while most semi-conductor makers have been increasing their overseas production in order to counter the effects on costs of the rising yen, Toshiba has decided to keep all semi-conductor production in Japan on the grounds that this is cheaper than going through the expensive process of setting up operations in new environments (*NW*, 6 September 1993, p. 8).

In terms of the amounts invested in fiscal years 1986–91, electrical machinery stands out as the largest of all branches of manufacturing, accounting for $18.9 billion or 7 per cent of the total, of which $9.7 billion (51 per cent) was invested in the US and $4.4 billion (23 per cent) in Europe. However, Table 4.2 shows that while North America and Europe were most prominent in money terms, Asia received the bulk of the cases, suggesting a division of labour between the more costly high-tech investments and the cheaper labour-intensive ones. It also shows that the reduction in FDI associated with the recession has not affected electrical investments in Asia anything like it has affected those in the advanced countries.

North American and European Zones

In the US and Europe, which have received the more costly higher-tech investments, not just to preserve Japan's market access in product areas where the advanced countries are themselves strong, but in order to gain access to the technology which feeds that strength, investment has been choked off much more abruptly by the credit crunch. But it is likely to be revived just as abruptly once the slump shows definite signs of coming to an end and domestic investment starts to pick up. Then, the need to expand markets in the advanced countries and to be close to cutting-edge knowhow will send Japanese companies back into the US and Europe. This latter purpose is of special importance in the electrical industry, in which fierce worldwide competition drives an ever-expanding race along the technological 'super-highway'. Some background to this race is necessary, especially the R&D records of the different advanced countries as well as the patterns of world trade in technology.

Table 4.2 Japan's FDI in electrical machinery, by region and fiscal years
($ million.)

		N. America	Latin A.	Europe	Asia	Oceania	Other*	Total
1981–	Cases	248	23	81	255	3	4	613
85:	$ million	1 493	94	272	289	15	5	2 166
1986–	Cases	388	12	134	613	5	1	1 153
89:	$ million	6 532	229	1 616	2 515	34	3	10 929
1990–	Cases	249	21	106	455	9	4	844
93:	$ million	5 466	238	3 658	3 122	65	8	12 559
1990:	Cases	89	6	48	121	5	–	269
	$ million	2 413	101	2 305	827	37	–	5 684
1991:	Cases	57	4	23	120	1	4	209
	$ million	868	46	501	871	2	8	2 296
1992:	Cases	50	7	26	95	1	–	179
	$ million	740	80	434	540	22	–	1 817
1993:	Cases	53	4	9	119	2	–	187
	$ million	1 445	11	418	884	4	–	2 762
1951–	Cases	1 103	151	378	2 092	26	19	3 769
1993:	$ million	14 152	775	5 675	6 471	132	31	27 235

* Africa and the Middle East

Source: Ōkurashō, 1991a, pp. 54–61; 1993a, pp. 46–53; 1994, p. 4.

Japan's total expenditure on R&D compares favourably with that of other advanced countries and continues to surge ahead of that of its European rivals and to catch up with that of the US, reaching almost ¥14 trillion in 1992 compared to almost ¥20 trillion (but worth ¥30 trillion in real terms) in the US and ¥6 trillion (¥7 trillion in real terms) in Germany. From capital's point of view, however, the money is managed more efficiently in Japan, with much larger proportions of the total coming from and going straight back into industry as opposed to government institutions and universities. Three main industries dominate the scene in Japan to an exceptional degree: in 1991 electrical machinery absorbed 34.7 per cent, chemicals 15.9 per cent and transport machinery 15.5 per cent, with all other industries together receiving the remainder of 33.9 per cent (of which just under a third went to general and precision machinery) (Kagaku gijutsuchō, 1994, pp. 97–8, 104–5, 108).

In spite of this tremendous concentration of Japan's R&D expenditure on electrical machinery, the country's overall deficit in technology trade, especially with the US but also with Germany and France, stems mainly from the large deficit in this industry, which almost wipes out the entire surplus earned from technology trade in transport machinery. In 1991, the ratios of Japan's technology trade (exports divided by imports) with these countries were 0.39, 0.53 and 0.5 respectively. The only surplus with a major country has been with the UK since 1987, and by 1991 this ratio had reached 2.27 (*Ibid.* p. 140). Each year the electrical machinery industry absorbs a larger proportion of the new cases of leading-edge technology to be introduced into Japan. In 1991 this had risen to 62.6 per cent, or 1988 out of 3117 cases (*Ibid.*, pp. 145–7). Table 4.3 shows the overwhelming weight of the US electrical machinery industry in Japan's imports of technology. Although trade with North America in this industry runs six to one in the latter's favour, much of this comprises royalties from technologies which were introduced some time in the past. The balance is a bit more equal than that if only the most recent cutting-edge technologies are considered. Needless to say, Japan imports almost no technology outside North America and Europe, and its largest export market is Asia. The importance of the electrical machinery industry to Japanese capital and of maintaining access to US technology is thus unquestioned.

Proliferating Strategic Tie-Ups

Because the electronic industry is the main one in which international capital from the different advanced countries will continue to act out their rivalries in the 1990s, it is simultaneously the most competitive and the

115

Table 4.3   Japan's technology trade by industry and region in 1991 (¥billion)

	Total	Asia*	Exports			Total	Imports		
			N. Am.	Europe	Other		N. Am.	Europe	Other
Construction	21.3	17.0	0.7	0.9	–	0.7	0.3	0.4	–
Mfg.	348.0	152.7	116.2	66.1	9.0	393.2	274.8	117.5	0.9
Chemicals	58.8	15.7	27.3	14.4	0.7	67.4	40.9	26.4	–
Elec. Mach.	105.8	62.2	19.5	21.8	1.1	161.3	123.3	37.9	–
Trans. Mach.	102.1	34.3	48.7	13.3	5.4	56.5	45.2	11.1	0.2
TOTAL	370.6	170.5	117.1	67.1	9.0	394.7	275.2	118.6	0.9

*Excludes western Asia.
Source: Kagaku gijutsuchō, 1994, p. 350.

most riddled with cooperative agreements among rivals. In contrast to the 'classical' technical alliances in which a more advanced country transfers technology to a less developed one, this new type of 'strategic alliance' among MNCs from advanced countries competing in the same market is both defensive and offensive (Burton and Saelens, 1994, p. 59). It is designed both to gain access to the technical advantages possessed by rivals, and well as to use one's own advantages to keep rivals in check. Because of the enormous R&D costs involved in developing new products in the electrical industry, these alliances are most numerous among Japan's leading electrical firms, which are being drawn to the advanced countries to further their productive strategies, and not just to maintain their markets.

Two broad types of firms are involved, each with its own preferred combination of marketing and technological requirements. The powerful vertical *keiretsu* with technology as their core competence, such as Hitachi, Toshiba, Fujitsu, Matsushita and NEC, are in search of partners with marketing strength as well as industrial strength, and they frequently agree to supply US firms on an OEM basis as a way of penetrating the US market. However, companies which began as consumer goods producers, such as Sony, Sharp and Sanyo, are stronger in marketing but weaker in heavy machinery technology, which constitutes their main need in the US (Burton and Saelens, pp. 61 ff). A range of examples from the three leading branches of electronics – microchips, computers and multi-media – are worth looking at in order to illustrate the depth and complexity of the alliances that are being forged. Even though the broad patterns into which they fall are similar to the ones revealed by the JETRO study cited in the previous chapter (Table 3.8), a view from within the electrical industry has its own story to tell. A large number of acronyms to express the idiosyncratic jargon of the industry are used in the following pages, such as DRAM instead of 'dynamic random-access memory', but it is not necessary to know exactly which technologies they refer to in order to follow the point of the discussion.

a) Microchips

The need to avoid excessive investment and to share risks has made strategic cooperation especially important among chip makers (Teece, 1992). This takes four main forms, two of which – complementary production and OEM supplies – are strongly motivated by marketing considerations, while the other two – technical cooperation and joint development – are more thoroughly motivated by the quest for technology.

i) Complementary Production

The first type of strategic alliance is the least frequent and can be illustrated through a typical example of complementary production between Toshiba and Motorola. The former supplies DRAM (dynamic random-access memory) technology while the latter supplies MPU technology, and production takes place in a new joint factory in Japan, Tohoku Semiconductor. In the latter half of the 1980s Motorola moved out of DRAM production and secured its supplies from this joint factory, selling them under its own brand. Within Japan, a fifty-fifty joint venture with Toshiba, Nippon Motorola Micro Electronics, is responsible for semiconductor sales. Toshiba, on the other hand, uses Motorola as a second source of MPUs in order to stabilise its supply. Motorola has been pursuing an aggressive strategy in Japan, particularly in relation to the cellular telephone market which was deregulated in April 1994, about the same time that Motorola opened up a semi-conductor design centre in Sendai. The relationship between these two giants covers a wide range of activities in which both sides have strengths that add to their existing strengths and help maintain their *even* development (Nihon bōeki shinkōkai, 1993a, p. 93; *NW* 28 June 1993, p. 8; 28 March 1994, pp. 1, 8).

ii) Original Equipment Manufacturing

Although OEM agreements typically tend towards the 'classical' rather than the strategic variety, in which an advanced country supplies technology and then receives OEM supplies which it sells under its brand name, there are also various OEM arrangements between the advanced countries that benefit both sides much more equally. For example, Texas Instruments receives CMOS-ASIC and logic goods from KTI Semiconductor, which is a ¥55 billion company it has jointly set up with Kobe Steel. Texas Instruments wanted to reduce its investment but expand its productive power, while Kobe Steel wanted access to its technology. Agreements among companies from the advanced countries also tend to have many dimensions which go back and forth and bind them together as a whole. Texas Instruments thus also receives OEM-supplies of 256KSRAM (static random-access memory) chips from Hitachi, while Hitachi receives OEM supplies of DRAMs from NMB Semiconductor, which had previously supplied another international company, Intel (Nihon bōeki shinkōkai, 1993a, pp. 92–4). Table 4.4 lists some of these and other recent OEM arrangements involving Japanese companies in the microchip industry. Agreements with less developed countries are few and far between in this industry, because even the ability to receive technology and produce OEM

Table 4.4   Examples of original equipment manufacturing agreements
in microchips

Japanese Company	Partner Company	Content of OEM Arrangement
NEC	National Semiconductor	NS receives 256KSRAMs
Toshiba	Motorola	T supplies DRAMs, M supplies MPUs
Hitachi	Goldstar Electronics	G provides DRAMs
Hitachi	NMB Semiconductor	NMBS provides DRAMs
Hitachi	Texas Instruments	TI receives 256KSRAMs
Matsushita	Intel	I receives EPROMs and FMs
Sanyo	Micron	M receives memory-goods
Sanyo	SGS Thomson	SGS T supplies chips
Sharp	Intel	I receives FMs
Oki	Catalyst	C receives EEPROMs
Oki	SGS Thomson	SGST produces DRAMs
Mitsubishi	SGS Thomson	M makes EPROMs
Matsushita	IBM	IBM supplies RS/6000 workstations

Source: Nihon bōeki shinkōkai, 1993a, p. 94; *NW*, 15 February 1993, p. 9;
6 September 1993, p. 8.

supplies requires a technological capacity which is rare outside the
advanced countries. The Hitachi arrangement with Goldstar is one of the
few to have been concluded in recent years. At the opposite end of
the spectrum, cooperation among advanced countries in exploiting Asian
labour is revealed by an agreement between Matsushita and National
Semiconductor, in which the latter supplies the former with bipolar and
MOSS chips from its factory in Malaysia (*NKS*, 13 June 1993, p. 7).

iii) Technical Cooperation

In the past, the technical superiority of US chip makers had made Japan
the main recipient of technical knowledge, but with the growth of Japan's
technical power in the 1980s, exchanges have become more reciprocal and
are now expressed in growing numbers of cross-licences. For example, in
October 1990, NEC and AT&T concluded cross-licensing agreements in
the field of ASICs, while Hitachi, which supplies 256KSRAM technology
to Texas Instruments, has also concluded an ASIC cross-licence agreement with VLSI Technology. Toshiba has also become a major supplier of
technology, particularly to European companies: Siemens receives DRAM

Table 4.5   Technical cooperation in microchips

Japanese Company	Partner	Content of Technical Cooperation
NEC	AT&T	ASIC cross-licenses
Toshiba	Siemens	S receives DRAM and LSI technology
Toshiba	Zilog	Z supplies MPU technology
Toshiba	SGS Thomson	SGS T receives CMOS logic technology
Toshiba	LSI Logic	Gehtoa ray technology cross-licenses
Hitachi	Texas Instruments	TI receives 256KSRAM technology
Hitachi	Goldstar Electronics	Goldstar receives DRAM technology
Hitachi	VLSI Technology	ASIC cross licenses
Sanyo	Vitelic	EPROM, EEPROM technical cooperation
Sanyo	Micron	Sanyo receives DRAM technology
Sony	AMD	AMD receives SRAM manufacturing technology

Source: Nihon bōeki shinkōkai, 1993a, p. 95.

and LSI technology, while SGS Thomson receives CMOS logic technology (Nihon bōeki shinkōkai, 1993a, pp. 94–5). Table 4.5 summarises these and other recent cases of technical cooperation in the semi-conductor industry. Once again, companies from less developed countries are conspicuously absent, not just because they have little to offer Japanese companies, but because they do not have the capacity to absorb very much either. The sole example is the agreement between Hitachi and South Korea's Goldstar.

iv) Joint Development

Massive development costs in the microchip industry have made joint development particularly necessary in recent years. In next generation DRAMs, for example, Toshiba cooperates with IBM and Siemens, and Hitachi works with Texas Instruments, while in next generation SRAMs, NEC works with AT&T, and Fujitsu with Motorola. In the field of FMs (flash memories), the cooperation is between NEC and AT&T; Toshiba & IBM; Fujitsu and AMD; and Sharp and Intel (Nihon bōeki shinkōkai, 1993a, pp. 94–5; *NW*, 19 April 1993, p. 9). The NEC relationship with AT&T is one of the most extensive, and involves developing production technology in 21 areas for cell-based ASICs. But NEC also works with

Table 4.6   Joint development in microchips

Japanese Company	Partner Company	Content of Cooperation
NEC	AT&T	FM, SRAM, ASIC
Toshiba	IBM, Siemens	next generation DRAM
Toshiba	IBM	FM
Hitachi	TI	Next generation DRAM
Fujitsu	AMD	FM, in US & new Japanese factory in 1995
Sharp	Intel	FM
Matsushita	Intel	Etching of next generation ICs
Sanyo	SGS Thomson	MPEG-based chips for multimedia

Source: Nihon bōeki shinkōkai, 1993a, p. 95; *NW*, 19 April 1993, p. 9; 24 May 1993, p. 9; 21 June 1993, p. 8; 28 June 1993, p. 8; 27 September 1993, p. 8; *NKS*, 22 June 1993, p. 10.

America's Mips Technology, with which it developed a new RISC chip in 1993 (for handheld computers) which is twice as fast as those of its competitors. The 1990s will see growing strategic agreements of this kind among Japanese and US companies in particular. Joint development exemplifies the equality of power between the two sides: for example, Matsushita independently developed the basic technology for etching next generation ICs (integrated circuits), but it has worked jointly with Intel, which sent researchers to Japan in 1992, to refine the technique (*NW*, 24 May 1993, p. 9; 27 September 1993, p. 8). Table 4.6 lists some of the main recent cases.

b) Computers

Since technological development in computers is also difficult to achieve independently, multiple alliances that include most of the world's leaders are emerging in the 1990s. Japan's main rival, IBM, has forged many international links in main frames, personal computers and workstations, and it has undergone one of the largest rationalisations the industry has ever seen. Beginning in 1986 with the expedited closure and amalgamation of many factories, by 1990 the emphasis shifted to developing new technology, particularly through international technical cooperation, and strengthening price competitiveness through using OEM suppliers. The next year saw plans for large worldwide layoffs, 40 000 in 1992, and further quests for international allies in order to capitalise on the spread of personal computers by entering the multi-media market. The company is also shifting from large to small machines and to making greater use of independent companies (Nihon bōeki shinkōkai, 1993a, pp. 51–53). Table 4.7 documents some of the most important tie-ups achieved by IBM in this period.

A European company to have experienced almost as great a transformation is Phillips, which in the 1980s had 400 subsidiaries in over 60 countries with a total of 400 000 employees. But growing internationalisation, technological change and maturation of certain products has required radical restructuring. In 1988–89 the white goods business was sold to the US company Whirlpool, while the military section of the industrial electronic section was sold to France's Thompson, leaving Phillips to focus on consumer electronics products like microchips, computers and communications equipment. By 1991 consumer electronics comprised 47 per cent of production, office machines and systems 22 per cent, lighting apparatuses and components each 13 to 14 per cent, while the number of employees had fallen to a mere 240 000. In areas where it was weak, the company found established allies: AT&T in digital exchange machines and Siemens in microchip development. Phillips' international strategy has been to reorganise and simplify by product and by country, for example, strengthen computer production in North America and improve price

Table 4.7   IBM's Main cooperative linkages

Date	Partner	Agreement
4/1988	Super Computer Systems	Develop parallel super computers
8/1991	NEC	Supply super computers
4/1991	Mitsubishi Electric	Obtain OEM supplies of large computers
1/1992	Bull	Obtain 5.7 per cent of Bull shares
3/1990	Sun Microsystems	Workstation cross license contract
4/1991	Hitachi	Obtain OEM supplies of note-type computers
7/1992	Hitachi	Jointly develop next generation printers
10/1991	Apple	Set up company to develop multi-media technology
6/1991	Wang	Obtain OEM supplies of large scale computers

Source: Nihon bōeki shinkōkai, 1993a, p. 53.

competition by shifting labour intensive activities to Mexico and Asia (Nihon bōeki shinkōkai, 1993a, pp. 54–6).

Japanese companies too have been keen to associate themselves with the recent reorganisation of the industry and to find allies. For example, in April 1991, IBM agreed to supply Mitsubishi with large-type computers, the first time it has supplied another company with its product to be sold under that company's brand name. IBM and Hitachi, which had developed close ties over the years, agreed in July 1992 to cooperate in the development of next generation printers and, the following year, jointly to produce a number of new products for IBM to sell world-wide. Apart from continuing to strengthen its ties with IBM, Hitachi bought America's National Advanced Systems in April 1989, and since 1991 has been selling large-type universal-use computers under its own brand name. It also works with Hewlett Packard in developing DCEs (distributed computing environments), that is, operating systems that permit networking among different kinds of computers. NEC is also a company which actively cultivates international links and has even closer ties with IBM in product development than Hitachi. In January 1992 it formed a business alliance with America's CDC, whose European network it uses in order to sell its own machines in the region. In July 1992 it bought 4.7 per cent of Bull, with which it had cooperated since the mid-1980s. Fujitsu is a further Japanese company which has considerably advanced its international alliances: in November 1990 it bought 80 per cent of Britain's ICL to combine Japan's strength in hardware with Europe's in software. It also bought a 45 per cent interest in America's Amdahl to strengthen its line-up of manufactures, joint development and sales in the US. Amdahl has since been procuring key components from Fujitsu (Nihon bōeki shinkōkai, 1993a, pp. 96–7; *NW*, 2 August 1993, p. 8;14 March 1994, p. 8).

To complete the circle of tie-ups, in January 1992 IBM bought into Bull to cooperate in the field of workstations: it would supply Bull with RISC-type processors, while Bull would produce the workstations and supply them to IBM on an OEM basis. About the same time Digital Equipment (DEC), which had been lagging in the trend towards downsizing, bought into Olivetti as well as the whole computer section of Phillips, in order to strengthen itself in the European market and to enhance its technology in mini-computers. This was also when DEC Japan and Seiko Epson began to cooperate in the field of small-type machines and to build LANs (local area networks) for personal computers (Nihon bōeki shinkōkai, 1993a, p. 96).

c) **Multi-Media**

Multi-media could well be the field in which the winners and losers of the 1990s are determined by the nature and strength of their strategic alliances, not just among Japanese companies, but between Japanese and US companies aiming at the post-2000 world-wide multi-media market which is expected to exceed ¥450 trillion. In October 1991, IBM attracted world attention with its agreement with key rival Apple to set up a multi-media subsidiary in which IBM relies on Apple for the development of software. The purpose of this alliance was to achieve world-wide unity in multi-media through mobilising the resources and power which only a consortium involving the leaders in the various relevant fields could muster. The Clinton Administration has vigorously promoted the 'information super-highway' and a range of US companies have started providing such services as online shopping and video on demand (Nihon bōeki shinkōkai, 1993a, pp. 95–6).

The Japanese market, however, remains regulated, with only about 700 000 households having cable TV compared to about 70 per cent of US households. The largest US CATV operator, Tele-Communications Inc., made a move into the Japanese market by purchasing 18 per cent of Cable Soft Network in 1993, a Sumitomo subsidiary which markets CATV programmes. Alliances like this are expected to shake up and eventually lead to the de-regulation of the market in Japan (*NW*, 14 June 1993, p. 8).

Among the first developments in the field of multi-media was CD-I (conversation compact disk), a multi-media product developed by Phillips and sold in the US since 1991 and in Japan and Europe since 1992. It is a progression from CD-ROM (compact disk read-only memories), which resulted from a Sony and IBM combination of computer and CD technology. Unlike hitherto CDs, which are for listening to music, CD-I has various *users,* including machines, and uses: music from software, photographs of singers, karaoke, games, art and encyclopaedia. Computer companies are moving into alliances with household electronics firms to take advantage of this development. Phillips US has joined a twelve-firm joint development company in the US, where the leaders in the field are IBM, Apple and Microsoft. Japanese electronic and computer firms are involved in joint developments with such companies as Apple, AT&T, IBM, Tandy, Microsoft, HP, Motorola, Eastman-Kodak and Corning. Both Toshiba and Sony have formed close ties with Apple and IBM, through which they hope to overcome some of their disadvantages on the software side (Nihon bōeki shinkōkai, 1993a, pp. 97–8; *TB*, Jan–Feb 1993, pp. 38–9).

General Magic is a new Apple-led joint venture firm which is in the forefront of the technology to store information digitally, whether it be data, graphics, sound or pictures. It is also a leader in certain technologies for handheld personal communication devices. For this reason, it is the target of investment tie-ups by a whole range of US, European and Japanese companies: Motorola, Phillips, Apple, AT&T, Sony, Matsushita and NTT. NTT, which had been prevented by regulations from pursuing a global strategy, has also bought into Nextel Communications, whose network is to provide the US's first advanced digital cellular phone services. Since Motorola provides Nextel with mobile licenses and systems in 21 states, the agreement, signed in December 1993, was very attractive to NTT. In March 1994, NTT also announced an agreement with Microsoft to develop multi–media software for use through its telephone lines and on CD-ROMs (*NW*, 28 March 94, p. 8). With Fujitsu and NEC as part of the 'NTT family', the Japanese presence is considerable. In April 1994, NEC was proposing to buy directly into General Magic to get access to that company's 'Telescript' and 'Magic Cap' technologies (Figure 4.1).

Other key alliances in the field include Kaleida Laboratories, which is a research firm jointly set up by Apple and IBM in an attempt to rally manu-facturers behind a single software standard for multi–media devices known as Script X. While it has won support from Hitachi, Toshiba and Mitsubishi, General Magic is the favoured strategy of most Japanese heavyweights. Mitsubishi, which is far behind the others in forging such links, recently (1994) teamed up America's Northern Telecom in order to get access to its ATM (asynchronous transfer mode) switching systems, which allow for simultaneous multi-media transmission (*NW*, 15

Figure 4.1   Strategic alliances in multi-media surrounding General Magic

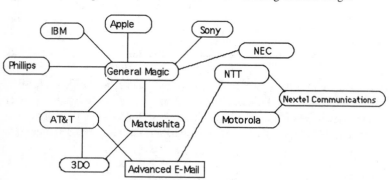

Source: *NW*, 31 January 1994, p. 8; 28 March 1994, p. 8.

November 1993, p. 8; 31 January 1994, p. 8; 28 June 1993, p. 8; 4 April 1994, p. 8; 25 April 1994, p. 8).

In a related development, Toshiba and Apple are planning to develop products using Apple's Newton technology, that is, handheld devices whose features include electronic mail, fascimile, pen-based data input and on-line data base access. Sharp, which has a similar arrangement with Apple, released its own Expert Pad in the US in 1993, and Casio and Tandy have linked up to develop their version of the product. *Nikkei Weekly* (31 January 1994, p. 8) commented:

> International alliances are blossoming as companies jockey to reduce risk and expand horizons by pooling technology and marketing might in the battle to set standards in the emerging market for handheld devices – a market seen by some as having the same growth potential in the 1990s as PCs did in the 1980s.

On a potentially even grander scale, the second largest American software house, Oracle Corporation, has been trying to set standards in multimedia software through allying with key Japanese manufactures, such as Sharp, Pioneer, Kyocera and Sega. Game machine makers like Nintendo and Sega, which linked up with Hitachi in late 1993 to develop multimedia equipment, stand a good chance of making the change to this market once it is clear which standards are winning out. In the meantime, the competition is tremendous and involves proliferating tie-ups to minimise risk and provide the needed breakthroughs (*NW*, 27 September 1993, p. 8; 21 February 1994, p. 8).

Another area in which Japanese strength in hardware production combines with US technology is in that of videophones: in April 1994 AT&T signed licensing agreements with Sanyo, Hitachi, Sharp, JVC, Sony and Canon in the expectation that the Japanese makers will be able to develop products cheap enough to be available for a mass market (*NW*, 25 April 1994, p. 8).

A highly ambitious and risky global telecommunications project currently being planned aims to link the world's portable phones by means of satellites. The Motorola consortium, in which a Japanese consortium Nippon Iridium is to own 15 per cent, leads the field with plans to commence service in 1998. The Japanese group includes Kyocera, Sony, DDI and a number of partners whose main function is to supply finance rather than hardware, such as the Long Term Credit Bank of Japan and Sanwa Bank (*NW* 3 May 1993, p. 8; 12 April 1993, p. 8).

In most of these attempts to keep up with cutting-edge technology, Japanese companies have been forced into strategic alliances with leaders in the field from the US and to a lesser extent Europe. However, an exclusively Japanese effort which combines NEC, Hitachi, Fujitsu and government resources is Ultra-High Speed Network and Computer Technology Laboratories, which was set up in early 1994 to develop multi-media communications technology (*NW*, 4 April 1994, p. 1). Figure 4.2 is a recent attempt to map out the mire of connections and alliances that characterise the field. Since so many of these have already been spelt out, and since new developments occur almost daily, no purpose is served by spelling out more of the details or even translating more of the original into English. The visual impact should be sufficient to make the point that the field is so littered with strategic alliances among MNCs from the advanced countries that these companies now constitute an increasingly united system of power. It is no longer possible to separate the power of any one, or even those of any one country, from the power they collectively achieve through their alliances. The less developed world is in no sense part of this system.

Because of the interdependency of their fortunes, capital in the electronics industry in the advanced countries has had to go through a painful process of restructuring and building alliances in an attempt to overcome recession and compete in the 1990s. The radical rationalisations undertaken by American and European corporations have helped put the US into the lead and Europe into second place in reviving accumulation. In 1994 Japan alone among the great powers lingered on in recession. In the wake of global restructuring by its competitors and of the collapse of Japan's bubble economy, Japanese companies have been forced to follow suit and conclude strategic technical agreements in order to reduce risks and to spread costs. This has applied particularly to industries with very high entry costs, such as the technology-intensive ones like computers and chips, or mature large-scale ones like motor vehicles. However, before this latter is examined, the other half of the story needs to be told, although in less detail.

Asia Zone

Asia's role in Japanese capital's global division of labour in the electronic industry is to produce cheaply whatever can no longer be cost-effectively done in Japan. Although the most labour-intensive assembly functions in the household 'white goods' industries, such as fridges and washing machines, were the first to be assigned to this region, during the 1980s assembly in other less basic industries, such as black and white TV sets, radiocassettes and other audio equipment were also relocated. At the same time, the assembly of a growing number of relatively unsophisticated

127

Figure 4.2 A bird's eye view of MNC alliances in multi-media

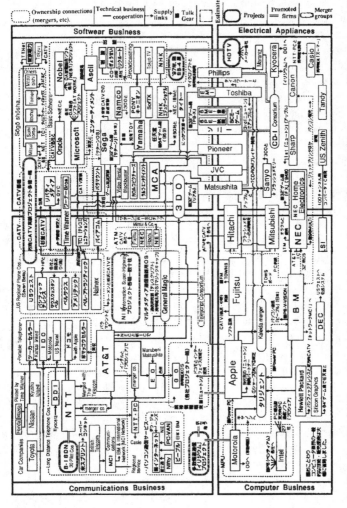

Source: Tsuchiya, 1994, pp. 230–31. Due to limited space and the conciseness of Chinese characters, only the names of the main companies and fields of cooperation have been translated.

components like 4KDRAMs also began to be produced in Asia, and then around the turn of the decade the tide moved towards an even higher level of component and product. By the early 1990s these included disk drives, VCRs and computers. If the kind of product no longer distinguished the role of Asia, at least the functions of assembly and component manufacture have remained fairly constant.

According to a list of a total of 369 FDI cases recorded by the Japan Electronic Machinery Association in the period 1985–89, 60 per cent went to Asia, and of the 208 that were in electronics components, 65 per cent went to Asia (Nihon bōeki shinkōkai, 1993a, pp. 67–8). At that time, the move to the region tended to centre on electronics components because the rise of the yen had made the wages even of Japan's low-paid work-force at the bottom of the sub-contracting system, too high for the giant electric companies (*NKS*, 21 June 1993, p. 19). Since then, although the recession might have squeezed corporate liquidity, a much wider range of industries have been shifting their labour-intensive operations into Asia where costs are lower and through which both profitability and liquidity can be restored. A full 87 per cent of Japan's investment in the electrical industry in Asia was made since 1989, and the amounts continue to increase each year, regardless of the recession. But it is not only assemblers and parts makers which are having to shift to the region. Many small retailers are securing their cheap supplies by producing overseas and importing the more competitive goods into Japan. Table 4.8 summarises the circumstances surrounding some of the main moves by Japanese companies into Asia in 1991–92: almost all were in the electrical industry.

Relative costs, it seems, constitute the overwhelming reason why, in addition to the manufacture of components for use all over Asia, as well as for export to Japan, the US and Europe, the production of a growing number of lower-end household electrical and electronics goods is also part of Japanese capital's Asia-zone strategy. With most household white goods long since having been relocated to the region, what are now these lower-end products are things like colour TVs, VCRs, hi-fi equipment and a range of computer-related products. By 1993, 70 per cent of the colour TVs produced by Japanese companies were being made overseas, compared to 30 per cent of VCRs and 20 per cent of hi-fi equipment, all mainly in Asia. For example, NEC, whose overseas production accounts for almost 40 per cent of the company's total output, decided in 1993 to cease production of colour TVs in Japan altogether, and to almost double the capacity of its Thai subsidiary to 800 000 units. These will be exported to the rest of Asia, including Japan, and will account for 70 per cent of the company's total sales. Already in early 1993 Japan became a net importer

Table 4.8 Major moves to produce in Asia by Japanese companies in 1991–2

Company	Product	Scale	Country	Reason	Domestic Influence
Chinon	Compact cameras		Taiwan	High personnel costs	Shift into FDD & printers
Hitachi	Projection TV	Raise by 1000 a month	Taiwan	Increase in production costs	Specialise in S-VHS, hi-fi video, etc
Hitachi	Wind-type air conditioners	100 000 a year within 3–4 years	Malaysia	Increase in personnel and liquidity costs	Specialise in high value added products like inverter types
Hitachi	VTR	50 000 a month, 10 per cent for Japan	Malaysia	Regional division of labour to suit value added	Shift 200 out of 3000 workers to heavy electrical section to make personal faxes
Hitachi	2-tub washer	Double production power to 100 000 p.a.	Thailand	High personnel costs	Focus on high value added fully automatic machines
Hitachi	Compressors for fridges	Expand from 130 000 to 140 000	Thailand	Stabilise quality and international competitive power	
Matsushita	FDD	Double production to 600 000	Philippines	Increase price competitiveness	
Canon	Compact cameras	By 1993 triple 1991 output to 1 680 000	China	Regional division of labour to suit value added	Shift to high class (EOS100) cameras, 20 000 a month
Kita Nippon Seiki	Agricultural machinery bearings	Raise output to 1 million a month	China	Raise efficiency through regional specialisation	Produce high class goods for European and US markets
TDK	Audio tape	Produce 10 million by 1994	Thailand	High personnel costs; expand market in SE Asia	Cut output; shift to high value added DDC and next generation tape
JVC	Small colour TV	Raise output from 12 to 13 or 14 million p.a.	Thailand	Falling profit due to rising costs	Shift to wide TV & big screen TV with inbuilt BS tuners

Source: Nihon bōeki shinkōkai, 1993a, p. 88.

of colour TVs as a result of the rapid relocation of the industry to Asia (*NW*, 7 June 1993, p. 9; 12 July 1993. p. 9; 6 September 1993, p. 8).

The same development is occurring in VCR production, as illustrated by Mitsubishi Electric's decision in 1993 to transfer to Malaysia the production of all overseas-bound VCRs, and Hitachi's decision to shift all low-end production from its Haramachi plant to Malaysia. Even what might have appeared to be higher-end electronics goods, such as disk drives, printers and personal computers, are now also being shifted to Asia. Fujitsu broke its tradition of keeping these products at home in 1993 when it decided to get entry-level personal computers from Taiwan on an OEM basis and to produce disk drives and printers in Thailand. At the same time NEC decided to design some of its low-end computers in Hong Kong, with almost 80 per cent of the components coming from nearby Asian countries. Fujitsu and Seiko Epson are two more companies which have decided to cut PC costs by moving production to Asia (Steven, 1990, pp. 114–5; *NW*, 7 June 1993, p. 9; 23 August 1993, p. 8; 11 October 1993, p. 9; 15 November 1993, p. 8).

Also in the computer industry, chip assembly is one of the favourites of Japanese companies in search of cost reduction, and Malaysia is the most preferred location for this activity, with most leading companies having set up or consolidated their operations in that country during the wave of FDI that followed the high yen recession. Matsushita's fifteen affiliates alone account for 4 per cent of Malaysia's total exports (Abegglen, 1994, p. 38). Japan's largest PC maker, NEC, decided in 1993 to set up what was only its second overseas chip-assembly plant, this time in China, and to commission a Taiwanese firm to produce advanced computers for it to export to the US on an OEM basis (*NW*, 23 August 1993, p. 8).

Quite a few of the shifts to Asia have been occasions for the closure of Japanese plants. Alps Electrical, which makes parts in a number of large factories in Asia, including a fifty-fifty joint venture with South Korea's Goldstar that employs 3200 workers, decided in 1993 to close three factories in northern Japan which employ over 600 workers. Around the same time Matsushita Communication decided to close its Hanamaki plant which assembles disk drives, a highly labour-intensive process, and to expand hiring at its new Santa Rosa plant near Manila to enable the latter to produce the entire Matsushita *keiretsu*'s floppy-disk drive output (*NW*, 7 June 1993, p. 9; 30 August 1993, p. 8; Shūkan tōyō keizai, 1993a, p. 581).

Teac was already at this time assembling 60 per cent of its disk drives overseas, half of them in Malaysia, while Sony was getting over half its total drives from its factory in Penang. Teac's other main overseas supplies come from Thailand on an OEM basis via Minebea, which has, along with its towering presence in ball bearings, a massive disk drive capability in that country (*NW*, 30 August 1993, p. 9; Steven, 1990, p. 179).

The stories could go on, mapping the low-cost production networks of individual Japanese companies, tracing the countries most favoured by these companies for each of the different branches of the industries or following a product from the sourcing of its labour-intensive components from various countries around the region, its sophisticated components from Japan and its assembly in one or more Asian countries, to its final market, local, regional or to an advanced country, including Japan. The details of the stories might vary, but the message would be the same. The Asia-zone has become a vast hinterland for low-cost production by Japanese electrical companies, a hinterland they are increasingly penetrating with their *keiretsu* networks to pile up layer after layer of crisscross patterns of production and marketing within the industry. Low-cost does not, however, mean low productivity or in combination with low technology. On the contrary, it means low unit-costs because of the absolute competitive advantage achieved by the combination of Asia's cheap labour with Japan's advanced technology. What are referred to as 'low-end' goods are simply ones whose final assembly is more labour-intensive than so-called sophisticated goods, since in each case Japan's most sophisticated plant and equipment is set in operation and at least some of Japan's most sophisticated components are also used. What is really at stake in classifications of high- and low-tech goods is the issue of technology transfer, or rather its opposite, technology control. To call an industry low-tech means that the people in whose country it is located will have low control over it, since the technology involved, that is, mainly the plant and equipment, will be controlled by the Japanese investors.

Technology Transfer

The previously discussed JETRO analysis of the technology tie-ups concluded by Japanese companies in 1991–92 has already revealed the overall pattern of the alliances with local companies in Asia. Since the only possible exceptions to the ubiquitous technology gap between Japanese and Asian companies are to be found in the South Korean electronics industry, which leads the less developed world in R&D spending with a total of $4.5 billion in 1991 (compared to $5.8 billion spent by GM alone), a few examples from that quarter are worth examining (*FEER*, 8 April 1993, p. 61). Most chip manufacture in Asia, especially the assembly stages of production, have more in common with bicycle assembly than the information super-highway.

OEM arrangements are among the most common, but these tend to differ from the ones concluded between companies from the advanced countries. For example, the agreement between Hitachi and Goldstar Electronics, whereby the former supplies technology for 1M, 4M and 16MDRAMs and receives OEM supplies which it sells under its own brand name, is much more one-sided, since the Korean partner's only bargaining card is the low production costs it offers. From Hitachi's point of view, the deal provides cheap supplies with the minimum of fuss: 'Hitachi says it views its alliance with Gold Star as a means of reducing the impact of the yen's appreciation' (*NW*, 18 October 1993, p. 10). Although much the same could be said of the agreement between Fujitsu and Hyundai, the case of Samsung is possibly different, since Samsung has much more clout in the electronics industry than the other Korean companies combined (*NW*, 18 October 1993, p. 9; Nihon bōeki shinkōkai, 1993a, pp. 92–4).

If volume of production is anything to go by, then Samsung ranks among the world's leaders, even challenging Toshiba for the position of the world's largest maker of DRAM chips. It was this 'muscle' (*FEER*, 7 January 1993, p. 57) that persuaded Toshiba, the inventor of flash memory chips, to license the technology to its Korean rival in the hope that the latter might help establish FM chips as standard for the industry. But if Samsung's offering to Toshiba was little more than that of mass producer, then its recent deal with NEC came closer to the kind of strategic alliance which characterises tie-ups among companies from the advanced countries. Both NEC and Samsung had done independent research on 256MDRAM chips, had become leaders in the field and concluded the agreement in order to 'put a lid on soaring development costs' by sharing the results of both past and future research (*NW*, 7 March 1994, p. 8).

Although we seem to have found an unambiguous case of strategic alliance between a Japanese and an Asia firm, the overall argument is not affected by this discovery, for a number of reasons. First, such strategic alliances are sometimes possible for LDCs because their *uneven* strength always gives them the potential to become leaders in limited fields. What they are not easily able to do is accumulate the across-the-board productive power that comes with a more *even* development. It is significant that the South Korean state has attempted to support a wide range of technological innovations in an attempt to achieve more balanced growth, an attempt referred to by the *Far Eastern Economic Review* (8 April 1993, p. 61) as 'South Korea's Wish List'. Second, the gaps in the country's industrial capacity require it to import from Japan some 'high-tech' items (which in effect means, 'controlled by Japan') without which chip production is impossible, such as the wafers needed to fabricate chips in commercial quantities. Finally, it should be remembered that since the new world order is ruled more by networks than by the rigid regulations of governments, the possibility, however remote, of a less developed country moving from one camp to the other is always there. Samsung's success might well bring with it other successes that could feed into the networks of South Korean capital to lift the whole to a new level of technological independence. But the prospects for this are not great (*NW*, 18 October 1993, p. 9; Steven, 1990, p. 157).

Analysis of a wide range of technical tie-ups among the advanced countries and a few with the most advanced less developed country confirms the elusiveness of technology transfers which also actually transfer control over production. It seems that the power needed to avoid control by those who provide technology comes first, a power that allows technical tie-ups to be 'strategic' rather than 'classical'. *Control* over technology is thus the real measure of the *level* of technology a country has achieved, and control has a way of accumulating when networks can spread over a wide range of activities. Similarly, control is lost when the networks have few places to go and few paths to connect.

Herein, as one might have expected, lies the key to the success of Japan's car industry, which is the hub of the country's industrial structure in terms of the numbers of people employed in it, the range of forward and backward linkages that tie its fortunes to those of other industries and the real technological lead that Japanese capital has established in it. Space permits examination of only the broad outlines of the relevant issues through a few selected examples.

TRANSPORT MACHINERY

In 1986–91, Japan's FDI in transport machinery was $9.5 billion, which within manufacturing was second only to electrical machinery. A full $4 billion (42 per cent) went to the US, $2.2 billion (23 per cent) went to Europe and the rest went to Asia, Latin America and Oceania. To a qualitatively greater degree than in the electrical industry, this investment is driven by a self-conscious obsession that low-cost production should not shoot itself in the foot by ignoring market considerations when selecting suitable locations, especially for motor vehicle production, which is the focus of this discussion. In the case of the advanced countries, these considerations have constituted the overriding motive, and when the ventures have run into problems on the cost side, wider regional and even global strategies have had to be mobilised to secure cheaper components. But even in Asia, partly because of the increasing rigidity of the limits on market expansion in the advanced countries, Japanese companies are investing with an eye firmly fixed on market shares.

By January 1991, a total of 543 component makers had moved abroad, of which 66 per cent had done so since 1985, in most cases close on the heels of their parent company: 183 to the US, 276 to Asia and Oceania, and 46 to Europe. In addition, many companies associated with the car industry shifted at the same time, such as tyre manufacturers (Bridgestone, Yokohama Rubber and Sumitomo Rubber) and glass makers (Asahi Glass and Japan Sheet Glass). Many of the moves by tyre companies to the advanced countries involved takeovers (such as Bridgestone's of Firestone and Sumitomo's of Dunlop), while those by glass makers tended to involve both joint ventures and takeovers (Nihon bōeki shinkōkai, 1993a, pp. 65-67). Table 4.9 shows the regional distribution of Japan's FDI in transport machinery from 1981–93 .

By the early 1990s, Japan's car companies had carved out a central role for Asia in their increasingly internationalised production networks, with the ASEAN countries in the forefront of the region in both assembly and

Table 4.9   Japan's FDI by in transport machinery, by region, 1981–93 ($ million)

	N. America	Latin A.	Europe	Asia	Oceania	Other	Total
1981– Cases	69	20	21	112	3	3	228
85: $million	1 126	447	361	426	26	9	2 395
1986– Cases	264	25	50	163	16	1	519
89: $million	3 237	291	932	633	539	2	5 635
1990– Cases	136	23	55	146	2	–	362
93: $ million	2 747	492	2 344	1 172	432	–	7 187
1990: Cases	38	6	20	35	1	–	100
$ million	577	214	546	373	161	–	1 872
1991: Cases	21	1	16	21	1	–	60
$ million	688	158	719	191	240	–	1 997
1992: Cases	25	6	6	23	–	–	60
$ million	594	37	385	171	2	–	1 188
1993: Cases	52	10	13	67	–	–	142
$ million	888	83	694	437	29	–	2 130
1951– Cases	415	84	119	479	32	12	1 141
93: $ million	5 718	1 442	2 618	1 890	1 187	21	12 877

Source: Ōkurashō, 1991a, pp. 54 –61;1993a, pp. 46–53; 1994, p. 4.

135

Table 4.10 Japan's three-zone strategy in automobile production, 1993–97 (1000 cars)

		Toyota	Nissan	Honda	Mitsubishi	Mazda*	Suzuki*	Total*
Domestic capacity:	1993	4 544	3 132	1 428	1 412	1 240	720	14 417
	1997	4 744	2 662	1 428	1 412	1 240	720	14 147
Overseas capacity:	1993	1 237	1 288	792	600	284	515	5 284
	1997	1 757	1 568	817	850	284	675	6 700
North America:	1993	605	450	610	240	240	200	2 505
	1997	820	450	610	240	240	200	2 720
Europe:	1993	222	400	90	10	–	85	962
	1997	322	435	100	210	–	125	1 377
Asia-Pacific:	1993	397	188	92	350	–	230	1 516
	1997	584	433	107	400	24	350	2 302
1994 Projections of:								
Domestic production:		3 510	1 750	1 094	1 330	1 104	769	10 779
% change over 1993		–1.5	–3.5	–5.1	–1.8	+7.3	–2.5	–4.2
Domestic sales		2 170	1 200	610	750	440	560	6 400
Exports		1 410	550	484	580	670	209	4 130
% change over 1993		–8.4	–19.6	–15.7	–8.9	–1.6	–18.9	–11.8
Overseas production:		1 020	1 100	805	590	n.a.	702	5 050

*Notes: Mazda refuses to disclose overseas production projections. Totals include figures for the remaining five companies, the largest of which are Toyota's affiliate Daihatsu and Nissan's affiliate Fuji Heavy Industries, which makes Subaru. Since Suzuki's domestic and overseas production projected for 1994, according to these figures, exceeds the capacity it was estimated to have, some adjustments are needed. Also, since the projections were made, Suzuki's joint project with Volkswagen, which was crucial to its European strategy, collapsed (*NKS*, 26 July 1991 p. 1; *NW*, 2 August 1993, p. 9).

Source: NW, 21 June 1993, p. 9; 31 January 1994, p. 9.

component manufacture. Although more money was still being invested in North America and Europe, in 1993 Asia accounted for a larger number of FDI cases in transport machinery than any other region, confirming its increasing importance to Japan's smaller component makers. Even the amount soared to a record $437 million that year, more than five times the Latin American amount and fifteen times what went to Oceania. The role that has emerged for Asia is thus to serve as a low-cost producer of components, but also assembly in or close to places with future market potential to compensate for the stalemate encountered in the advanced countries over market access and trade. Table 4.10 reveals the zone strategies of Japan's leading automakers by showing their projections for production capacity in 1997 in each zone, the increases in that capacity over 1993 levels and 1994 projections of domestic production, domestic sales, exports and overseas production.

Nissan plans to cut heavily at home and expand abroad, especially in Asia, while Toyota plans an across-the-board expansion, with the largest percentage increase in Asia. The only planned expansion in North America is by Toyota, while only Mitsubishi intends to increase its European presence by more than its Asian presence. By 1997, capacity in Asia will almost catch up to that in the US, while one million more cars could be produced in Asia than in Europe. If anything, these projections greatly underestimate the role of Asia, since they do not include assembly of what are essentially Japanese cars by local companies in Asia under licence, which is especially common in China. Foreign investment in South Africa had long been concealed by the expedient of using trade in knockdown kits and licensed assembly to circumvent restrictions on investment. Since all Japan's automakers are rapidly replacing exports with overseas production, the latter was expected to surpass the former for the first time by about 20 per cent in 1994. Almost a million fewer vehicles were exported in 1993 than in 1991.

North American and European Zones

In the motor car industry the need for cooperation among the advanced countries is not so much driven by the speed of technological change and the cost of keeping up with rivals as by the size of the markets for cars in the three core regions and the simultaneous desire of each to protect its own market while gaining maximum access to those of its competitors. The US, Japan and Europe account for three-quarters of the world car market, but their shares have fluctuated widely since 1980, when Europe took ten million vehicles, the US seven million and Japan three million.

Although the US market had increased to twelve million by 1985, six years later it had slumped back to its previous level of seven million, causing unprecedented losses to America's 'big three' car makers, especially General Motors, whose market share fell from 46 per cent in 1980 to 33 per cent in 1991. The company's response has been a spectacular plan to restructure by cutting white collar staff by 26 per cent, or by 25 000, and blue collar by 24 per cent, or 79 000, in the period 1990–95 alone. The downsizing involves closing 21 factories (including 11 component factories) and reducing capacity from 6.7 million to 5.4 million (Nihon bōeki shinkōkai, 1993a, pp. 57–8). In an attempt to reverse a similar decline, Ford has also recently made major changes, one of which was to move into Europe's luxury car market, which it did by buying Jaguar in 1989, a move which was matched by GM's takeover of Saab. Chrysler's strategy has also included the purchase of some top luxury producers, such as Maserati and Lambourgini, and heavy reliance on OEM supplies from its Japanese ally, Mitsubishi (Nihon bōeki shinkōkai, 1993a, pp. 36–7).

Cooperation between Japanese and US car companies has a twenty-year history, beginning with the purchase by Ford and Chrysler of interests in Mazda and Mitsubishi respectively. Thereafter, Japanese companies began to supply the big three with small trucks, small cars and parts such as engines. Eventually these and other exports to the US resulted in so much trade friction that from the mid-1980s local production, in many cases jointly with US companies, was stepped up as a means to curtail Japanese exports. By 1991, Japan had expanded its motor vehicle production capacity in the US to 1.55 million, including 1.36 million automobiles. The Toyota-GM (NUMMI) effort turned out 100 000, Nissan's Smyrna factory 200 000, and Toyota's Kentucky factory a further 200 000. Of Japan's eight car makers, only Daihatsu does not currently make cars in the US, having decided in 1992 to shut down an operation which stood little chance of moving into the black (Nihon bōeki shinkōkai, 1993a, pp. 31–2).

Since the US market remains the single largest for this volume-dependent industry with its world-wide overcapacity in 1993 of some eleven million cars, Japanese capital's global strategy still rests most heavily on the North American zone. The emphasis is now on growing local production to take the place of exports, which fell by close to half a million in the two-year period 1991–93. Toyota is the most ambitious of Japan's automakers in the region, with plans almost to double its Camry capacity to 440 000 in the next few years and to create half that for a new luxury three-litre car, the Avalon. The latter is to be the first example of full integration of development, production and marketing of a model as required by the new zone strategy. Honda, which derived almost 42 per cent of its consolidated income from the US market in 1992 (compared to only 33.4 per cent from the Japanese market), remains the most dependent on North America and dedicated to preserving its shares. Of the 794 000 vehicles (down 16.7 per cent from the previous year) sold in North America in fiscal 1992, 500 000 were locally produced. By 1994 Japan's transplants had helped restore the US to the position of the world's largest producer of motor vehicles which it lost to Japan in 1980. As recently as 1991, Japan had produced 4.43 million more vehicles than the US. An ongoing consequence of the shift has been the loss of jobs in Japan: in 1993 alone, Nissan, Honda and Mazda announced cuts involving 12 000 workers. Nissan's closure of its Zama plant and Honda's decision to substitute local production for all exports of the Accord were the main culprits (Tsūshō sangyōshō, 1993b, 1994b; *NW*, 21 June 1993, p. 9; 18 October 1993, p. 8; 8 November 1993, pp. 1, 23; 6 December 1993, p. 9; 24 January 1994, p. 9; 31 January 1994, p. 9).

Local procurement of parts has also risen in the US, but the proportion needs to be 75 per cent if the vehicles are to count as local production rather than imports and so avoid retaliatory action. Honda's Accord with its 82 per cent local procurement is the sole fully sanction-free zone, but since this only applies to about 40 per cent of its production, it shares with other Japanese car makers the urgent need to step up the local procurement of parts. However, the ongoing difficulty of US suppliers to meet Japanese standards of control, expressed in terms of timely delivery and willingness to shoulder more of the costs of development, has meant that the problem is best solved for Japanese capital when its own *keiretsu* suppliers take on the task overseas. Nippondenso, Toyota's giant affiliate which has eleven subsidiaries in North America alone as well as its own network of subcontractors in tow, is the most outstanding example of this process, while Calsonic is Nissan's equivalent but in no sense Nippondenso's equal. Nissan's preferred alternative to US suppliers when its own group members are not at hand is from affiliates in Mexico, which has the advantage of wages that compare to ASEAN's as well as a lower local-content requirement, allowing more tariff-free imported inputs. In 1994 Nissan even opened a parts design centre in Mexico for use by 170 local firms (*NW*, 1 March 1993, p. 9; 24 May 1993, p. 9; 6 September 1993, p. 9; 24 January 1994, p. 9; *FEER*, 26 December 1991; pp. 72–3; Shūkan tōyō keizai, 1993a).

A very similar, although shorter, story could be told in relation to FDI in Europe by Japan's automakers in order to secure that market as well as obviate conflicts with their European rivals. Mainly because of an increase in demand in Germany, the market in Europe rose to about 14 million in

1991, but competition intensified due to the slump in demand in Britain, France and Italy, as well as due to the growing ability of Japanese companies to penetrate this market. The result was rationalisations, personnel cuts and reorganisations similar to those which had occurred in the US. BMW bought the 80 per cent of Rover which Honda did not own, much to the latter's annoyance, since Rover had been groomed to fulfil a variety of strategic purposes for the Japanese company; Saab was taken over by GM to give it a prestige name plate; and Volvo and Peugeot combined forces by exchanging stock. The only remaining independent large-scale luxury car makers in the region were Mercedes Benz and BMW. The outcome of growing Japanese investment in Europe to substitute for restrictions on exports was also similar to what had emerged in the US: greatly rejuvenated and more powerful local industries (Nihon bōeki shinkōkai, 1993a, pp. 29–31; Australian *Financial Review*, 18 August 1993, p. 23; *NW*, 2 February 1994, p. 9; 7 February 1994, p. 1; 28 February 1994, p. 9).

Japanese companies have received the added incentive of growing European unity, which threatens to raise even further the level of protection against Japanese imports, in order to expand their production capability in the region. The voluntary quotas negotiated between the European Community and Japan's Ministry of International Trade and Industry (MITI) in effect make the market share in Europe of Japanese car makers depend on their local production capacity. Hitherto, the leading presence in the region has been Nissan, which has had large production facilities in Spain and Britain for some time, but both Toyota and Honda have also established themselves quite firmly, and in 1992 both began producing passenger cars in Britain. Honda's long association with the Rover group, initially producing engines for its ally, had been part of its preparation for this move. Of Japan's other major car makers, Mazda, following a three-year feasibility study together with its US ally Ford, decided in March 1993 that it would abandon joint production with Ford in Europe, while Mitsubishi's main regional strategy depends on joint production with Volvo and the Dutch government in the Netherlands from 1995. Mitsubishi is also involved in large-scale agreements, mainly in relation to environmental protection, with Daimler-Benz. With the collapse in August 1993 of the agreement between Suzuki and Volkswagen to develop and produce 1000 cc vehicles in Spain, Suzuki joined Mazda as one of only two major Japanese car makers without a firm European strategy. So although levels of local production in Europe lag behind what has been achieved in the US, a strong upward trend is projected over the next few years. The special strength of European companies in the kinds of cars introduced by Japan is also putting added pressure on Japanese companies to strike strategic deals with their European competitors, often in the form of joint ventures (*NW*, 8 March 1993, p. 9; 6 December 1993, p. 9; *NKS*, 26 July 1993, p. 1; 7 February 1994, pp. 1, 23; Shūkan tōyō keizai, 1994b, pp. 27–8).

Strategic Alliances

Strategic moves by Japanese car companies in North America and Europe have clearly centred on the market place, and included the shift by Japanese companies of large proportions of their productive capacity to the US and Europe, often in joint ventures with rivals. Growing exports from Japan of components to what were initially dubbed 'screwdriver factories' then elicited a counter-move by the latter in the form of rising local-content requirements. Now the state of play is moving in the direction of growing numbers of strategic alliances, since both sides are simply too strong to succumb to competition from the other, but actually thrive on it. For example, the increased competition resulting from Japan's trade and investment in the US, which in 1989 sent Honda's Accord into the position of America's best selling car, helped Ford take over two years later with a re-styled Taurus (*NW*, 6 September 1993, p. 9). MNCs of such calibre have no alternative to finding some accommodation, particularly in their own markets.

Within the US this originally took the form of 'voluntary' quotas on imports from Japan, but now the emphasis is on OEM agreements. By the end of 1993, over 12 per cent of the vehicles produced by Japanese subsidiaries were being marketed by the 'big three' under their own brand names. However, since the latter's main gripe is not over what happens in the US but Japan, attention has shifted to deals that give them access to the Japanese market. And so the 1990s have for the first time seen a movement in the opposite direction: the supply of cars and parts to Japan from the US, again a consequence of conflict and negotiation over market shares. Japanese capital is trying to exploit this by exporting its own cars from the US (Nihon bōeki shinkōkai, 1993a, pp. 31–2; *NW*, 6 December 1993, p. 9).

Four main developments have resulted from the conflict and negotiations with the US. The first has been the supply of cars and parts by the big three for sale in Japan under Japanese brand names, beginning with Ford's supply of multi-purpose vehicles to Mazda in 1990. This was followed in 1992 with an annual provision by Ford of 50 000 jointly-developed mini-vans to Nissan and a proposal to furnish Mazda with pick-up trucks in 1993. Chrysler's contribution came in early 1993 with the proposal to provide Mitsubishi with pick-up trucks, and in November Toyota came on board with an agreement with GM to sell 20 000 Chevrolet Cavaliers annually under its brand name. The second development comprises plans, in relation to the joint-venture companies in the US, for Ford to supply Mazda with engines and transmissions and Chrysler to supply Mitsubishi with engines. Thirdly, there have been agreements by Japanese companies to expand the purchase of parts made by the big three, an issue discussed further in the next chapter. Finally there are agreements to sell cars made by the big three under their own brand names, for example, Mazda's plan to sell 4500 Ford vehicles a year from 1992; Nissan's also to sell Ford vehicles; Honda's to expand the sale of Chrysler jeeps to 1200 in 1994; and Mitsubishi's to sell 6000 Chrysler vehicles in 1995 (Nihon bōeki shinkōkai, 1993a, p. 100; *NW*, 14 June 1993, p. 9; 22 November 1993, p. 9; 17 January 1994, p. 1).

Asia Zone

In sharp contrast to the market-sharing alliances between Japanese car companies and those of the other advanced countries, Japan's FDI in less developed countries involves either no need at all to ally with a local partner, or where the local upper class has been more nationalistic, to conclude alliances which license the use of Japanese technology in the classical fashion. In South Korea and Taiwan the tendency has been more towards licensing local companies, while in ASEAN countries, Japanese capital has itself assembled vehicles, though often in joint-venture factories. Since no one Asian country has hitherto – China is the first real exception to this – had the potential to become a mass market for Japanese cars on the scale of an advanced country, production strategies have frequently had to include inter-regional and in some cases even global considerations.

Component makers have been brought to Asia not just to have parts close at hand, but to procure low-cost supplies for the whole region, and even for export to the advanced countries, including back to Japan. The aim has thus been to find production sites from which exports can be launched, both of components and of fully assembled vehicles. Since the conclusion in October 1988 of the BBC (Brand to Brand Complementation) agreement among ASEAN countries (excepting Indonesia which has since come under heavy pressure to participate), import tariffs were reduced by 50 per cent for participating companies – so far Toyota, Nissan, Mitsubishi, Daimler-Benz and Volvo, with Honda expected to do so – which means that all components imported from within the region are included in local content.

Toyota's BBC scheme, which began operation in the second half of 1992, uses Thailand to make diesel engines, pressed parts and electronic apparatus; Malaysia to make steering gears, shock absorbers and radiators; the Philippines to make transmissions; and Indonesia to make gasoline engines and pressed materials. All are being used for one type of assembly or another, and most export at least something back to Japan as well. Everything has been carefully planned and designed to fit Toyota's pet project in the region, the ASEAN car. Mitsubishi has a similar project focusing on component manufacture in Malaysia, Thailand and the Philippines as well as Australia, with the export of vehicles to the UK and Canada and transmissions back to Japan. Nissan has always been more willing to procure supplies from wherever they are the cheapest, and has a regional strategy that focuses heavily on Thailand, especially for engines, but also includes the Philippines and Malaysia for engine parts and trim parts and Taiwan for body panels. Nissan also has a highly developed global strategy that uses Mexico, where it has produced engines since the 1960s (Ichie, 1993, pp. 66–80; Shūkan tōyō keizai, 1994a, 1994b).

Since the recent increase in FDI in Asia by Japanese car makers has been strongly motivated by these regional and global strategies, ASEAN rather than the NICs has received the most attention. Taiwan and South Korea continue to produce cars under licence for their own as well as for export markets, although the trickle of Japanese parts makers behind them remains as regular as ever. Edward Lincoln captured the relationship very well (1993, p. 179–80):

> Every Korean and Taiwanese automobile manufacturer has some rela-
> tionship with a Japanese firm, and virtually every Japanese automaker
> has a tie with a firm in either South Korea or Taiwan. . . Overall, some
> two-thirds of all the technical agreements of the Korean auto firms are
> with the Japanese.

The most important of these ties is perhaps Mitsubishi's 15 per cent ownership of Hyundai, which it also supplies with sophisticated components and which it uses to compete at the low end in world markets, particularly the advanced countries. Cooperation is thus of the 'classical' rather than the 'strategic' variety. Such production under licence of what are in varying degrees still Japanese cars is not normally included in assessments of the global capacity of the Japanese industry. Since Table 4.10 excluded it, the current rush into Asia could be greatly underestimated. Nissan certainly sees its 1994 plan to license technology to Samsung Heavy

Industries, to enable the latter to enter the 'country's' two-million-strong car industry, in this light (*NW*, 25 April 1994, p. 8):

> The proposed venture is expected to strengthen Nissan's Asian strategy by helping it regain ground in South Korea, where the company has been trailing. . . Nissan is likely to transfer some production facilities from its Zama plant near Tokyo, which the company will shut next spring, to the new factory.

Clearer examples of the way technology licensing can give Japanese capital even greater benefits than it could derive from participating in ownership come from China. Toyota has found that exporting semi-knocked down and completely knocked-down kits of its Deluxe mini-buses to Jinbei (Gold Cup) – a 50 000 employee conglomerate of component makers – for assembly under licence has enabled it to avoid the kinds of problems GM has had with interference from the Chinese government. Toyota gets in return for Chinese control over the problems of ensuring uninterrupted production, a guaranteed market which is the envy of GM (*FEER*, 27 May 1993, pp. 54–6).

Technology licensing as a method of securing market access is analogous to the kind of production control which Japanese workers get from management's use of quality control circles. Workers are given the responsibility to take over the exercise of managerial prerogatives so long as they do so in accordance with management's requirements, for example, to work harder and longer. What they therefore get is not freedom from managerial control, but the added burden of having to exercise that control themselves (Katō and Steven, 1993).

All the Chinese seemed to have gained from the agreement with Toyota was control over the process which guarantees Toyota access to the Chinese market, since the possibility of substantially limiting the components supplied by Toyota is extremely remote. Toyota might, in response to 'pressure' from the Chinese government in the form of tariff cuts if it does, yet have to buy into Jinbei or increase local procurement, perhaps by having its own affiliates do the job. This might also be Toyota's way round China's 'three big, three small, and two mini' policy, which has limited the number of passenger car makers to eight: two large projects with Volkswagen and one large one with Citroen; one small venture with each of Chrysler, Peugeot and Daihatsu; and one mini with each of Suzuki and Fuji Heavy Industries. Early 1993 projections by the *Nikkei Weekly* (1 March 1993, p. 9) for production in China by 1995 were close to half a million vehicles: 'Nissan Diesel, Daihatsu, Suzuki bank on limitless demand, lack of local competition' ran the headline. All of Japan's automakers are finding ways of entering the Chinese market through one or other form of local production, Nissan Diesel in the largest venture to date (*NW*, 15 March 1993, p. 9; 2 August 1993, pp. 1, 23; 22 November 1993, p. 9; 7 March 1994, p. 9).

Much more could be said of what is beginning to look like another 'rush' by Japanese automakers into Asia, by parts makers and assemblers alike, into traditional areas like Taiwan and South Korea, into areas entered during the previous rush following the high yen recession and since then 'conquered', such as ASEAN, and now into newer frontiers such as China. Daihatsu, an affiliate of Toyota that was often made to test new waters, is doing all of these things simultaneously: withdrawing from the US to focus on Asia, linking up with the Malaysian government to produce that country's second national car (perhaps Japan's second, since the first, Proton Saga, was essentially a Mitsubishi vehicle) and occupying a leading position in relation to China's 'limitless' market (Steven, 1990, pp. 196–7; *NW*, 15 August 1994, p. 9). As a managing director of the firm put it: 'We withdrew from the U.S. market and cannot expect substantial growth in Europe either. We will therefore concentrate investments of people and money in Asia' (*NW*, 14 June 1993, p. 9).

Asia is thus being used once again by Japanese capital as a place on which to displace the malfunctioning of Japanese capitalism. Rising Japanese wages remain the central problem of Japanese automakers, one which sent their investments in the region sky-rocketing during the late 1980s to leave behind a solid network of low-cost assembly and component-making facilities. These have remained ready to be expanded and linked together in preparation for an onslaught on the currently most important problem: the need to reorganise markets on a regional level, away from Japan and the other advanced-country zones towards Asia, a task best achieved by relocating production close to the new markets to be opened up.

Technology transfers and other agreements in this industry have had little effect on the technology gap between Japan and Asia, because the former has always managed to retain its *control* over the technologies that really matter. Mabuchi Motor is a Japanese company whose whole strategy is to eliminate all production in Japan by licensing technology to local producers throughout the Asian region (especially China) and retaining only management and R&D at home. What it thus consigns, much in the way that OEM arrangements do, is the dirty-work of production to enable it to supply half the world market in magnetic motors, which are used by both the electrical and car industries (Abegglen, 1994, pp. 28–9; *TB*,

February 1994, pp. 26–7). What is essentially political, under capitalism always somehow has a way of presenting itself as 'technical'. Since the point hardly needs further illustration, Japan's remaining overseas investments in the manufacturing industry will be looked at only in broad statistical terms.

Other Manufacturing

The other key manufacturing industries in which Japanese capital has invested heavily abroad are general machinery, metals and chemicals. In 1986–91, $7.2 billion went into general machinery, $6 billion into ferrous and non-ferrous metals, and $8.6 billion into chemicals. However, the FDI booms in the latter two industries are associated with those in the machinery industries already examined, since the main source of demand for metals has been the car industry and of demand for chemicals has been both the electrical and car industries. Japanese capital wanted to secure overseas production bases for the materials needed by its machinery companies, in many cases by means of takeovers – in 1990 in the chemical industry alone there were 37 in the US and eleven in Europe – but it also wanted to advance specific technologies, particularly in chemicals (Nihon bōeki shinkōkai, 1993a, pp. 68–70). Table 4.11 provides a regional breakdown of Japanese FDI in the above three industries in 1981–89 and the most recent period 1990–93. The shift towards Asia is once again the most remarkable development: by 1993 investment in general machinery and metals in the region even exceeded the amounts that went into either North America or Europe, and Asia towered over Latin America by a long way in both metals and chemicals, industries in which the latter had previously played a major role. The decline of investment in the US was occasioned by the drop in motor vehicle investments in that country and the growing need to find markets *elsewhere* and not just by *other means*, as FDI in the US car industry had attempted to do. In the chemical industry, investment in Asia was more than double what went into either the US or Europe in 1992, but the next year the advanced countries were ahead again, mainly because of the need for strategic investments and alliances in order to keep up with rivals in this high-tech industry.

If one sets aside the fall in investment in US manufacturing, which resulted more from the limits on what FDI could do to help sell Japanese goods, particularly in the motor vehicle and related industries, it is clear that the current recession has not slowed the flow of Japan's FDI to any great extent. The slump's main impact seems to have been on the regional distribution of FDI and on the consolidation of the three key zones, almost

Table 4.11   Japan's FDI in general machinery, metals and chemicals, by region, 1981–93 ($ million)

		N. America	Latin A.	Europe	Asia	Oceania	Other	Total
General machinery								
1981–85:	Cases	195	19	92	186	8	2	502
	$ million	555	106	95	307	15	1	1 078
1986–89:	Cases	311	13	128	348	15	1	816
	$ million	2 502	40	1 125	807	33	–	4 507
1990–93:	Cases	169	13	115	234	11	–	542
	$ million	1 844	120	1 819	1 164	64	–	5 013
1993:	Cases	34	5	28	79	3	–	149
	$ million	399	29	300	434	9	–	1 171
1951–93:	Cases	874	147	401	1 235	48	9	2 714
	$ million	5 122	512	3 158	2 551	135	12	11 491
Metals								
1981–85:	Cases	84	10	27	141	80	6	348
	$ million	667	917	105	666	109	107	2 571
1986–89:	Cases	193	9	53	348	9	1	613
	$ million	2 619	357	134	882	65	15	4 072
1990–93:	Cases	126	8	45	285	17	1	482
	$ million	1 596	184	415	1 071	249	18	3 532
1993:	Cases	29	1	7	68	–	1	106
	$ million	225*	52	77	339	43	18	754
1951–93:	Cases	475	105	407	1 215	133	39	2 374
	$ million	5 252	2 194	811	3 649	676	211	12 794

Table 4.11 Continued

	N. America	Latin A.	Europe	Asia	Oceania	Other	Total
Chemicals							
1981– Cases	132	18	42	279	1	5	477
85: $ million	426	56	111	570	6	186	1 356
1986– Cases	214	12	81	297	4	5	613
89: $ million	2 911	45	895	785	22	11	4 666
1990– Cases	137	13	99	232	3	10	494
93: $ million	2 994	306	1 523	2 612	15	200	7 651
1993: Cases	18	3	20	51	1	2	95
$ million	652	39	626	408	10	6	1 742
1951– Cases	576	147	276	1 309	26	46	2 380
93: $ million	6 575	907	2 632	4 690	142	1 354	16 300

Source: Ōkurashō, 1991a, pp. 54–61; 1993a, pp. 46–53; 1994, p. 4.

to the total exclusion of others. It has forced overseas investors to focus more on costs and, when market considerations have entered, to ensure that costs are not inflated to the point of making losses, as had been the rule in the US, or reduced to the point of losing markets, as had been the rule in Japan. The result has been a huge leap in the importance of Asia, increasingly to the point of overshadowing that of the US and Europe. However, in the unproductive industries, such as finance and real estate, the recession has had a tremendous impact, and sent into indirect or portfolio investments monies that previously went into FDI projects associated with the purchase of assets.

UNPRODUCTIVE INDUSTRIES

A notable feature of worldwide FDI in the 1980s was the tremendous expansion of investment in finance and real estate by all the advanced countries, mainly in other advanced countries. Investment in the finance sector resulted largely from developments in communications, from continued internationalisation of industry and from world-wide de-regulation, while the extra interest in real estate resulted chiefly from the boom in travel and tourism. The non-manufacturing share of the top four foreign investors (US, Japan, UK, Germany) grew from 33.2 per cent in 1982 to 50.2 per cent in 1990, the share of finance doubling from 11.5 per cent to 21.5 per cent and the shares of services rising from 8.3 per cent to 13 per cent and of real estate from 0.6 per cent to 4.4 per cent (commerce fell from 12.2 per cent to 10.8 per cent). In 1986–90 almost 60 per cent was in the non-manufacturing industries (Nihon bōeki shinkōkai, 1993a, p. 9).

If one compares the amounts of Japan's FDI in the four main unproductive industries in the periods 1986–89 and 1990–93 as a whole, the only unambiguous fall is in the finance industry (Table 4.12): commerce actually expanded substantially, particularly in Asia (because of the re-structuring of Japanese markets) and Europe (because of impending European unity); real estate held its own because the falls in the US (largely because of a slump in the industry) and Asia were more or less matched by rises in Europe and Australia; in services there was a sizeable overall increase, particularly in the advanced countries of Europe and North America and in Latin America, although there was a slight fall in Asia and Australia. The only drastic almost all-round falls were thus in finance, beginning abruptly in 1991 and becoming sharpest in the tax havens of Latin America, in Europe, in Australia and in the US. Asia, however, was quite steady and if anything showed signs of attracting growing interest in the industry.

Since commercial investments are closely connected with trade, the changing patterns of FDI in commerce reflect Japan's steady shift into Asian markets, particularly if one looks at the number of cases rather than the amounts of money, because the same amount of money buys more in Asia than it does in the US or Europe. The more or less equal importance of Asia is reflected in the increasingly similar number of commercial investments in the three key zones.

FDI in real estate is most fully associated with speculation and surplus distribution in the advanced countries, where real estate prices can receive the kinds of boosts that make speculation worth while. In 1986–91, $52.2 billion (19.4 per cent of the total) was invested in this industry, overwhelmingly in the US, Australia and Europe. In the peak year of 1989 alone, $14 billion found its way mainly into office buildings, hotels and resorts. The large amounts of money and concentrations in places like Hawaii, California and Australia provoked some strong anti-Japanese outbursts. In Australia, Japan's share of real estate investment in 1986–91 was between 30–40 per cent. However, the slump in US land prices confirmed the precarious nature of the investments, whose profitability sank into the red in 1991 and ended the speculative boom as abruptly as it had begun (Nihon bōeki shinkōkai, 1993a, pp. 71–2).

In 1980–85, Japan's FDI in services was $3.5 billion, whereas in 1986–90 it increased tenfold to $35.4 billion, by over $10 billion in each of 1989 and 1990. The increase was part and parcel of the general FDI boom, particularly in the US, spearheaded by the main manufacturing investments, with 61 per cent of it ($21.7 billion) going to the US. The service industry is more like the commercial sector in that it provides backup for the productive sector, although some branches, such as hotels and resorts, are similar to real estate. Of the 266 cases in the US in 1986–90 recorded by the Commerce Department, about half were of this latter type, while over a third were in business, engineering and accounting services, and the rest were in education, film and automobile maintenance. A full 149 were also M&A cases, with over 70 per cent in 1990 falling into this category. Spectacular examples include the purchase of Columbia Pictures by Sony in 1989 for $3.4 billion and MCA by Matsushita the next year for $6.1 billion (Nihon bōeki shinkōkai, 1993a, pp. 72–3).

Direct investment in the finance industry was the most sensitive of all to the ups and downs of Japan's trade cycle, since recessions sooner or later express themselves in credit crunches, which sap the life blood of the industry. However, much of Japan's FDI in finance during the late 1980s was of the same speculative nature as real estate, involving as it did some costly mergers and takeovers. And so the general asset deflation that triggered and

Japan and the New World Order

Table 4.12   Japan's FDI in unproductive industries, by region, 1981–93 ($ million)

	N. America	Latin A.	Europe	Asia	Oceania	Other	Total
Commerce							
1981– Cases	1 955	128	675	739	208	23	3 728
85: $ million	3 928	664	1 669	658	339	12	7 269
1986– Cases	1 635	81	722	816	184	9	3 447
89: $ million	6 726	658	2 918	1 517	631	32	12 481
1990– Cases	998	117	682	683	143	17	2 640
93: $million	8 733	1 410	5 655	3 388	985	33	20 206
1993: Cases	150	41	132	176	14	3	516
$ million	1 805	632	1 763	704	178	14	5 096
1951– Cases	7 967	738	3 172	3 606	790	110	16 383
93: $ million	22 879	3 169	11 059	5 963	2 203	91	45 364
Real Estate							
1981– Cases	381	20	12	48	55	–	516
85: $ million	2 076	14	57	307	79	–	2 533
1986– Cases	2 837	32	221	499	692	5	4 286
89: $ million	22 562	185	3 612	2 043	3 738	69	32 209
1990– Cases	2 169	16	246	360	664	–	3 555
93: $ million	17 973	79	6 597	1 617	4 958	–	31 224
1993: Cases	283	4	34	57	63	–	441
$ million	4 285	37	808	359	581	–	6 071
1951– Cases	5 387	68	579	907	1 411	5	8 357
93: $ million	42 611	279	10 265	3 967	8 774	69	65 966
Services							
1981– Cases	291	104	74	447	61	60	1 037
85: $ million	617	474	154	1 272	157	614	3 293
1986– Cases	1 206	75	306	409	307	23	2 326
89 $ million	10 951	687	2 234	2 914	1 827	74	18 688
1990– Cases	1 404	75	575	539	249	29	2 871
93: $ million	17 652	1 504	3 481	2 410	1 693	38	26 777
1993: Cases	207	11	107	105	32	–	462
$ million	1 889	87	928	494	143	1	3 542
1951– Cases	3 480	349	1 035	1 708	681	135	7 388
93: $ million	29 690	2 775	5 967	7 225	3 743	752	50 152
Finance & Insurance							
1981– Cases	107	55	155	83	24	7	431
85: $ million	3 244	1 458	2 873	515	277	67	8 433
1986– Cases	243	294	438	193	29	16	1 213
89: $ million	12 802	11 959	17 563	2 807	1 215	67	46 414
1990– Cases	166	163	227	192	26	10	784
93: $ million	8 185	3 047	9 419	2 799	390	158	24 000
1993: Cases	22	57	48	53	3	7	190
$ million	2 520	1 028	2 079	676	42	56	6 402
1951– Cases	606	590	953	626	106	57	2 938
93: $ million	25 181	16 763	30 677	6 387	1 945	319	81 271

Source: Ōkurashō, 1991a, pp. 54–61; 1993a, pp. 46–53; 1994, p. 4.

was triggered by the end of Japan's bubble economy sent more of the monies available for speculation into the hands of institutions which specialise in *zaiteku* (financial engineering), thus transferring them from direct into indirect investments, which are examined more fully in Chapter 6.

M&A Boom of late 1980s

Although most of the slump in the amounts of Japanese FDI in the early 1990s is accounted for by falls in unproductive investments in the advanced countries, we have seen that there was also a significant fall in manufacturing investments in the US, chiefly because of a large reduction in new motor vehicle establishments. However, the plunge in M&A activity, which has a speculative element regardless of the industry it targets, resulted from the shortage of finance following the end of Japan's bubble economy and affected FDI in a wide range of industries and locations. In 1991, M&A by Japanese companies fell to only one-third (¥958.4 billion) of its 1989 level, while in 1992 it dropped by another 44 per cent to ¥550 billion (Shūkan tōyō keizai, 1993, p. 10). Table 4.13 shows the change in the numbers of cases in the main regions as well as the top five acquisitions in 1991.

Table 4.13   Japan's overseas mergers and takeovers, 1989–92

Zone	1989 Cases	%	1990 Cases	%	1991 Cases	%	1992 Cases	%
US	190	46.9	215	48.9	124	42.2	79	43.2
EC	103	25.4	113	25.7	89	30.3	44	24.0
Asia/Oceania	78	19.3	81	18.4	67	22.8	42	23.4
Other	34	8.4	31	7.0	14	4.7	18	9.8
Total	405	100	440	100	294	100	183	100

Best 5 Acquisitions in 1991

Buying Companies	Acquisition	Bought Company	Amount (¥bil.)
Itochu/Toshiba	12 per cent of shares	Time-Warner (US)	130.0
Mitsui & Co.	business takeover	Monsanto (US)	40.8
Fukutake Shoten	51 per cent of shares	Berlitz International (US)	30.0
Ricoh	share acquisition	Gestetner (UK)	28.0
Nippon Shinpan	business takeover	Mirage Resort (Aus.)	26.0

Source: Nihon bōeki shinkōkai, 1993a, p. 62–3.

The M&A boom among Japanese companies at the end of the 1980s was part of a more general M&A boom involving the advanced countries in the late 1980s, particularly in Europe and America. Enormous amounts of money were involved in the US: in 1988, 2258 cases chalked up $247 billion; in 1989, 2366 cases $221 billion; in 1990, 2074 cases $108 billion; and in 1991, 1877 cases $71 billion. This was the 20th century's fourth but largest ever merger boom. Its characteristics were the huge amounts involved in each case, the massive borrowings made in order to secure the takeovers, the increase in hostile takeovers, the expansion of the range of industries involved and the increase in takeovers by European and Japanese firms. Since 1987, takeovers by foreign firms have comprised almost a third of the amounts involved in all US M&A activity, while after 1988, M&A has comprised about 80 per cent of FDI amounts in the US. The main countries to participate were the UK, Japan, Canada, Germany and Switzerland, in that order. The manufacturing industries they targeted were chemicals, pharmaceuticals, publishing, printing, computers and office machines, while outside manufacturing they went for financial services, films, hotels and retail outlets (Nihon bōeki shinkōkai, 1993a, pp. 9–10).

In Europe, British and US companies led the boom, with the number of cases rising from 303 in 1987 to 622 in 1990. Half the total were internal and half were cross-border, of which 622 were from other European countries and 265 were from outside the region. By far the largest number of cases were in chemicals, followed by food and foodstuffs. The reasons were diverse, though for foreign firms the impending European Union was the most important broad consideration. The frenzy of activity from the US and UK began to subside in 1990, mainly because mounting bad debts and 'junk bonds' choked off the supply of finance. In Britain, M&A subsided as the domestic recession deepened with Britain's approaching fuller entry into Europe. Germany played only a minor role, bogged down as it was in the former Eastern Germany. Japanese takeovers in Europe fell from an average of around one hundred a year in 1989–91 to a mere 24 in the first nine months of 1993. One of the most eye-catching was Sumitomo Metal's ¥216 billion link up with America's LTV in the iron and steel industry, but this was small by the standards of the late 1980s (*NW*, 22 November 1993, p. 2; Nihon bōeki shinkōkai, 1993a, pp. 10–11; 1994a, p. 44).

CONCLUSION

Although the three regions of Asia, North America and Europe also received the majority of Japan's investments during the FDI boom of the

late 1980s, in terms of both money and number of cases, the absence at
that time of any conscious regional strategy or any recognition of the
need for one allowed parts of other regions to assume considerable
importance in a limited range of industries: Liberia in shipping, Brazil in
manufacturing, South Africa in motor vehicles – the fiction of an investment boycott was preserved with the help of 100 per cent locally-owned
assemblers – the Cayman Islands and Panama in tax-cutting projects and
Australia in raw-materials, motor vehicles and speculation in real estate
and resorts. It also meant that links among the diverse activities in the
different parts of the world were at times haphazard and at others even
non-existent.

Since the current wave of investment that is building up in the 1990s
has had to take place in a much tighter financial climate, everything has
had to be planned much more carefully so that the advantages gained by
each project could accumulate through more effective linking with other
projects. Because this required the development of zone strategies, which
were only feasible in the three main regions of North America, Europe
and Asia, interest either tended to fall away from other parts of the world
or became narrowly focused on even more limited ranges of activities than
before. These zone strategies have since been developed most comprehen-
sively within Japan's leading export industries, electrical and transport
machinery, the ones which had to export, first the excess goods resulting
from the uneven development between Japan's productive power and the
power of its consumers, then the problem of Japan's rising wages due to
the revaluations of the yen – which stemmed from a refusal by the other
advanced countries to import the first problem – and now a growing
attempt to export both the first and second problems to a region with less
power to resist.

It has been repeatedly emphasised that one of the distinctive features
of Japanese capitalism is the very high degree to which production and
marketing are institutionally linked through tight networks, which can
guarantee markets to a qualitatively greater degree even than the most
monopolistic arrangements found elsewhere. The *keiretsu* structure is
simultaneously a system in which technical divisions of labour are
institutionally separated but then coordinated, both horizontally and
vertically, as well as a system of highly planned marketing. Japan's FDI
is thus very consciously and tightly linked to its trade, so that projects
tend to fall into one of two categories: to establish, extend or protect
markets (and thus linked to exports), on the one hand, or to secure
supplies (and thus linked to imports), on the other. The traditional
pattern of Japan's FDI has always been to do both of these. But is

Japanese capital as capable of manipulating external markets through its *keiretsu* networks as it is of tying up domestic markets? Under the new world order, the answer to this question lies in the strengths of those networks.

5 Trade: From Patriotic Duty to Corporate Strategy

Traditionally, Japanese capital traded in order to acquire products which could not be obtained domestically. The historic task of the state, especially MITI and its predecessor, was to encourage the development of export industries in order to earn the required foreign exchange, from which Japan suffered a continuous and chronic shortage throughout its transition from feudalism to advanced capitalism. Japanese capital has thus seen trade, particularly exporting, as a kind of patriotic duty which happily also solved a very basic problem, that of marketing its output. Today, a more illuminating window through which to view Japan's trade is the latter's relationship with foreign investment, since with the rise in the 1980s of the consumer goods industries to the heights of international competitiveness, especially in the production of cars and electronics goods, the traditional problem of trade deficits and their solutions through export promotion has given way to a new problem which has towered over all policy-making and discussion in Japan: the chronic trade surplus with the US resulting from the need to export the cars and electrical goods which the domestic market could not absorb. Having inherited a bureaucracy and production system that knew only how to promote exports and curtail imports, the attempts by recent Japanese governments to do the opposite have made very little impact on the current problem, which in almost all respects is the mirror opposite to the traditional one.

The focus of this chapter is first of all on that problem, particularly its domination over Japan's trade relations with the advanced countries, in which its zone strategy now has the limited and defensive objective of simply maintaining what it already has. Next, the attempts to shift the trade imbalance onto the Asian zone, in which markets are being aggressively expanded, is examined as a possible solution to that problem. Finally, through the separate windows of Japan's exports and then imports, the coherence of the various zone strategies is assessed, both in terms of how far they combine to constitute a coherent global strategy, and the links between trade and investment, especially in the Asia-zone. The overall focus is thus on the ways Japanese capital's cross-border purchases and sales are linked to its overseas production and contribute to its zone and global strategies to maintain accumulation and profitability.

ADVANCED ZONES: STRUCTURAL CRISIS

It has not been possible so far for the directions or even the 'administrative guidance' of successive Japanese governments to make much impact on the country's 'excessive exports', because once the consumer goods industries had stepped into the driver's seat of Japan's economy, exports have solved the fundamental market problem that arose from 'excessive' reliance on low-cost production. Unlike having a surplus of producer goods, for which domestic demand can be expanded by raising levels of capital investment, a surplus of consumer goods cannot be disposed of domestically without radically redistributing income in favour of wage earners, whose higher earnings then raise costs and undermine profitability. Surplus consumer goods *have to be exported* because there is nowhere else for them to be sold.

Mainly since the oil crisis of the early 1970s that provoked Japan's restructuring out of the raw-material processing industries into manufactured consumer goods, a growing number of key industries have become predominantly dependent on exports, and Japan's exports have become heavily dependent on these industries. By 1993 machinery (general, electrical, transport and precision) contributed a full 76 per cent of Japan's exports, and over half the output of the core machinery industries must now find markets outside Japan.

Table 5.1 shows how the export dependence of some of Japan's key industries has changed over the years. For example, motor cars, which began as a purely domestic industry but which by 1980 came to depend on foreign markets for almost 60 per cent of production, once again became more domestically dependent as large sections of it were relocated, mainly

Table 5.1   Export dependence of some of Japan's key industries (volumes)

	1980	*1985*	*1988*	*1990*	*1992*	*1993*
Motor cars	59.2	57.9	54.1	45.1	47.0	46.0
Motor cycles	53.5	62.8	49.4	61.0	72.8	81.4
VCR	77.6	90.1	78.7	80.7	75.4	72.9
Machine tools	39.5	37.6	36.1	34.0	38.7	50.1
Cameras	79.3	83.0	76.6	81.1	80.0	81.6
Televisions	51.6	77.5	31.9	42.2	44.5	36.7

Source: Tsūshō sangyōshō, 1986b to 1994b.

in the US. A similar story could be told of TV sets. However, the persistent inclination of Japanese capitalism towards finding export markets, especially for its consumer goods industries, continues to express itself, often through rapidly growing exports of revolutionary new products, such as VCRs.

Japan's traditional orientation towards exporting has thus received a structural boost through the growing dependence of its key industries on overseas markets. The state, chiefly MITI, has come under this dual pressure not simply to promote exports, but also to protect the leading industries from any imports which might eat into their domestic markets. Because the US and Europe boasted the world's largest buying power, these regions became the primary targets of the policy. The consequence has been the growing international competitiveness of the protected industries and mounting trade imbalances with the US and to a lesser extent Europe. By the mid-1980s these imbalances had become a source of chronic conflict which continues to manifest itself in rising values of the yen. In spite of repeated calls for structural changes to solve the problem, these are ruled out by the very foundations on which Japanese capitalism is built, low domestic wages. The problem remains, but it has been exported.

We have already seen how the trade imbalance behind the appreciating yen has sent Japan's manufacturing industries into foreign ventures, in the advanced countries to sharpen their technologies and protect their markets, and into the less developed world first of all to cut their costs but now also to promote sales. Having to export in order to compensate for the absence of raw materials has thus given way to trade which is directed more by the profit-making strategies of individual corporations, which have had their international competitiveness eroded by the rising yen and so have had to find international strategies to restore that competitiveness.

Structural Imbalance

After a brief period when it seemed that a trade balance was being struck with the US, these profit-restoring strategies sent Japan's balance of payments in 1992 to a record surplus of $117.6 billion. The US accounted for $43.6 billion ($38.2 billion in 1991) of the *trade* surplus of $106.6 billion and the EC $31.2 billion. In only a few years Japan had travelled a full circle from the chronic surplus of the mid-1980s. The main reason, once again, was the ongoing success of Japan's export drive in the machinery industries to compensate for the shortfall at home, an effort which more than offset the fall in motor vehicle exports resulting from increasing local

production, especially in the US. So even though the US share of Japan's
machinery exports fell from 37.5 per cent in 1988 to 32.1 per cent in 1993
and Southeast Asia's share climbed from 21.1 per cent to 26.2 per cent,
the deeper structural problem between the two advanced countries
remained. Europe's share, rather than North America's, was falling in line
with the expansion into Asia (Tsūshō sangyōshō, 1992b, 1993b, 1994b).
Table 5.2. shows the changing regional destinations of the different categories of machinery exports since 1991. Apart from transport machinery,
overseas markets for the output of these industries have also become more
exclusively associated with the three strategic zones.

The high-yen recession of the mid-1980s, which itself resulted from the
attempt to export Japan's domestic imbalance between production and
consumption, seemed so easy to deal with at the time, since within a year
or two it was over. However, all the conditions which worked towards that
solution had disintegrated within a couple of years, and the problem
rebounded back onto Japan with increased stubbornness. The main difference between the two recessions is that because the boom following the
short-lived high yen recession of 1986 included substantial upper-class
consumer-spending, huge volumes of imports could be sucked in without
eroding the market of Japan's own producers, whereas the chronically
deficient domestic demand which has characterised the current slump
turns imports into something that feeds the recession and therefore something to be discouraged. In 1991 real imports from Germany and the US
fell, those from South Korea, Taiwan and Thailand barely held their own,
while only those from Malaysia showed any real increase. During the high
yen recession real imports from all these countries had expanded considerably, in line with upper-class consumption and equipment investment
(Nihon bōeki shinkōkai, 1993b, pp. 45–6, 60–2).

We saw in Chapter 2 how by 1992 a massive 60 per cent of Japan's
growth rate had come to depend on foreign demand, a proportion almost
three times as high as 1985. In order to deal with the recession it thus
became necessary to complement the export drive – with all its normal
costdown measures to keep export prices down – with *limits* on imports,
since they now competed with domestic producers for a chronically
deficient spending power. So although the Japanese government kept up
the appearance of working for a solution to the trade imbalance, the less
visible but more powerful networks of Japanese capital openly put all their
energies into increasing exports and very little into encouraging imports.
In fact a lot of the blame for the continuation of the recession well into
1994 was put on a surge in imports earlier that year. By August the *Nikkei
Weekly* (29 August 1994, p. 2) had come to believe that 'the tide of

Table 5.2   Japan's machinery exports, by region and industry, 1991–93 (%)

	General			Electrical			Transport			Precision			Total		
	1991	1992	1993	1991	1992	1993	1991	1992	1993	1991	1992	1993	1991	1992	1993
N. Am.	31.9	32.3	35.2	28.7	28.6	29.1	43.3	38.4	37.4	32.4	33.2	34.8	34.7	33.3	34.0
SE Asia	34.2	32.0	31.0	34.7	36.9	40.4	11.1	12.0	14.5	26.0	27.0	29.8	26.2	26.4	28.5
C. Asia*	2.3	3.9	5.7	2.7	3.4	3.8	0.8	1.5	2.5	1.0	1.1	1.6	1.8	2.7	3.8
Europe	21.5	21.7	18.2	24.3	21.4	17.5	22.9	22.7	19.5	31.8	30.1	25.6	23.5	22.5	18.9
Other	10.1	10.1	9.9	9.6	9.7	9.2	21.9	25.4	26.1	8.8	8.6	8.2	13.8	15.1	14.8

*Communist Asia, largely China.

Source: Tsūshō sangyōshō, 1992, p. 101, 1993, p. 99.

imports could drain the economy'. It went on to quote a MITI official as having said that 'the rapid growth in imports is considered a main reason for the decline in domestic consumer products shipments'. So a large part of the structural problem that preserves Japan's trade surplus with the US is a problem in the structure of Japanese capitalism, that is, the uneven development between its productive power and its market capacity: exports *have* to be encouraged and imports *have* to be discouraged.

Not just conditions within Japan, but also those within its main trading partners have also played their part in swelling Japan's trade surplus. Following the upturn in the US economy in 1991, imports from that country soon more than offset the decline in German imports, soaring by 11.6 per cent in 1992 in comparison to a 0.6 per cent rise the previous year (Nihon bōeki shinkōkai, 1993b, p. 10; *NW*, 31 January 1994, p. 3). Certain structural features of US capitalism thus also tend to stimulate imports whenever economic growth picks up, making their volumes less sensitive to price increases resulting from the rising yen. The most important is the high degree to which domestic industry has been 'hollowed out' by its high level of internationalisation, with approximately 24 per cent of corporate America's total productive power having been sent abroad in comparison to Japan's six or seven per cent. A great deal of what allows countries like Taiwan and South Korea to run trade surpluses with the US actually stems from the power of US companies in these countries.

Unable to alter its own industrial structure because its entire social system is built on it, each side demands that the other changes its structural problem. Thus the US wants numerical quotas for its products in the Japanese market, while Japan wants a quantitative increase in exports from within the US. Neither can oblige the other, because Japanese capital would collapse if it actually allowed the foreign quotas to increase and to eat away at its structurally-deficient market, and US capitalism would collapse if it tried to bring back into the country the productive power which it long ago had to relocate. The long and continuously revised lists of demands and counter-demands, accusations and counter-accusations, that have been presented by both sides to the increasingly difficult talks they have held, especially in 1993 and 1994, can be best understood in this light. The detailed allegations of closed markets and price fixing in Japan, or of deficient competitive power in the US do not really matter, since at best they conceal the structural conflict that lies behind the allegations. From the point of view of Japanese capital what matters is its need to maintain market shares in the US, if necessary by means of increasing local production, and to resist any substantial intrusion into its own market by US capital. These then are the central axes of its strategy in the North

American zone (*NW*, 24 May 1993, p. 7; 17 May 1993, pp. 2–3; 14 February 1994, p. 2; 28 February 1994, p. 1; 7 March 1994, p. 1; 14 March 1994, p. 2; 4 April 1994, pp. 1, 23; 18 April 1994, p. 2; *TB*, February 1994, pp. 44–7).

In Europe, although Japanese export volumes tend to be a bit more responsive to the higher yen, they have not fallen very much either, also in part for reasons relating to that region's industrial structure, which as a *whole* has fewer gaps the Japanese are able to fill, even though some parts of it have been all but de-industrialised. In the car industry, for example, since the market is still gripped by recession and centres on the VW Golf – in contrast to the three-litre Ford Taurus in the US – Japan's export drive is spearheaded by one- to two-litre cars. The result is that the prices of the smaller cars destined for Europe are only about two-thirds of those of the larger cars that go to the US. Moreover, Japanese transplants in the US have grown so rapidly that fewer cars are being exported than before, whereas the limited number of transplants in Europe means that sales rely mainly on exports. Since the quality of Japanese cars also compares less favourably with local products in Europe than it does in the US, Japanese companies concentrate more on the lower end of the market. They have also been more successful than expected because the yen has not risen as much in relation to the European currencies as it has in relation to the dollar.

However, because the new European Union is making it harder rather than easier for Japanese capital to maintain its exports in this zone, the rearguard action needed simply to preserve markets depends even more heavily on local production than it does in the US, not just in the car industry, but also in the electrical industry in which local production also lags behind what has been achieved in the US. Japan's trading strategies in Europe thus rely even more on the success of its investment strategies in the region, and so long as the trade surplus does not grow to proportions that provoke excessive retaliatory action, the two can function in reasonable harmony with each other much in the way that they do in the US. In Europe Japanese capital has also so far been able to avoid the main problem that arises *within* the North American zone strategy, that is, the overall lack of profitability of so many projects.

However, the task of maintaining markets in the two advanced capitalist zones has not been easy for Japanese capital, since successful export drives in the territories of its equals have required constant changes in product quality and price. Unfortunately, many of the changes were so swift that the export drives became too successful, so that the weight between preserving markets by means of local production and by means of exports shifted too much in favour of the latter. The result was another surge in the trade surplus and a fresh round of conflict with the advanced capitalist zones.

Prices, Volumes and Exchange Rates

Changes in Japan's export prices and to a lesser extent the volumes of its exports and imports have therefore made the recent surplus even more difficult to deal with than before and the recession in Japan therefore harder to end. While in 1985–86 there was some reduction in both yen-based export prices and the yen-value of Japan's exports, in 1992–93 neither of these has fallen significantly, partly because of Japan's restructuring into higher value-added exports (notably higher-priced luxury cars) in the late 1980s. On the import side, largely due to a plunge in oil prices, yen-based import prices have also fallen more heavily in the 1990s and caused a sharper reduction in the value of Japan's imports. Both price movements therefore contributed to the widening of the surplus in the 1990s. The volumes of trade have also differed in the two periods. From late-1986 to mid-1988, a substantial rise in the volume of imports accompanied a fall in the volume of exports, both helping to reverse the surplus. But in the early 1990s import volumes rose much more slowly – even falling by 0.2 per cent in 1992 – while export volumes actually increased – by 0.2 per cent in 1992, and so the imbalance was exacerbated. Although in 1993 export volumes fell somewhat and import volumes increased, their positive effects on the trade balance were, as will be seen below, eroded by changes in *dollar*-based prices due to the rise of the yen.

Compared to the other advanced countries, Japan still continues to rely overwhelmingly on increasing its volume of exports rather than on selling higher-priced goods, mainly because this continues to reflect Japan's social and industrial structure. However, since 1985 a number of changes have begun to affect this pattern. First, there has been an increase in the proportion of exports whose prices and volumes have both risen, such as chemicals, general machinery and electrical machinery. Particularly in electrical machinery, the production of lower value-added goods (household electronics goods such as fans, stoves, tape recorders, radios, small colour TVs, telephones) has shifted abroad and Japan has raised the sophistication of its components (microchips, disk drives) as well as its finished goods (compact disk players, large colour TVs, cordless telephones, computers, fax machines). These tend to contribute most to Japan's burgeoning surplus, because the effects of their higher prices are multiplied by the effects of having to find mass markets for them outside

Japan. Second, there are goods, such as automobiles, whose prices have risen steadily but whose volumes have not changed greatly, mainly because more have been produced by overseas subsidiaries. Since they still constitute a large proportion of Japan's trade with the US, the fall in volumes has been insufficient to reduce their values to any noticeable degree (Nihon bōeki shinkōkai, 1993b, pp. 70–3).

In the context of these changes in the volumes and prices of Japan's exports over the past few years – shown more fully in Table 5.3 – the rise of the yen has produced substantial changes in their *dollar* values: a 0.2 per cent increase in real exports in 1992 translated into a full 8.0 per cent surge in their dollar value, while a similar fall in real imports reduced their dollar value by only 1.3 per cent. The result was that Japan's trade surplus soared to a record $106.6 billion (Nihon bōeki shinkōkai 1993b, pp. 45–6). For the same reasons, in 1993, a 2 per cent fall in export volumes and a rise twice that size in import volumes translated into a mere 0.8 per cent decline in the yen-based trade surplus, but a rise in the dollar-based surplus of 12.8 per cent to a record $120.2 billion (Tsūshō sangyōshō, 1994b, p. 1).

Whatever adjustment had been gained by the yen's revaluation in the mid-1980s had by the early 1990s been totally lost, for the same reasons that the problem had developed in the first place. In spite of the higher value-added products that have been exported in the 1990s, the cost-down which the recession made necessary has kept yen-based export prices firmly in check and allowed export volumes to rise in spite of the higher yen, which actually became the immediate cause of the sudden escalation in dollar-based export prices and the surge in the dollar-value of exports.

Table 5.3   Volume and price indices of Japan's trade, 1985–93 (1990 = 100)

	1985	1986	1987	1988	1989	1990	1991	1992	1993
Exports									
Volumes	87	86	93	91	95	100	103	104	102
Yen-based prices	116	99	93	90	96	100	100	100	95
Dollar-based export prices	70	85	93	101	101	100	107	114	123
Imports									
Volumes	63	68	74	88	95	100	104	104	108
Yen-based prices	145	94	86	81	91	100	91	84	74
Dollar-based prices	87	79	86	91	95	100	97	96	95

Source: Tsūshō sangyōshō, 1994b, p. 1.

On the import side, even though the higher yen lowered the yen-based prices of imports, the recession checked the volume of imports sufficiently to prevent any substantial rise in the dollar value of imports. The monetarist 'solution', that is, exchange rate adjustment, to the international problems created by Japan's international displacement of its domestic problems, turned out to be no solution at all. During the recession, Japanese capital has been taking all the usual measures to protect its own shrinking market and to expand its foreign markets, not least in the rejuvenated US.

For a short period following the rise of the yen in the mid-1980s it seemed that exchange rate adjustments might reverse the trend of Japan's growing trade imbalance with the US, but by 1992 the surplus was once again on the increase and by 1993 it reached record levels. The main reasons were the heavy costdown programme to deal with the recession and the higher yen, the resulting need to step up the export drive to compensate for falling domestic demand, the networks which Japanese capital uses to create non-tariff barriers to protect its own market and conquer foreign markets, and the continued dependence of the US on Japan for certain high value-added products due to the different ratios of overseas production of the two powers.

It has been argued (Takeuchi *et al.*, 1987, p. 19) that if one considers all the sales that take place between Japanese and American companies, irrespective of where in the world these are located, the trade imbalance tends to disappear, since US companies sell as much to Japanese companies as vice versa. The problem is not different levels of productive power, which certainly is the main factor behind Japan's surplus with less developed countries, but different levels of internationalisation and protection of the home base. Of all the advanced powers with more or less equal technological power and international competitiveness, Japan stands out for the large degree to which its productive power is located within Japan and so expressed in terms of Japanese exports. American, German, French, British and Italian productive power has been internationalised to a qualitatively much greater degree, and in each case it expresses itself in sizeable exports from a wide range of countries. But since Japanese capital cannot wait until it has relocated a fifth of its productive power overseas before its conflict with the US and Europe is resolved, in the meantime it must do whatever it can to maintain its existing markets in the advanced countries.

Because of the very high proportion of Japan's trade with the US that is conducted in dollars, as shown in Table 5.4, the greatest impact of the rising yen on Japan's price competitiveness has been on trade with the US. However, as Table 5.4 also reveals, Japanese companies have managed to

Table 5.4   Currency of Japan's exports in 1991

Currency	Region	Share of Total Value
Yen	World	39.4
	US	16.5
	EC	42.0
	Southeast Asia	50.8
US $	World	46.8
	US	83.4
	EC	6.8
	Southeast Asia	45.9
Other	World	13.8
	US	0.1
	EC	51.2
	Southeast Asia	3.3

Source: Nihon bōeki shinkōkai, 1993b, p. 68.

denominate more than half their exports to Asia in yen, thereby preserving the profitability of their export contracts from exchange rate fluctuations by shifting the cost onto those without the bargaining power to determine the currency in which prices are contracted. The other ways Japanese capital compensates for its failures in the advanced countries by taking it out on Asia must now be examined as well.

ASIA-ZONE: STRUCTURAL SOLUTION?

In order to resolve the market problems which have plagued it so stubbornly, Japanese capital has re-directed its attention to the three main zones that dominate world trade as a whole – the advanced regions of North America and Europe, and less developed region of East Asia – which are also the centres of the world's productive power and the main recipients of Japan's FDI. The task facing Japanese capital is both to consolidate the linkages between its trade and investment within each zone as well as somehow to combine the zone strategies into a coherent global strategy. Table 5.5 shows how world trade fluctuates widely in association with changes in real economic growth, especially in the advanced countries, but also in Asia. After falling from its previous peak growth rate of 9.1 per cent in 1988 to 2.3 per cent in 1991, world trade expanded by 4.2 per cent in 1992 and an estimated 5.2 per cent the next year. However, the

Table 5.5 Economic growth and increases in volume of world trade (%)

	1984	1985	1986	1987	1988	1989	1990	1991	1992
Advanced countries GDP growth	4.5	3.3	2.8	2.6	4.4	3.2	2.1	0.2	1.5
Advanced country exports growth	9.6	4.1	2.7	4.1	8.2	6.6	5.7	2.9	3.2
World trade volume growth	8.3	3.4	4.0	6.0	9.1	7.0	4.4	2.3	4.2
LDCs GDP growth	4.5	5.3	4.9	5.6	5.3	4.0	3.7	4.2	6.1
LDCs exports growth	5.5	0.5	7.8	11.8	13.6	6.2	6.0	7.7	8.4
Asia real GDP growth	8.4	7.2	7.1	8.1	9.1	5.5	5.7	5.8	7.9
Average real GDP growth	4.4	3.8	3.6	3.9	4.6	3.3	2.0	0.6	1.8
'Socialist' countries	3.3	2.0	3.2	2.6	4.4	1.9	-3.6	-10.1	-15.5

Source: Keizai kyōryoku no genjō to mondaiten, 1993, pp. 3, 5, 11.

current recessions in Japan and Europe have left the US, where capital accumulation picked up briskly in 1992, and Southeast Asia as the main engines behind increases in world trade in the first half of the 1990s. Both remain the main targets of Japanese companies desperately looking for markets, even though their relative weights in Japan's overall global strategy are being altered (Nihon bōeki shinkōkai, 1993b, p. 9).

The most rapid increases in trade over the past decade have been among the East Asian countries, between East Asia and the advanced countries, and among the advanced countries, especially *within* Europe. However, in all cases, the leading force has been the tremendous productive power of international capital as it consolidates its hold over the whole range of elements that jointly constitute its distinctive power, such as almost limitless finance, leading-edge technology, cheap labour, a global division of labour and strategic positioning in the global market place. In recent years, the geographical loci in which that power most vigorously expresses itself have increasingly clustered round selected areas of the East Asian region: the NICs in the 1970s and early 1980s, ASEAN in the latter half of the decade and China in the early 1990s. Trade statistics of nations states are thus quite misleading, since at best they help reveal the location of this driving force, at worst they give the misleading impression that international commodity exchange is governed by the comparative advantages of nations rather than the technical-industrial power of capital, in particular international capital and its world-wide networks. Changing shares of world trade thus mainly point to international capital's changing strategies, which must take into account the whole range of influences on money making, not least political economic alliances with ruling elites in less developed countries.

In 1985–92, the period in which East Asia received the largest single wave of FDI in the history of capitalism, that region's share of world trade soared by 4.57 percentage points to 13.73 per cent (almost two and a half times that of Japan and only half a percentage point behind the US). In the same period, Africa's share fell by 0.69 percentage points to a mere 2.2 per cent, that of the Middle East by 0.92 percentage points to 4.52 per cent, while the Latin American share crept up by just 0.13 percentage points to 4.61 per cent. Japan's share of world trade has zigzagged unevenly to produce its widening imbalance: on the export side, the period 1981–91 saw an increase from 8.3 per cent to 9.1 per cent, but on the import side there was a decline from 7 per cent to 6.3 per cent. The US performance remained fairly constant, with export shares falling from 12.7 per cent to 12.1 per cent and import shares remaining at 14.2 per cent. Table 5.6 shows the changes in more rounded figures (Nihon bōeki shinkōkai, 1993b, p. 25; Tsūshō sangyōshō, 1993a, p. 20).

Table 5.6   Regional shares of world trade, 1982–92

	Exports		Imports	
	1982	*1992*	*1982*	*1992*
East Asia (NICs, ASEAN and China)	9	14	9	15
Japan	8	9	7	6
US	12	12	14	14
EU (external)	17	15	18	17
EU (internal)	19	25	18	23
Other	35	24	33	25

Source: Tsūshō sangyōshō, 1994a, p. 16.

Table 5.7   Intra-regional and inter-regional shares of world trade, 1980–92

	1980	*1985*	*1990*	*1991*	*1992*
Intra-North America	4.04	6.38	5.35	5.23	5.25
North America ↔ Japan	3.11	5.41	4.62	4.45	4.29
North America ↔ East Asia	2.97	4.56	4.88	5.12	5.26
North America ↔ Europe	6.60	7.95	7.45	7.02	6.78
Japan ↔ East Asia	3.22	4.10	4.38	4.81	4.81
Japan ↔ Europe	1.56	1.94	2.91	2.93	2.81
Intra-East Asia	1.65	2.64	3.98	4.71	5.09
East Asia ↔ Europe	2.23	2.56	3.79	4.08	4.19
Intra-Europe	28.27	27.08	33.87	32.83	32.33
Sub-total	53.65	62.62	71.23	71.18	70.81
East Asian exports	7.47	10.32	12.55	13.76	14.15
East Asian imports	7.44	9.16	11.47	13.04	13.73

Source: Nihon bōeki shinkōkai, 1993b, p. 11.

The dominance of the advanced countries and their satellites in East Asia is perhaps more starkly revealed by the growing proportions of world trade that are conducted amongst themselves, since the networks through which this trade is conducted help link the centres of power together and so further consolidate their strength. Table 5.7 shows that in a little more than a decade this trade skyrocketed from just over a half to nearly three-quarters of the world's total.

East Asia has been international capital's chief target for FDI and FDI-related trade for well over twenty years, a trend which has been greatly accelerated by the liberalisation of foreign investment regulations and the shift to policies encouraging export-led growth (ELG), so that FDI and ELG have become two sides of the same coin. International capital, which has been the leading force behind the export of manufactures from East Asia, has thus been the driving force behind the region's high rates of accumulation and its increasing shares of world trade.

However, parallelling the shift of Japan's FDI and trade from the advanced countries towards East Asia, there were growing signs that the trade surplus was also being successfully displaced in the same direction. The countries which have been absorbing the largest amounts of Japanese FDI are running the largest trade deficits with Japan. And the more rapid the rate of economic growth of each Asian country, the larger is Japan's trade surplus with it, because the main exports to these countries comprise the capital goods which drive their economic development. The NICs, Thailand and Malaysia are notable examples.

Table 5.8 shows that while in 1989 the surplus with Southeast Asia was less than half the surplus with the US, by 1992 the former had soared into the top position. Even the trade balance with the ASEAN region, which used to serve mainly as a source of raw materials for Japan's traditional industrial structure, has moved from a large deficit to a surplus, as individual countries become more dependent on Japanese capital goods for their industrial transformations, goods whose prices have risen sharply with the appreciation of the yen. For example, while Japan's exports of semiconductors to the NICs leapt by 42 per cent in fiscal 1993, its exports to ASEAN sky-rocketed by 64.4 per cent, partly in response to the steady shift by Japanese subsidiaries from the NICs to ASEAN. A broader restructuring of FDI from the recession-ridden advanced countries (particularly in Europe) to the more rapidly growing Southeast Asian countries has helped boost the region's imports from Japan by double figures each year since 1987 (*NW*, 1 March 1993, p. 27; 12 April 1993, p. 4; 2 August 1993, p. 24; 17 January 1994, p. 1; 25 April 1994, p. 1).

FDI-Linked Trade

According to a recent JETRO survey, the rise of the yen in 1992–93 has had a much larger, but also much more diverse, impact on Japanese managerial strategy than did *endaka* in 1988. A full 60 per cent of 775 responding companies found the 1993 rise to be harder to deal with, over 80 per cent faced falling exports and 41 per cent had to accept the cancellation of export orders. The most heavily affected industries were precision machinery, electronics parts, pulp and paper (over 80 per cent in all

Table 5.8   Japan's trade balance, by country and year ($ billion)

	1985	1986	1987	1988	1989	1990	1991	1992	1993
Japan's total trade surplus	46.1	82.7	79.7	77.6	64.3	52.1	77.8	106.6	120.2
US	39.5	51.4	52.1	47.6	44.9	38.0	38.2	43.6	50.2
EU	11.1	16.7	20.0	22.8	19.8	18.5	27.4	31.2	26.3
Southeast Asia	3.0	12.3	14.4	19.3	20.6	28.1	37.4	46.9	56.8
NICs	12.6	17.6	20.7	24.8	25.6	30.7	39.5	46.5	53.5
South Korea	3.0	5.2	5.2	3.6	3.6	5.8	7.7	6.2	7.4
Taiwan	1.6	3.2	4.2	5.6	6.4	7.0	8.8	11.7	12.4
Hong Kong	5.7	6.1	7.3	9.6	9.3	10.9	14.3	19.7	20.7
Singapore	2.3	3.1	4.0	6.0	6.3	7.1	8.8	9.9	13.0
ASEAN	-9.4	-6.3	-6.8	-6.0	-5.1	-2.2	-1.5	0.5	3.7
Thailand	1.0	0.6	1.1	2.4	3.0	5.0	4.2	4.4	5.8
Malaysia	-2.2	-2.1	-2.6	-1.7	-1.0	0.1	1.2	1.5	2.0
West Asia (Middle East)	-18.0	-8.8	-11.6	-11.1	-15.2	-21.7	-17.5	-14.4	-14.0
Latin America	2.2	3.3	2.4	1.0	0.5	0.4	3.0	7.1	8.6
Africa	1.1	0.5	1.8	1.8	1.1	1.8	2.2	3.1	3.6
'Socialist' countries									
China	6.0	4.2	0.8	-0.4	-2.6	-5.9	-5.6	-5.0	-3.3
USSR/Central Europe	1.6	1.5	0.5	0.4	0.0	-0.7	-1.1	-1.2	-1.3

Source: Nihon bōeki shinkōkai, 1993b, pp. 52–4; Tsūshō sangyōshō, 1994b, p. 774–5, 781 ff.

these found the 1993 *endaka* worse), non-ferrous metals (over 75 per cent), transport machinery and components and electrical machinery (both around 70 per cent). The main reason given for the greater difficulty in 1993 was the limit on further rationalisations, costdowns and shifts into domestic demand, which had saved the day in 1988 (Nihon bōeki shinkōkai 1993b, pp. 78–80).

Nevertheless, Japanese capital's main anti-recessionary strategies did not change much since 1988, the key ones being further rationalisations of production at home and export promotion of higher value-added products in order to compete more through product quality than through price. Since both strategies lie at the very heart of Japan's current structural problem, there is little reason to believe that their consequences in the 1990s are likely to differ from those in the late 1980s. In 1988 as well as in 1993, the proportions of firms surveyed by JETRO which selected these two strategies were close to 70 per cent and close to 50 per cent respectively. The next most favoured strategy, selected by about a third of respondents on both occasions, was to put the blame on dollar-based export prices and to seek out new markets. Also on both occasions, about a quarter of the firms favoured increasing overseas production or setting up new overseas ventures. However, the main change since 1988 centred on international trading strategies, particularly on the import rather than the export side, namely, securing cheaper overseas supplies of parts and intermediate goods (from 19 to 31 per cent) and increasing 'reverse imports' from Japanese subsidiaries overseas, or *gyaku yunyū* (from 9 to 19 per cent). Japanese companies are now moving more and more away from simply securing market shares in export markets and towards using trade, notably their import strategies which they are linking more to their investment strategies, to maintain and expand profitability. The functions of the *sōgō shōsha* (the trading companies that control most of Japan's trade) have also been shifting away from managing the 'barter' between the raw materials that Japan lacks and the manufactures of which Japan produces a surplus. Now these behemoths act less for 'the nation' and more to consolidate the zone strategies of the *keiretsu* groupings they represent, performing a whole range of functions which further cement together the links between industrial, financial and commercial power (Nihon bōeki shinkōkai, 1993b, pp. 82–3).

The profit-making strategies of Japanese manufacturing companies have singled Asia out for two closely related trading roles that are gradually being brought together as the zone strategy takes shape. Both centre on the growing importance of FDI in the region. First, with the relocation of so much productive power to low-cost countries, what once were domestic transactions within a company or *keiretsu* have been transformed into cross-border transactions, as the Japan head office imports supplies which have become too expensive to produce at home. Second, as the local production of consumer goods in Asia substitutes for Japanese exports and enhances the overall zone strategy, the structure of Japan's trade changes because the local subsidiaries now import sophisticated plant, machinery and components from Japan.

All this trade has little to do with high principles like comparative advantage or bartering manufactures for raw materials, but varies with the different internationalising strategies of the companies concerned and of the *keiretsu* to which they belong. Its greatest advantage to the *keiretsu* is that they now get repeated bites at the cherry: low-cost production of components or finished consumer goods to be sent back to Japan, local markets for these consumer goods through the growing income of the urban middle classes, and new export markets for Japan's high-tech industries which supply the local subsidiaries with plant, equipment and components. Table 5.9 shows that by 1991 over half the exports of Japan's manufacturing companies were to their overseas subsidiaries, and that the industries with the highest proportions of turnover that must be exported – especially machinery – have the highest proportions of their exports going to their own subsidiaries. On the import side it shows that while import dependence was still relatively low in the machinery industries, the proportions of these companies' imports that came from their subsidiaries were high, for example, 36 per cent in electrical machinery. Trade is thus linked to investment through the purchases and sales of the subsidiary companies, transactions that tend to be concluded within the *keiretsu* networks.

Because this kind of connection between Japan's trade and its FDI in the manufacturing industries is organised through vertical *keiretsu* networks, the industries with the highest levels of international production, such as electrical machinery, are also the ones in which intra-industry trade is greatest: Japanese subsidiaries are requiring constant supplies of plant and equipment, materials and sophisticated components, and they are manufacturing other components as well as finished goods for their parent companies in Japan.

An acute observer of Japan's trade and power has recently argued that East Asia's trade is increasingly being conducted autonomously within the region itself and that only a part of this intra-regional trade can be accounted for in terms of the growing cross-border activity among the subsidiaries of Japanese corporations (Lincoln, 1993, p. 174). The remainder, it is argued, stems from real independent capitalist development and independent regional integration. Intra-regional exports have grown from

Table 5.9   Trade between Japanese companies and their overseas subsidiaries, March 1992

	Exports		Imports	
	As % of turnover	% to subsidiaries	As % of turnover	% from subsidiaries
Agriculture	5.2	10.7	29.5	41.7
Mining	3.2	11.0	50.0	10.2
Construction	5.1	18.7	1.4	12.1
Manufacturing	22.0	53.7	12.2	26.5
Food	0.7	19.6	13.9	27.8
Textiles	11.2	6.3	7.5	28.2
Wood/Pulp	6.3	4.7	26.0	23.8
Petroleum/Coal	1.8	17.9	51.6	29.9
Chemicals	10.5	29.2	16.2	7.2
Iron & Steel	17.2	5.2	23.4	4.5
Non-ferrous metals	6.9	29.1	18.4	8.7
General machinery	22.5	39.4	3.8	23.6
Electrical machinery	28.6	59.0	9.0	36.1
Transport machinery	33.1	55.1	2.9	21.3
Precision machinery	46.2	77.1	11.1	43.8
Other	13.2	53.0	8.3	30.7
Commerce	12.0	27.3	15.4	28.8
Services	1.8	13.1	0.5	16.7
Other	4.2	10.2	1.6	55.9
TOTAL	16.1	48.9	13.5	27.4

Source: Tsūshō sangyōshō sangyō seisakukyoku kokusai kigyōka, 1993a, pp. 6–7, 49, 50.
Table 5.8 is based on a MITI survey of 1 789 head offices and 8 505 subsidiary companies at the end of March 1992.

22 per cent of the total in 1980 to 36 per cent in 1992 (Japan's share falling from 12 per cent to 8 per cent), while intra-regional imports grew from 22 per cent to 37 per cent in the same period (but Japan's share also grew, from 13 per cent to 16 per cent) (Nihon bōeki shinkōkai, 1993b, pp. 24–5).

However, while it is true that the cross-border sales of Japanese subsidiaries located in East Asia are modest relative to East Asian trade as a whole, the dynamism that Japanese capital injects into the region has many more manifestations than this. For example, joint ventures between Japanese car makers and Thai conglomerates can lift the fortunes of the latter in many other ways which promote intra-regional trade. If the key position occupied by Japan's leading-edge technology in this process is recognised, the real basis of growing intra-regional trade within Asia can be assessed more accurately. And if FDI in East Asia from the other advanced countries (especially the US) and its links with Japanese capital is also taken into account, there is little doubt that international capital is the powerhouse behind the region's internal as well as external trade. The distinctive power of Japanese capital to direct and to appropriate for itself activities that are located in nominally separate institutions or regions must never be lost sight of. Sales among Japanese subsidiaries within the region or the latter's trade with Japan, especially the growing imports from Japan of plant and equipment, are only some of the manifestations of this power. Japan's trade and investment thus constitute the centre of gravity around which the explosive capitalist development in the region is occurring.

Keiretsu Networks

The role of links among *keiretsu* companies and other channels which bind Japan's investment and trade together can also be seen by comparing the trading patterns of Japan's overseas subsidiaries with the overall trading patterns of the countries in which the subsidiaries are located. Table 5.10 provides such a comparison on the basis of 1988–89 data, which are recent enough to capture the trends that established themselves mainly in the 1980s. On the export side, while there is little difference between NICs' exports to Asia and those of Japanese companies located in the NICs, the exports of Japanese subsidiaries to Japan are almost three times those of NICs' exports to Japan, suggesting the operation of very powerful networks linking Japanese investment to trade with Japan. On the import side, the influence is even greater, with Japanese subsidiaries in the NICs importing from Japan almost four times what the NICs import overall. A similar, although possibly slightly weaker, influence on ASEAN trade with Japan is also apparent, especially in the manufacturing industry.

The only real power in Asia to export to Japan lies in raw materials and light manufacturing, and with Japanese networks. According to one estimate, 30–40 per cent of Japan's total trade with ASEAN comprises internal transactions within Japanese parent companies and their overseas subsidiaries (*FEER*, 3 June 1993, p. 48). These same networks also enhance Asia's internal trade, as revealed by the higher levels of exports to Asia by Japanese companies in both the NICs and ASEAN than total NICs and ASEAN exports to Asia. Asia's dependence on Japanese technology is also strikingly revealed by the very high levels of imports which

Table 5.10   Markets of Japanese firms in Asia and of the regions generally, 1988–89 (%)

All Industries (1988)	Japan	Trading Partner Asia	N. America	Elsewhere
Exports of:				
NICs (total exports)	12.4	25.5	33.4	28.7
Japanese firms in NICs	**34.4**	26.6	22.2	16.7
ASEAN (total exports)	24.6	27.0	20.7	27.7
Japanese firms in ASEAN	33.7	32.7	19.8	13.8
Imports of:				
NICs (total imports)	23.8	27.4	18.0	30.8
Japanese firms in NICs	**83.1**	13.6	0.6	2.6
ASEAN (total imports)	23.7	34.0	14.1	28.2
Japanese firms in ASEAN	**67.5**	25.7	2.4	4.4
Manufacturing (1989)	*Japan*	*Asia*	*N. America*	*Europe*
ASEAN's total exports	13.1	27.2	27.8	17.8
Japanese firms' exports	38.7	30.1	12.9	5.3
ASEAN's total imports	31.2	17.3	17.5	16.6
Japanese firms' imports	75.1	7.4	1.8	1.2
Electrical machinery				
ASEAN's total exports	5.6	32.7	41.7	15.7
Japanese firms' exports	26.9	38.6	19.2	4.6
ASEAN's total imports	27.4	21.8	30.5	12.6
Japanese firms' imports	61.4	16.7	0.3	0.0
Transport machinery				
ASEAN's total exports	8.3	23.2	48.7	8.6
Japanese firms' exports	23.6	7.8	0.9	0.0
ASEAN's total imports	79.5	1.4	2.0	12.8
Japanese firms' imports	99.8	0.0	0.0	0.0

Source: Urata, 1992, p. 58 for 1988 data, and Tsūshō sangyōshō, 1993d, pp. 187 for 1989 data.

come from Japan in the leading electrical and motor vehicle industries, whether or not Japanese networks are directly involved. An important change that has taken place since 1989 when these data were created is the rapidly growing use of ASEAN countries to make parts for Japan's ASEAN cars. However, one thing that Japanese companies have not done, as it once seemed they might, is themselves use Asian countries as export bases to the US or Europe, in order to displace trade friction, to the same degree that other companies in Asia have. Nevertheless, the region has clearly performed such a function for Japanese capital even without the direct mediation of its own networks.

Although Japanese networks in the NICs might have been stronger than they were in ASEAN in the early 1980s, growing FDI since then in ASEAN manufacturing has created a more similar influence in both regions: the effects of Japanese networks on the exports and imports of both the NICs and ASEAN countries are being very powerfully felt via the links they forge between investment and trade in the region. Table 5.11, which relies on a 1986 MITI study, confirms that the sales to Japan and imports of supplies from Japan by overseas subsidiaries are overwhelmingly transactions within the same *keiretsu*. What might seem surprising are the high levels of intra-group trading that are involved in transactions with third countries, particularly by Japanese subsidiaries in the US, but since production is almost entirely for the domestic market in that country, this is not significant. Transport machinery in Asia (notably the NICs) is another case of high *keiretsu* regulation of transactions with third countries, but this is because the car industry is dominated by a few tightly organised interlocking corporate networks.

Since these networks were first set up in Free Trade Zones in the 1960s and 1970s, when they simply comprised imports of supplies from and exports to Japan and elsewhere, they have developed over the years into increasingly complex patterns, especially in Asia. The most typical of these comprise multiple sources of supply – from Japan, from local and regional Japanese subsidiaries and from non-Japanese companies worldwide – and multiple sales outlets, consisting of the local market, exports back to Japan, sales to local and regional subsidiaries (including assembly) and exports to other countries (Aoki, 1992, pp. 80–3).

Much of the coordination among the Asian networks is carried out from Singapore by what its government calls the companies' International Procurement Offices (distribution centres), of which there were 44 in 1992, 35 of which were electrical companies (Aoki, 1992, p. 85). The Singapore government grants special tax concessions to companies which bring to the country a comprehensive range of activities, such as distribution, manufacturing and R&D. By March 1991, of the 37 foreign companies which had been granted this status, seven were Japanese (Anazawa, 1992, p. 99).

Although from the point of view of each of the three main zone strategies, and even Japanese capital's global strategy, it might seem that the central problem of Japan's domestic economic structure is being dealt with satisfactorily in the international arena, the persistence of recession within the country is the most powerful evidence to the contrary. Japan's growing shares of Asian markets simply require Asia to export more to the US,

Table 5.11 Market shares of overseas subsidiaries which are within the same *keiretsu*, 1986

	Markets				Supplies			
	Local	Japan	Other	Average	Local	Japan	Other	Average
Asia								
Manufacturing	8.9	76.5	23.7	24.0	6.8	66.6	34.3	37.3
Electrical Machinery	9.6	73.0	32.1	31.6	6.2	78.1	55.9	49.9
Transport Machinery	9.1	46.0	62.8	22.0	4.0	56.1	67.9	42.0
ASEAN								
Manufacturing	9.2	78.5	17.0	18.5	8.2	66.7	30.5	33.9
Electrical Machinery	13.4	57.7	16.5	18.2	19.6	77.6	59.8	57.1
Transport Machinery	13.8	45.0	37.5	20.1	7.0	70.3	39.6	48.2
US								
Manufacturing	3.1	87.0	20.8	6.0	30.1	70.6	42.8	58.8
Electrical Machinery	1.3	97.4	67.0	2.4	92.0	70.9	83.5	73.6
Transport Machinery	48.8	96.7	100.0	58.0	68.4	73.6	0.0	49.5
Manufacturing	19.0	99.2	17.8	19.6	42.7	87.1	32.8	64.4
Electrical Machinery	29.4	100.0	53.1	32.6	79.2	88.8	26.0	77.2
Transport Machinery	0.0	100.0	10.4	2.0	0.0	56.4	51.6	21.8

Source: Urata, 1992, p. 59.

which is then forced to put its barriers up against Asia. The extent to which Japan languishes in recession is thus a measure of US power to contest that of Japan in the region and to send Japan's domestic problems right back to where they came from. The US has gradually been raising its protection against Asian imports and, along with its escalating FDI in the region, has been increasing its exports to the point that Asia (including Japan) surged ahead of Europe as its leading export market in 1993 (*NW*, 20 September 1993, p. 27). The degree to which Japan can make Asia pay the full price of its domestic imbalance will increasingly depend on the degree to which it has to share the exploitation of Asia with its powerful American rival. The lingering recession is a reminder that Japanese capital cannot have everything its own way in the wider world, although if stagnation is a measure of international powerlessness, then the stagnation that surrounds the lives of the majority of Asian peoples is a stronger reminder of who the chief victims of the new imperialism really are.

Economic revival in the US must not therefore be seen as the American Achilles heel which sucks in 'excessive Japanese imports', since it expresses the continued strength of US capitalism and the state system which champions its interests so effectively in the outside world. The role of the US in the post-war world order of super-power rivalry produced a state that was as vigorous in 'defending' US interests abroad as it was negligent in protecting US capitalism from internal onslaughts, notably the cheap imports from America's overseas subsidiaries that have hollowed out key sectors of US industry. The Japanese state has functioned in almost exactly the opposite way: having no military cards to play in a world order dominated by force, it focused almost exclusively on the home front, offering protection from internal and external attacks alike. However, as we will presently see, Japanese capital lacks the kind of state that can effectively integrate its different zone strategies into a coherent global strategy, with the result that while the US economic revival owed much to its government's aggressive overseas policy, not least towards Japan, Japan's recession owes as much to its government's inability to respond.

Although East Asia derives most of its market strength from the productive power planted within it by Japan and other advanced countries, as far as Japanese capital is concerned this helps rather than hinders the region's capacity to absorb Japanese goods and to resolve once and for all the problem which bedevils accumulation in Japan. If the US and Europe can always strengthen their barriers against Japanese goods and resist the full displacement of Japan's domestic problems into their backyards, then the more deeply entrenched Japanese networks of power within Asia should be sufficient to prevent any similar fate from occurring in that region. However, although it is unlikely that even US networks in Asia will, for some time to come, achieve sufficient breadth and depth to offer a serious challenge to 'their Japanese counterparts, who consider Asian markets their turf' (*NW*, 20 September 1993, p. 27), Asia cannot run permanent trade deficits with Japan unless it can run permanent surpluses with the US. And this latter is something the US is not prepared to tolerate, even though in the short term it might be. And so in the short term at least, Japanese capital has been determined to step up its export drive into Asia as a way of counteracting the ever deeper depression into which the domestic market has been sinking in the early 1990s. The real challenge is thus for Japanese capital to blend together into a coherent global strategy its two main zone strategies. In the advanced countries it must at least hold onto its market shares by blocking the 'Japan bashing' that is bowled its way and by replacing as many exports as possible with local production, while in Asia it must use its networks to tie up and to expand markets in close relation to its cost-cutting investment strategies. To see how far these two imperatives can be coherently combined requires looking at them through the more general windows of Japan's exports and imports.

JAPAN'S EXPORTS

Since so much of Japan's FDI in the advanced countries was propelled by the need to maintain markets which were coming under increasing protection, the profit-making strategies of Japanese companies in the US and Europe have put further limits on the exports these markets can absorb. Local production for the local market might help preserve overall corporate profitability, but it makes it harder rather than easier to market what is produced in Japan, unless production in Japan is in turn reduced to what the local market can absorb. The current recession and further hollowing out of Japanese industry is a painful reminder that this is exactly the kind of alternative that looms more permanently should the problem no longer be capable of being exported. The rush into Asia is thus all the more desperate. Fortunately for Japanese capital, the kind of FDI being sent to the less developed countries has a much greater tendency to stimulate Japanese exports than FDI in the advanced countries, and the most attractive production sites in Asia are also the most rapidly expanding markets for both exports from Japan and for the output of local Japanese firms: China, ASEAN and the NICs, in that order – but also Latin America –

mainly *because* these are the areas in which investment has grown most rapidly. In 1991, as revealed by Table 5.12, Southeast Asia overtook the US as Japan's top export market.

Table 5.12   Japan's exports, by product and destination, 1989–93 ($ billion)

Industry	1990	1991	1992	1993
Foodstuffs	1.6	1.8	1.9	2.0
Raw Materials	2.4	2.4	2.9	3.3
Heavy Manufactures	250.5	275.2	297.3	317.5
Machinery	215.1	236.6	256.8	274.4
General	63.5	69.5	76.3	82.8
Electrical	65.9	73.7	77.4	84.5
Transport	71.8	77.9	87.1	90.4
Motor vehicles (excl. parts)	51.0	54.8	60.5	58.4
Ships	5.6	6.7	7.9	10.2
Precision	13.8	15.5	16.0	16.7
Metallic goods	19.5	21.1	21.3	22.9
Iron and Steel	12.5	13.6	13.3	14.5
Chemicals	15.9	17.5	19.1	20.2
Light Manufactures	27.8	30.1	32.2	32.0
Textiles	7.2	7.9	8.6	8.2
Non-ferrous metallic goods	3.2	3.5	3.9	4.0
Re-exports etc.	4.6	5.0	5.4	6.1
TOTAL	286.9	314.5	339.6	360.9
Destination				
Advanced countries	170.0	176.9	184.8	187.6
US	90.3	91.5	95.8	105.4
EU	53.5	59.2	62.5	56.4
Other	26.1	26.2	26.5	25.8
Developing countries	107.1	125.6	140.3	152.9
Southeast Asia	82.7	96.2	104.4	117.4
NICs	56.7	66.9	72.6	80.5
ASEAN	22.2	25.3	27.6	32.9
Communist Asia	6.5	9.1	12.7	18.2
China	6.1	8.6	11.9	17.3
West Asia*	9.7	12.0	14.9	13.3
Latin America	10.3	12.8	15.8	16.9
Africa	5.7	6.0	6.8	7.5
Russia and Eastern Europe	3.3	2.9	1.9	2.3

*Mainly the Middle East, but excluding North Africa.

Source: Nihon bōeki shinkōkai 1993b, p. 47; Tsūshō sangyōshō, 1994b.

The well-worn reason for this change is the stubbornness of the trade imbalance with the US and its continual intrusion into almost every area of policy-making in Japan. This problem has meant that Asia is increasingly being cultivated as much for the growing market potential offered by its prospering upper and middle classes as for the low-cost production offered by its urban and rural poor. Table 5.13 shows the enormous potential of Asia, chiefly the ASEAN countries and China, to substitute for the advanced countries as markets for the consumer goods produced by Japan's leading electronics firms.

The shift to Asian markets does not, however, simply reflect the attempt to avoid trade friction with the advanced countries, but also the cumulative links companies have forged between their overseas investments and their foreign trade. By definition, overseas production means that the output is not marketed from Japan and so is not recorded as 'Japanese exports', but the extent to which overseas production actually *substitutes* for exports depends on the degree to which it is matched by production cuts in Japan, since if there are no corresponding cuts the overseas subsidiaries *erode* the export markets that producers in Japan still require. Other effects on trade of foreign investment include the *generation* of exports, when supplies of plant, equipment and components are needed by the subsidiaries, and *gyaku yunyū,* or 'reverse imports', when the output is marketed back to Japan by these subsidiaries. The actual consequences depends on the type of project as well as its location.

Particularly since the large cost-cutting wave of Japanese investments that took place in the late 1980s, there have been growing forward and backward linkages like these between FDI and trade. In the car industry, for example, shifting the stage of assembly closer to the market (as in the advanced countries) or to cheap labour sites (as in Thailand) initially resulted in large exports of intermediate goods from Japan. However, either in response to local demands to increase the domestic content of the cars (as in the US) or the need to reduce the cost of imported components because of the high yen (as in Southeast Asia), many subcontractors shifted from Japan either to the countries where their components were required or to neighbouring low-wage countries in the same region. This move by component makers has contributed most to the higher levels of local or regional supplies of parts and materials over the past five years. For example, the number of Japanese firms supplying the Japanese electrical machinery industry in Malaysia soared from 78 in 1987 to 406 in 1989 (Aoki, 1992, p. 77). In the US the full cycle of this kind of development has taken place most rapidly in transport machinery, while in Europe the pace has been quicker in electrical and general machinery.

Table 5.13   Growth rates of markets for electronics goods, by region, 1987–97

	Colour TV		VCR		Video Camera		VD Player		CD Player		Tape Recorder		Car Stereo	
	1987–92	1992–97	1987–92	1992–97	1987–92	1992–97	1987–92	1992–97	1987–92	1992–97	1987–92	1992–97	1987–92	1992–97
Asian NICs	3.0	2.6	8.5	4.1	39.8	10.5	–	12.2	33.5	10.0	1.6	1.5	18.3	3.4
S. Korea	5.8	2.7	21.9	6.8	151.2	14.9	–	26.2	127.9	14.6	1.4	1.9	31.2	5.1
Taiwan	2.4	3.3	5.4	-0.3	32.0	20.0	–	16.5	127.9	14.6	0.8	1.4	21.7	3.1
Hong Kong	-6.3	0.0	-9.7	-1.0	24.9	3.7	–	12.7	12.2	1.7	-0.9	1.9	0.5	-5.0
Singapore	1.3	3.0	-0.4	4.8	20.6	5.5	–	3.7	24.0	6.8	5.6	0.9	-6.5	4.6
ASEAN	16.6	8.1	22.4	12.9	14.9	27.2	–	24.6	56.6	18.0	12.1	4.0	30.5	7.2
Thailand	11.2	8.0	12.3	12.5	43.1	33.0	–	24.6	51.6	13.4	2.3	1.6	32.7	9.1
Malaysia	22.9	8.4	32.0	15.6	3.4	21.2	–	14.9	109.1	17.6	7.2	4.8	28.0	1.8
Indonesia	22.9	8.9	33.9	13.2	–	27.2	–	38.0	–	38.0	25.1	5.1	58.5	47.6
Other	8.1	3.3	56.9	7.7	0.0	24.6	–	14.9	4.6	3.7	6.6	4.3	35.1	9.2
China	5.5	11.2	43.6	7.0	35.1	81.9	–	14.9	–	58.5	2.4	8.6	28.3	10.4
Japan	-1.8	0.8	-6.2	-1.8	3.7	3.6	2.9	5.1	3.9	-14.0	1.7	-15.3	4.0	-6.8
US	2.6	1.3	1.0	-0.9	11.9	3.8	28.5	18.0	15.5	3.0	-0.2	0.4	4.7	-2.9
Western Europe	4.5	2.7	5.4	3.9	32.2	0.5	–	38.0	22.5	2.6	0.7	-0.3	5.1	-0.4

Source: Survey conducted by the Japan Electronics Association in April 1993, cited in Nihon bōeki shinkōkai, 1994, p. 29.

Table 5.14 shows that in the machinery branches of manufacturing, that is, ones unrelated to natural resources, the *local* and *regional* procurement of components and materials is highest where Japanese suppliers have also set up operations, for example, in the general machinery industry in Europe, the transport machinery industry in the US, or in both of these in the Asian NICs, because Japanese companies still overwhelmingly prefer to secure supplies from within their own *keiretsu*. However, they are increasingly not only using suppliers from low-wage neighbouring countries within each of the three main regions (e.g. Mexico in North America, Spain in Europe), but ones from Asia for all regions (these companies are then the same as Asia's 'regional suppliers'). So in those industries in the advanced countries where the share of local suppliers has fallen in recent years (e.g. electrical machinery in both Europe and the US), an expansion in supplies from within the region or from Asia accounts for most of the decline.

There are some other interesting new developments in the networks through which Japanese subsidiaries secure their supplies of intermediate goods. First, the proportion obtained locally by companies in Asia, particularly in the machinery industries, has been decreasing in recent years, while imports from both Japan and other Asian countries have been increasing. We have noted that the growing importance of Asian supplies reflects the success of the regional strategies of Japanese companies, which produce different parts in different Asian countries (rather than all parts in all countries). However, the rise in imports from Japan reflects the consolidation in the home country of the production of high-tech sophisticated components, which have become the staple of Japan's current exports to Asia. The other development, which is similar, has been encountered before: low (and slightly falling levels) of local procurement in Europe, but very high (and increasing) levels of regional procurement, also a result of the improvement of zone strategies in Europe as a whole and the development of a division of labour in the region. However, while Asian subsidiaries have been importing more from Japan, those in Europe have been importing less, because the required sophisticated technology can be more easily transferred to the advanced countries of Europe than it can to the less developed countries of Asia. The same factor lies behind the general fall in imports from Japan by subsidiaries located in the US. The most important exception to this, apart from the materials-related industries, is in electrical machinery, although even here the fall in local supplies in the US has been matched more by the huge rise in imports from Asia than by the minor rise in imports from Japan.

The advanced countries' greater technological power thus crucially determines the patterns of Japan's intra-industry trade resulting from the

Table 5.14   Supplies of components and materials for Japan's overseas manufacturing subsidiaries, by zone and selected* industries, 1991

	(a) Local Supplies		(b) Imports i) from Japan		ii) from 3rd Country		of which from: within Region		Asia	
	1987	1991	1987	1991	1987	1991	1987	1991	1987	1991
North America	44.3	47.1	52.9	47.1	2.8	5.7	30.2	33.7	34.7	54.8
Food	86.7	96.3	7.3	0.6	6.0	3.1	14.2	18.8	0.4	81.2
Wood/Pulp	97.6	100.0	0.9	0.0	1.5	0.0	47.4	0.0	10.5	0.0
Chemicals	83.2	68.3	**16.2**	**31.0**	0.6	0.7	0.0	85.9	0.0	0.0
Iron & Steel	75.5	95.9	11.9	2.6	12.6	1.5	40.1	0.0	1.3	50.3
General machinery	23.8	33.0	76.0	58.8	0.3	**8.2**	24.4	24.9	6.7	25.8
Electrical machinery	**38.1**	**26.0**	60.0	65.0	1.9	9.0	38.5	25.5	**54.3**	**72.6**
Transport machinery	**27.9**	**56.0**	71.9	41.5	0.2	2.5	0.0	74.6	100.0	6.0
Europe	34.5	31.3	49.4	40.7	16.1	28.0	74.1	82.4	21.8	15.0
Chemicals	66.3	46.8	33.3	35.0	0.4	9.1	100.0	90.0	0.0	4.5
General machinery	**19.2**	**52.4**	**65.5**	**38.8**	15.4	8.8	80.6	92.8	19.3	5.0
Electrical machinery	**30.5**	**19.0**	62.3	45.6	7.1	**35.4**	53.2	**83.9**	**40.6**	**13.6**
Transport machinery	38.5	35.5	57.7	57.9	3.8	6.6	99.8	91.3	0.0	2.7
(Precision machinery)	23.9	22.3	63.0	68.7	13.0	9.0	52.7	**99.1**	**39.4**	**0.9**
Asia	53.7	44.5	33.6	38.8	12.6	16.7	65.4	69.3	65.4	69.3
NICs	53.4	49.0	35.1	38.9	11.5	12.1	66.8	71.6	66.8	71.6
Food	78.2	50.3	9.7	15.8	12.1	33.9	79.3	98.9	79.3	98.9
Textiles	**93.5**	**39.5**	**1.3**	**12.2**	**5.2**	**48.2**	99.8	56.9	99.8	56.9
Chemicals	31.6	59.3	39.9	19.5	28.5	21.2	1.9	31.6	1.9	31.6
Iron & Steel	42.4	44.3	48.8	22.4	8.9	33.3	98.7	39.2	98.7	39.2

Table 5.14 Continued

	(a) Local Supplies		(b) Imports i) from Japan		ii) from 3rd Country		of which from: within Region		Asia	
	1987	1991	1987	1991	1987	1991	1987	1991	1987	1991
Non-ferrous metals	**64.6**	**28.6**	**25.9**	**57.3**	9.5	14.1	**52.7**	**100.0**	52.7	100.0
General machinery	43.9	**48.5**	49.6	**47.6**	6.4	3.9	21.9	37.6	21.9	37.6
Electrical machinery	52.8	50.3	36.7	39.7	**10.6**	**10.1**	93.8	85.9	93.8	85.9
Transport machinery	63.7	57.9	34.3	39.8	2.1	2.3	95.9	7.8	95.9	7.8
Precision machinery	25.5	29.5	61.5	64.4	13.1	6.1	99.7	99.3	99.7	99.3
ASEAN	53.4	37.2	33.8	39.5	**12.8**	**23.4**	64.8	67.3	64.8	67.3
Food	78.6	85.0	11.8	8.0	9.6	7.0	79.5	54.4	79.5	54.4
Textiles	91.5	39.9	**1.5**	**30.0**	**7.0**	**30.1**	56.2	44.0	56.2	44.0
Chemicals	35.4	59.0	32.5	12.1	32.2	28.9	18.6	39.7	18.6	39.7
Iron & Steel	54.2	23.2	35.2	5.3	10.6	**71.5**	**59.6**	**98.7**	59.6	98.7
Non-ferrous metals	62.2	34.8	28.9	15.5	8.8	**49.7**	39.3	15.8	39.3	15.8
General machinery	41.8	31.2	53.0	52.5	**5.2**	**16.3**	**21.1**	**99.1**	21.1	99.1
Electrical machinery	51.6	31.2	36.7	41.1	**11.6**	**27.6**	92.6	92.4	92.6	92.4
Transport machinery	48.7	33.9	**43.1**	**59.5**	8.2	6.5	99.4	44.1	99.4	44.1
Precision machinery	23.4	23.9	63.9	74.6	12.7	1.4	94.6	100.0	94.6	100.0

*For each region, those industries requiring supplies worth less than ¥50 billion in 1987 have been excluded. Figures in bold type indicate significant market concentrations.

Source: Tsūshō sangyōshō sangyō seisakukyoku kokusai kigyōka, 1990a, pp. 192 ff. 1993a, pp. 24–5, 90–7.

internal networks of its MNCs. This point becomes even clearer when one examines the different degrees to which the capital goods required by Japanese subsidiaries can be obtained locally: the average in the advanced countries is between three and four times the ASEAN level. Regional supplies are also almost non-existent, because, with the partial exception of Europe, the regions are typically the low-cost peripheries which are receptive to component manufacturing but not to high-tech production. Hence what cannot be secured locally must come from Japan. Although the most recently available data come from a 1989 MITI study carried out in 1986 (Urata, 1992), the enormity of the technological gap between the advanced and the less developed countries makes it unlikely that very great changes have occurred since then. The Japanese suppliers of these goods have never been willing to shift production of such high-tech goods to LDCs, and they are unlikely to do so in the foreseeable future. Table 5.15 presents the results of this MITI study.

The different production strategies of Japanese companies in Asia and in the advanced countries have resulted in the generation of very different levels, not simply of exports from Japan to subsidiaries in the different

Table 5.15   Supplies of capital goods for Japanese overseas manufacturing subsidiaries, by zone and industry, 1986

	Local Supplies	*Imports from:*	
		Japan	*Third Country*
Asia			
Manufacturing average	47.4	51.3	1.3
Electrical machinery	47.0	53.0	0.0
Transport machinery	44.1	55.9	0.0
ASEAN			
Manufacturing average	24.9	75.1	0.0
Electrical machinery	35.5	64.5	0.0
Transport machinery	28.0	72.0	0.0
US			
Manufacturing average	66.4	33.6	0.0
Electrical machinery	52.8	47.2	0.0
Transport machinery	64.0	36.0	0.0
EC			
Manufacturing average	81.4	18.6	0.0
Electrical machinery	60.9	39.1	0.0
Transport machinery	85.9	14.1	0.0

Source: Urata, 1992, p. 56.

zones, but also of imports back to Japan because of the very different markets aimed at by these subsidiaries. In the advanced countries, the subsidiaries serve one another in joint efforts to maintain their shares of the local markets, while in the less developed countries they serve the parent companies in Japan, either by helping them cut the costs of products needed in Japan, or by contributing to regional production and marketing strategies which are also managed from Japan. The key to understanding both patterns lies in the way trade and investment are combined by the *keiretsu* networks of Japanese companies to form zone strategies.

JAPAN'S IMPORTS

In Asia, where Japan's low-cost production strategy is most fully developed, FDI stimulates trade in a number of ways through these *keiretsu* networks. In some industries, such as electrical machinery, the diverse markets of the output correspond to diverse production strategies. When cheap components are required by *keiretsu* members in Japan, which is a common production strategy in Asia, the effect is to create 're-imports' (or so-called *gyaku yunyū*) back to Japan. When the components are required in some other country, as is also a common production strategy in Asia, the effect is to substitute for Japanese exports to that country (so long as production in Japan is correspondingly curtailed, otherwise they would be *competing* with Japanese exports). When the output of the subsidiaries is sold in the local market, as is almost entirely the case in the advanced countries, the effects are the same as when it is sold to some other country: it either *substitutes* for or *competes* with Japanese exports, depending on what happens to production in Japan. Table 5.16 shows the actual marketing patterns of Japanese subsidiaries in each of the three main zones in 1987–91. Since the markets in the advanced countries are overwhelmingly local and thus relevant to the previous discussion on Japan's exports, the breakdown by industry is confined to Asia, from where Japanese subsidiaries are substantially engaged in production for export, mainly back to Japan to create 're-imports', but also to elsewhere *within* the region.

Production for export is greatest in the precision machinery and electrical machinery industries and in the ASEAN countries rather than the Asian NICs. For example, in fiscal 1991, the same source as the one used to compile Table 5.16 (Tsūshō sangyōshō sangyō seisakukyoku kokusai kigyōka, 1993a, pp. 78 ff.) reveals that only 10 per cent of precision machinery production and 25 per cent of electrical machinery production by Japanese companies in ASEAN countries was for the domestic market.

Table 5.16   Markets of Japan's overseas manufacturing subsidiaries, 1987–91*

	Local	*To Japan*	*Exports To 3rd Country*	*Of which Within Region*
North America				
1987	92.8	4.8	2.5	51.2
1991	89.4	4.1	6.5	43.8
Europe				
1987	66.0	1.5	32.5	87.6
1991	56.3	1.9	41.9	89.9
Asia				
1987	59.1	16.7	24.3	45.7
1991	54.5	15.5	30.0	52.0
Food	24.7	36.5	38.8	21.7
Textiles	55.5	11.6	32.9	55.9
Wood & Pulp	67.0	32.5	0.5	75.0
Petroleum/Coal	61.3	0.0	38.7	100.0
Chemicals	76.9	5.6	17.5	87.0
Iron & Steel	72.0	15.5	12.5	89.7
Non-ferrous metals	69.0	2.8	28.2	93.1
General machinery	76.3	12.2	11.5	58.4
Electrical machinery	34.6	24.0	**41.4**	**51.5**
Transport machinery	83.5	3.2	13.3	23.0
Precision machinery	33.5	26.2	**40.3**	**38.6**
Other	67.3	11.7	21.0	59.7
Agr./For./Fish.	1.7	98.0	0.3	0.0
Mining	26.3	51.4	22.2	27.1
Construction	95.4	0.2	4.4	90.3

* Figures in bold indicate significant concentrations.
Source: Tsūshō sangyōshō sangyō seisakukyoku kokusai kigyōka, 1990a,
pp. 180 ff., 1993a, pp. 78 ff.

The rest was for export, mainly back to Japan (2.6 per cent of precision machinery and 28 per cent of electrical machinery), but also to elsewhere within Asia (18 per cent and 20 per cent), to North America (13 per cent and 14 per cent) and to Europe (15 per cent and 4 per cent).

Trade is being used in three quite distinct but similar ways to complement Japanese capital's production strategies within Asia. First, production for export back to Japan gives the *keiretsu* networks tight control over the supplies of the cheap Asian imports it requires, a theme that is elaborated in the next section of this chapter. Second, Japanese companies in other Asian countries use the same networks to secure cheap supplies of the full range of imported components which the uneven development of any one of them makes it impossible for it to produce. Japanese capital's solution to having to use so many costly 'made-in-Japan' parts in its Asian factories is to rely on importing cheaper ones from within the region. Finally, low-cost production in Asia for export to the US or Europe is used to increase the competitiveness of Japanese goods in these markets, while at the same time minimising trade conflict with them by having the Japanese exports present themselves as imports from Asia.

The identical three broad trading strategies can be discerned from the marketing patterns of Japanese subsidiaries in industries other than manufacturing. For example, the output of Japan's mining investments in ASEAN is largely for export back to Japan (51 per cent), with a further 22 per cent being exported to third countries (largely North America) (*Ibid*, p. 82). Mining production in Latin America is more or less similarly marketed: 40 per cent back to Japan and 60 per cent for the local market, often as a source of cheap supply for local Japanese companies (*Ibid*, p. 80). In Thailand, over 85 per cent of Japanese companies export more than 80 per cent of their production, while in Malaysia such firms comprise almost 60 per cent of Japanese companies (Nihon bōeki shinkōkai, 1993b pp. 76–7).

In the case of manufacturing subsidiaries located in Latin America, the most important export market after Japan is the US. For example, although in 1991 the local market absorbed 71 per cent of transport machinery production and Japan received a further 17 per cent, most of the remainder went to the US (10 per cent) (Tsūshō sangyōshō sangyō seisakukyoku kokusai kigyōka, 1993a, pp. 80–3). In the case of subsidiaries located in Oceania (particularly Australia), there are wide variations across industries. A full half of all mining production in 1991 was exported to Japan and a further 37 per cent was exported to other countries, mainly Asia and the US, whereas 97 per cent of both electrical machinery and transport machinery production was for the domestic market (*Ibid*, p. 86).

Although Japanese subsidiaries in the advanced countries are there to further Japan's export strategies by focusing on the domestic market, in some industries there have been significant 're-imports' into Japan: 21 per cent of foodstuff production by Japanese subsidiaries in the US in 1991 was marketed in Japan as well as 31 per cent of wood and pulp production. In Europe, however, the situation is very different due to the distinctive structural features of European capitalism previously noted. Although about the same proportion of production in the region gets marketed within the region as North America, there are vastly more exports to other countries within the region and fewer sales within the producing country itself. In 1991, for example, only 44 per cent of chemicals produced in Europe were marketed locally in the same country, whereas 90 per cent of the exports to countries other than Japan (which took only 2.4 per cent of the total) were marketed within the region. Other industries in which European countries functioned as production bases for export to elsewhere in Europe were textiles, general machinery and transport machinery (*Ibid*, pp. 78 ff.).

Annual surveys by Japan's Export–Import Bank have detected some recent changes in the strategies of Japanese overseas subsidiaries in relation to the markets they consider the most important to them. Between the 1991 and 1993 surveys there has been a marked shift in favour of the ASEAN market and towards exports back to Japan (*gyaku yunyū*), mainly at the expense of NICs markets, which are increasingly to be targeted directly from Japan with higher value-added goods than before. For example, in the electrical machinery industry in 1991, 14 per cent of Japanese firms in ASEAN saw Japan as their most important market, 33 per cent preferred the ASEAN region, a further 24 per cent the NICs market and 22 per cent the North American market. However, by 1993, the proportion concentrating on exports back to Japan had almost doubled to 23 per cent, while those favouring ASEAN had leapt to 41 per cent and those favouring the NICs market had plummeted to 7 per cent (the North American share was largely unchanged). Similar patterns are coming from the subsidiaries in China: by 1993, 20 per cent of electrical machinery companies considered exports back to Japan as their most important market, while 56 per cent said they concentrated on the local market and 12 per cent on the North American market.

The NICs' markets are themselves becoming saturated with low-cost Japanese goods and finding it increasingly difficult to absorb the output even of Japanese subsidiaries located within them, let alone those in ASEAN. In 1991, also in electrical machinery, 63 per cent of Japanese firms in the NICs focused on the NICs markets, with only 9 per cent on exports back to Japan, 4 per cent on exports to ASEAN and 20 per cent on exports to North America. Two years later, however, the first group fell to 55 per cent, while those concentrating on exports to Japan leapt to 13 per cent and those on exports to ASEAN doubled to 8 per cent. The North American group fell marginally to 19 per cent. Another important change that took place during the two years was an increasing specialisation on these four markets by companies in both ASEAN and the NICs: the proportions that concentrated on other markets (such as Europe and elsewhere in Asia) fell into insignificance. In the same two years subsidiaries in the advanced countries all but ceased to focus on exports to the NICs: in 1991,

14 per cent of those in North America concentrated on the NICs, as did 4 per cent of those in Europe, but by 1993, 99 per cent of Japanese firms in both Europe and North America favoured the local market (Tejima *et al.* 1994, pp. 39–41).

The significance of these changes can hardly be exaggerated, since they reveal a rapidly increasing specialisation and division of labour among the different zones and as well as within the Asia zone. First, the shift from the NICs to ASEAN for both low-cost production and markets within Asia is leaving the NICs free to function as the main export markets for the higher value-added goods which Japan has kept at home but which it has difficulty in exporting to the advanced countries without further provoking them. Second, ASEAN and China are becoming increasingly integrated low-cost production zones in themselves for supplying both the US market as well as Japan itself. This latter, however, might become the thin end of the wedge for Japanese capital.

The Empire Strikes Back: *Gyaku Yunyū*

Overall, the most dramatic change in Japan's trade that has occurred since 1988 has been the rise in the proportion of production in Asia which has been destined for the Japanese market, the Achilles heel of Japanese capitalism which sent producers abroad in the first place to get away from the deficiency of domestic consumer demand. Now with rising re-imports from Japan's overseas empire, that weakness could turn into a cancer via the back door, just as rising exports to the US by Japanese subsidiaries in Asia can provoke further reactions against Japan from that imperial power.

Even in 1992, when Japanese imports from other parts of the world (including the Asian NICs) were falling, those from Asia as a whole continued to rise, propelled as they were by imports of textiles, machinery and miscellaneous goods from China and ASEAN. Table 5.17 shows that Japan's overall manufactured imports ratio skyrocketed from 31 per cent in 1985 to 52 per cent in 1993 – but it was still well below the 70 to 80 per cent for the other advanced countries – and that most of the increase occurred during the first four years, when import prices fell and import volumes grew rapidly.

There has actually been little change since 1988, when the ratio was 49 per cent, partly because import prices fell by only half as much in the early 1990s as they did in the second half of the 1980s, but also because of the very different economic conditions in the two periods: the short-lived high-yen recession ended in a boom, whereas the current underconsumption has affected imports along with everything else. Nevertheless, there

Table 5.17   Japan's manufactured imports ratios, by country of origin, 1985–93*

	1985	1990	1992	1993
World-wide	31.0	50.3	50.2	52.0
US	55.2	62.0	61.3	61.8
EU	82.7	88.1	85.4	85.1
Southeast Asia	25.3	46.6	49.3	53.6
Asian NICs	57.8	73.4	73.3	71.9
ASEAN	8.4	23.9	31.8	34.6
China	27.0	50.8	63.7	68.7
Vietnam	12.5	3.9	13.9	22.2
Southwest Asia	30.8	53.5	55.1	55.7
India	23.1	46.7	48.5	49.6
Pakistan	61.4	81.0	79.0	82.9
Bangladesh	15.5	42.9	52.1	41.3
Sri Lanka	20.2	52.7	61.8	63.6

*Figures for the advanced countries are not strictly comparable, since they include 're-imports' whereas the other figures only comprise 'processed manufactures'.
Source: Nihon bōeki shinkōkai, 1993b, p. 31; Tsūshō sangyōshō,1994b.

has been a continued rise in the proportion of manufactured imports from those low-wage countries of ASEAN, China and South Asia which had been targeted by Japanese companies keen to find new sites of low-cost production. Table 5.18 shows how in just a few years there have been almost total transformations in the suppliers of some goods to the Japanese market, and that the trend towards Asian suppliers has not fallen away with the recession as it has in the case of imports from the advanced countries (Tōyō keizai tōkei geppō, July 1994, pp. 9–12).

The ASEAN region with which Japan now conducts so much manufacturing trade comprises the very countries that Japanese capital first entered in the 1960s and 1970s in order to secure the bulk of the raw materials it consumes. However, since this theme has been written about extensively (e.g. Steven, 1990) and is pursued more fully in the final chapter, the discussion will continue to focus on Japan's manufactured imports, even though some important developments have been occurring in countries like Vietnam and in industries like crude oil, logging, plywood and food, especially rice (*TB*, January–February., 1993, pp. 58–9; *FEER*, 4 March 1993, pp. 43–4; *NW*, 25 October 1993, p. 2; 15 November 1993, p. 24; 21 February 1994, p. 15; 28 March 1994, p. 10; 11 April 1994, p. 20).

Table 5.18   Asian shares of Japanese imports, by commodity and country, 1988–92

	1988	1989	1990	1991	1992
Textiles ($ million from Asia)	8 132.9	9 989.9	8 835.8	10 017.5	11 741.5
Asia share of total imports					
(per cent)	76.6	75.3	64.7	73.4	76.6
NICs	59.4	55.5	48.9	42.1	33.6
ASEAN	3.2	4.5	6.6	7.3	8.6
China	29.9	32.5	36.2	42.2	50.1
Household elec. appliances					
($ million)	896.9	1 121.3	921.3	1 171.3	1 364.4
Asia (per cent)	80.3	80.1	73.6	78.3	79.5
NICs	90.0	79.8	69.2	58.0	50.7
ASEAN	4.9	10.3	19.5	29.8	32.4
China	5.0	9.3	10.8	11.7	16.3
Air conditioners ($ million)	26.2	41.6	43.0	200.0	174.1
Asia (per cent)	54.4	64.0	64.8	90.4	83.4
NICs	42.1	47.0	25.3	7.4	11.6
ASEAN	57.8	52.9	74.4	92.4	87.9
Colour TVs ($ million)	100.5	235.2	148.9	263.0	335.8
Asia (per cent)	89.8	94.8	93.9	92.1	87.6
NICs	99.9	99.7	90.6	73.3	55.1
ASEAN	0.03	0.05	7.9	26.3	39.8
China	0.01	0.2	1.3	0.3	5.3
Bags ($ million)	371.7	455.1	530.4	710.1	859.1
Asia (per cent)	48.0	44.0	40.0	47.8	52.0
NICs	84.4	80.2	71.8	64.8	56.6
ASEAN	1.9	2.9	4.1	5.6	6.8
China	13.0	16.3	23.6	29.2	35.9
Footwear ($ million)	889.3	853.2	959.7	1 209.7	1 390.9
Asia (per cent)	77.1	72.4	70.3	73.9	76.0
NICs	90.9	85.9	75.4	64.8	53.2
ASEAN	1.4	2.8	6.3	8.7	9.6
China	7.3	10.7	17.7	25.9	36.4

Source: Nihon bōeki shinkōkai, 1993b, pp. 32–3.

The composition of Japan's manufactured imports has also changed considerably since the mid-1980s. For example, clothing imports soared by an average of 27.9 per cent in 1985–92, almost doubling their share of manufactured imports (from 5.0 to 9.5 per cent), while electrical and transport machinery also increased their shares, from 9.7 to 12.5 per cent and from 6.4 to 8.7 per cent respectively. The biggest losers were chemicals, which fell from 20.1 to 14.8 per cent, and non-ferrous metals, which dropped to 6 per cent from 10.1, in both of which the US had been the main source of imports. The attempt to displace Japan's surplus onto Asia thus had contradictory consequences (Yasuhara *et al.*, 1994, p. 111; Tsūshō sangyōshō, 1994b, pp. 209, 246).

A more ominous change becomes apparent when Japan's manufactured imports are classified according to end use, since consumer goods almost doubled their share, rising from sixteen to 30 per cent, while that of intermediate goods fell from 56 to 40 per cent, also mainly because of the falling share of chemicals and non-ferrous metals. And while the US share of manufactured imports fell from 35.5 to 27.3 per cent of the total, that of the three key areas of Asia (NICs, ASEAN and China) jumped from 22 to 33 per cent, that of ASEAN and China more than doubling to 7.4 and 9.2 per cent respectively, having soared by an average of almost 30 per cent a year (Yasuhara *et al.*, 1994, April 1994, pp. 114 ff.)

This trade is intimately linked to Japanese investment in the region. Surveys by Japan's Export Import Bank (Tejima *et al.*, 1994, p. 23) have shown that securing imports back to Japan has been one of the most rapidly increasing motives for investments in China (mentioned by 9 per cent of firms in 1991 but 20 per cent in 1993) and ASEAN (from 9 per cent to 21 per cent). Firms looking for component supplies have soared from 6 per cent to 17 per cent in ASEAN and from 0 to 12 per cent in China. Other new motives propelling investments into China are also sales related and include opening up the local market (from 29 per cent to 45 per cent) and exporting to third countries (from 9 per cent to 16 per cent). Exporting to third countries has been the main new motivating force behind investments in the NICs (from 6 per cent in 1990 to 26 per cent in 1993) as well as in ASEAN (from 13 per cent to 32 per cent in the same period). The contrast with the advanced countries is striking and continues unchanged. While low-cost production remains a predominant motive throughout Asia, it is hardly mentioned in relation to the advanced countries, which continue to attract investments which 'maintain and broaden the local market'.

Since low-cost production in Asia does increasingly aim at the Japanese market, there are growing signs that the tide of re-imports could, if unchecked, undermine the domestic market in Japan as savagely as the re-imports from US subsidiaries hollowed out that country's industrial base. Already imports of colour TVs from the Asian transplants exceed Japan's exports and account for a good half of the domestic market. Similar developments seem to be occurring through the re-imports of a wide range of electrical goods, including VCRs, personal computers and microchips, and to a lesser extent motor vehicle components and even motor vehicles. Although the numbers are not yet very great, Japan imports more 'retros' (re-imported cars) from its subsidiaries in the US than it does vehicles made by US companies. Among the reasons for this is that marketing in Japan's labyrinthine distribution system is something the *keiretsu*-linked companies find relatively easy. As the real agents of Japan's new imperialism with power above the Japanese state, they might also be the source of an eventual trade balance through chipping away at Japan's productive base until it comes down in size sufficiently to match Japan's shrunken consumer demand. For all its efforts, the Japanese state has so far offered little more than knee-jerk reactions to the problem: it has welcomed the imports for their potential to smooth over trade friction with the advanced countries, but it has come up with as contradictory a set of traditional solutions to the recession as have individual Japanese companies.

CONCLUSION

Asia is clearly being required to function more and more as a panacea for the obstacles Japanese capital encounters in other parts of the world, beginning with those coming from within Japan itself and then moving to those which, although they had also originated in Japan, had been displaced to other parts of the world where they subsequently encountered growing difficulties of their own. The difference between what the developed and less developed zones have to put up with is a consequence of their power, that is, whether or not they too possess the networks of 'international capital'.

Japan's move into Asia soon after the war was to secure the raw material supplies it lacked, a strategy which was accelerated in the 1970s in response to the growing ability of Asian suppliers to influence commodity prices. To appropriate for itself these growing rents, the impact of which was greatest during the 1970s 'oil shocks', Japanese capital sent its sōgō shōsha into a wide range of raw material investments which their *keiretsu* networks forged into a tightly-knit system of trade (Steven, 1990). To this day Indonesia is Japan's number one supplier of wooden products, natural gas and shrimps (and prawns), it is second to Malaysia as a source of tropical wood and it is Japan's third largest supplier of copper ore, butane, coffee and crude oil. The Philippines remains Japan's top suppliers of many tropical fruits (pineapples, mangoes and bananas), as well as a major source of other foodstuffs and tropical wood. Japan also secures a number of foodstuffs and materials from Thailand, which ranks first in cassava, rubber, sugar, cuttle fish and spices. Malaysia's main exports in this regard are wood and palm oil (ASEAN Centre, 1993, pp. 50–4).

The next major obstacle encountered by Japanese capitalism at home resulted from the rise of the yen in the mid-1980s. Although this was a back-slap from the advanced countries for the attempt to make them absorb the consumer goods Japan could not, its effect was more on costs than on markets, which could be protected so long as production could be sufficiently cheapened. The 'rush' to Asia in the late-1980s was thus to help achieve this end, which the same *keiretsu* networks served by initiating a trade in low-cost manufactures to Japan. This was a classical example of 'unequal exchange' in Japan's favour, since the products of Asia's labour-intensive low-wage industries were now also made with high-tech plant and equipment from Japan, resulting in the generation of massive surpluses whose prices grossly undervalued the Asian resources that went into them. This combination of advanced technology with cheap labour also gave Japanese capital such competitive strength over local capital in Asia, that the choice facing the latter was either to find their proper place within the *keiretsu* networks or to suffer the consequences.

While costdown at home and through exploitation in Asia did resolve the immediate problem by keeping Japanese exports cheap enough to preserve their overseas markets, the detour had not prevented it from boomeranging right back again, this time not just in the form of an even higher yen, but also a more heavily-armed and aggressive regime in the US. If the predictable 'rush' back into Asia was less haphazard this time, involving as it did greater attempts by the *keiretsu* and the state to foster coordination and to plan regionally as well as globally, there are few signs that the extended diversion can do much to eliminate the basic problem. Japan still languishes in recession, and even if another round of rapid accumulation does emerge from the foundations which are being carved out in Asian markets, this will only increase the pressure for further expansions of Asian exports, to the US and Japan, in order to preserve trade balances in that zone. Either the US or Japan will have to face the recessionary costs of the floods of cheap imports that their own strategies in the region make necessary. The victims of imperialism in the present world order can no longer be confined to the less developed countries. The contradictory investment and market strategies required to preserve Japan's social system may take Japanese capital to very distant shores, but nowhere is far enough to escape from home.

Home is where the Japanese 'system' is of course on its strongest ground, and there have been sincere attempts by the state to coordinate a solution, if only it could work out what that could be. One consistent note has been the encouragement given to imports through removing regulations which the US alleges function as 'non-tariff barriers', but it is doubtful that this is very much more than an exercise in public relations, since the state has no intention, or ability, to dismantle the *keiretsu* networks which really lie behind market regulation in Japan. Besides, nobody really believes that the problem of market deficiency in Japan can be solved by flooding the Japanese market with imports. The power of *gai-atsu* (foreign pressure) to shift the Japanese system (Van Wolferen, 1989) into these uncharted waters has been floundering in the face of equally powerful forces that the 'system' brings together within Japan: profits and patriotism.

Import promotion is thus a popular strategy, cited by 47 per cent of firms in the previously-mentioned JETRO survey for solving the nation's problems, largely because of its potential to restore their profits. The most important reason for supporting the campaign, that is, 'profitability on the cost side' (mentioned by 37 per cent of firms), suggests that import promotion and *gyaku yunyū* are often seen as the same thing, although advantages were also said to flow from the high quality of imported products, the diversification of supply lines, establishing links with overseas firms, securing goods from Japanese subsidiaries abroad and overcoming the shortages of domestic supplies (mentioned by 8 to 13 per cent). Only about 5 per cent of the firms thought that import promotion could help avoid trade friction. Newspaper reports of actual increases in imports have revealed a similar range of motives: motor cycle parts (crank cases, cylinder heads and mufflers) from subsidiaries in Brazil in order to cut costs made intolerable due to the high yen, personal computers from Taiwan and South Korea in order to raise price competitiveness, a wide range of electronics parts from Southeast Asia in order to counter the high costs of Japanese labour and motor vehicles from the US in order to help US exports (Nihon bōeki shinkōkai, 1993b, pp. 84–5; *NW*, 12 July 1993, p. 9; 2 August 1993, p. 9; 16 August 1993, p. 9; 13 September 1993, p. 9; 4 October 1993, p. 9; 28 February 1994, p. 9; 28 March 1994, p. 2; 11 April 1994, p. 4).

It thus seems that if the Japanese state is ever called on to increase, rather than reduce, its protection of the domestic market, then the challenge will be to harmonise various sections of Japanese capital, not to mention the more difficult one of placating foreign capital. We have seen that the main sources of Japanese imports are shifting from the advanced countries to the developing countries, particularly the largest recipients of Japanese investment in Asia, and that the fastest growing manufactured imports comprise consumer and intermediate goods (components) from the labour-intensive industries of the low-wage countries in the region. In the years 1990 to 1992, China soared from the fifth to the second largest (only behind the US) source of Japan's manufactured imports and Thailand from twelfth to ninth position, while manufactured imports from all the other countries which had been in the top ten in 1990 fell in the years to 1992, notably the US, Germany, South Korea and Taiwan (Tsūshō sangyōshō, 1993b, 1994b).

Japanese capital has been happy to use its *keiretsu* networks to usher in selected ranges of low-cost imports which offer the least threat to the productive power it likes to keep within the country, since this is the most effective way to keep the real competition at bay while still complying with the formal demands for de-regulating the Japanese market which the US never ceases to press. The recent demands for quotas goes to the very heart of the matter, since it implies that the inability of US goods to penetrate the Japanese market is proof of that market's impenetrability, while the conclusion Japanese capital prefers to draw is that US goods lack the required qualities and price competitiveness. The repeated breakdown in 1994 of negotiations to resolve the impasse suggests that the reasons are no longer of any concern and that the crunch has finally come. Although this does not have to mean anything like a full-scale trade war, it does mean altering the balance between the use of carrots and sticks, again with the predictable consequences of recession, somewhere or other. It must be remembered that the effect of Japan's 'excessive exports' to the US is not the destruction of US industry – on the contrary, the US car industry's revival in the early 1990s owed a lot to the stimulus it received from having to compete with Japanese cars, both exports and locally produced models – but the trade imbalance. The standoff is about commercial rather than productive power.

If the Japanese state is allowing the outcome of the contest within Japan to be determined by the profit-making strategies of Japanese companies, then outside the country it is more vigorously using its influence in favour of regional trading arrangements. At the global level, the World Trade Organisation (the offshoot of the GATT) is more important for its moral than for any actual or potential role it has to play outside industries like agriculture, which do rely on tariff barriers to protect Japanese producers. Japanese politicians and officials actually like to point out how well Japan performs in relation to the legalistic criteria of market openness which this largely US-created initiative uses, but since the Japanese work more through their own *keiretsu* networks than the combination of military force and moral high-ground used by their rivals, the importance of the WTO is, for the moment at least, limited in comparison to that of the various regional trading blocks, such as the ones being built by rivals, NAFTA and the EU, as well as those being put together in Asia by a wide diversity of interests (*NW*, 17 May 1993, p. 2; 13 Decenber 1993, p. 1; 20 December 1993, pp. 1, 3).

Although there are some important differences in the ways these agreements function, they all enable the advanced powers to protect their own markets while at the same time imposing free trade on the less developed countries within their regional spheres of influence. NAFTA is a free trade agreement which is to eliminate tariffs among members while preserving the autonomy of each in relation to non-members, thus giving the US free access to Mexico's low-cost labour and Canada's resource-rich environment as well as their markets. Japanese capital is also happy to prepare for NAFTA by shifting more of its productive power into Mexico in order to combine the advantages of low-cost production with high levels of consumer demand that the region offers. The EU, on the other hand, is a customs union which requires common tariffs towards non-members, and its sheer size and diversity allow most of the production and marketing needs of its leading power, Germany, to be met from within the region. While the threat of NAFTA to Japanese capital will be the greater competitiveness its US rival can achieve, the wall being raised by the EU gives across-the-board advantages to any who can scale it and permanently discriminates against outsiders. Production within Europe is thus the only way to meet the European threat (*NW*, 24 January 1994, p. 7; 5 September 1994, p. 8).

APEC (Asia–Pacific Economic Cooperation Conference) is the largest attempt in the Asia–Pacific region to promote free trade, but for this very reason as well as for its dominance by the US, the support it gets from the less developed countries in the region as well as from Japan fluctuates widely. AFTA (ASEAN Free Trade Area), however, is an arrangement like NAFTA and has had more success, with the initial aim of lowering tariffs among members to below 5 per cent within fifteen years (of January 1993) but with the ultimate intention of abolishing them altogether. Since AFTA's main purpose was to create economies of scale and stimulate foreign investment, it is confined to capital goods and manufactures, including processed agricultural goods but excluding unprocessed agricultural products. The Japanese companies surveyed by JETRO in 1992 generally saw considerable merits in the initiative: between 30 and 50 per cent of those in ASEAN countries as well as those in Singapore and South Korea felt it would strengthen their division of labour in the region, help them furnish regional supplies of components and assist their cost-down strategies. Helping with economies of scale was also cited by approximately 20 per cent of the firms (Nihon bōeki shinkōkai, 1993b, p. 21; *FEER*, 15 April 1993, pp. 48–50; *NW*, 15 November 1993, p. 1).

Japanese capital hopes to manoeuvre its way through the web of protection its rivals are weaving by escaping into its own sphere of influence, where it can shape rules that allow it to preserve the overall strategy which it has embraced ever since it restructured into consumer goods, that is, to export the surplus goods rather than re-shape its social fabric by redistributing income in favour of wage earners. This means that the trade imbalance cannot really be eliminated without a lot of pain – abroad through juggling around the countries which must absorb the surplus, at home through the recessions that result from the power of rivals to say 'no'. Although the new world order still allows most of the costs of imperialism to fall on the peoples of the less developed countries, some of them have always rebounded back again. Perhaps the complexities of the new world order can also come to the rescue with some temporary solutions. For example, although trade has become a source of division and rivalry, the production strategies of the different advanced countries have been a source of unity, even if the alliances among them are motivated by 'strategic' considerations. But, apart from its effect on the value of the YEN, the flow of finance among the advanced countries has helped soothe these troubled waters even more.

6 Finance for the Rich, 'Aid' for the Poor

Money is the most flexible of all forms of capital. This is because quantity is the sole feature that distinguishes different parcels of money from one another and because these quantities can be so easily expressed in the form of bank notes, promissory notes of one kind or another or even electronically. Money can move across national borders with greater speed than either traded commodities or relocated factories, and it can be transformed into and out of either of these in an instant. The capitalist system functions through its movements, into and out of other forms of capital and from one part of the world to another, in response to fluctuations in profit, which are in turn all expressed in terms of quantities of money. Since on its own, without constant transformation into productive and commodity capital, money is no more than an idle hoard, its apparent magical power to multiply itself and to command whatever it fancies stems from its relationships with trade and investment. Indeed the special feature of Japan's international finance is the exceptional tightness of the networks which preserve close relationships between trade, investment and finance. Apart from the brief period of the bubble economy in the late 1980s, when Japanese money seemed to fly in all directions into and out of almost anything, often with little apparent purpose or monitoring, these same networks have spearheaded Japanese capital's international onslaught into world money markets. The purpose of this chapter is to analyse this internationalisation and its relationship with trade and investment. Space precludes discussion of Japan's domestic financial system and its gradual liberalisation, a topic which is adequately dealt with elsewhere (Düser, 1990).

With both world trade and FDI so thoroughly dominated by the advanced countries, it should come as little surprise to find that the movement of money, in all of its many forms, also takes place predominantly among the three regions of the developed capitalist world. In addition to bank loans, these financial flows comprise the buying and selling of the various 'products' put together by governments, such as bonds to cover fiscal deficits, and by highly specialised financial managers, such as securities houses which boast a myriad of ways to earn the highest rates of return involving the lowest possible risks: shares, bonds, debentures, options, swaps and so on. The Japanese word *zaiteku* (financial engineering) superbly captures the essence of this activity of making money out of money, or what are usually called portfolio or indirect investments, although government regulation of the Japanese financial sector has made Japanese investors rely quite heavily on a more limited range of products, especially bonds. But this regulation has not prevented the movement of money in and out of Japan to the degree that even less formal regulations prevented the movement into Japan of traded goods or foreign investment. Yet the greater ease with which finance flows among the advanced countries says more about the nature of money than it does about any openness of the Japanese financial system.

Internationally, Japanese banks and fund managers have tended to work closely with the institutions that have spearheaded the country's foreign investment and trade, especially the *sōgō shōsha* and the giant industrialists which together with the banks constitute the core members of the big six *kinyū keiretsu* (financial *keiretsu*). However, whereas in the case of bank loans the links among money, productive and commercial capital are institutionally preserved through the full complement of *keiretsu* ties, in the case of portfolio investments computerised information systems ensure that big money goes to big producers and traders, and vice versa. There are thus fewer *institutional* reasons why the indirect investment of Japanese money should head as exclusively towards Japanese FDI projects or trading activities. However, the tendency for Japanese money to follow only the most profitable productive and trading activities of other Japanese corporations has greatly reinforced the uneven developments that exist between and within countries. Most money goes to the advanced countries, while the bulk of the rest goes to Asia, mainly to the same countries in which foreign investment and trading networks are already most fully established, and within these countries only to the flourishing sectors, and within them to the most profitable firms. The movement of money is thus guided by whatever will ensure that the result is more money at the end, and that requires tight links with productive and commercial activity.

The tremendous power of finance due to its relationship with trade and investment means that bank loans and portfolio investments from Japan have very different effects on the advanced countries from what they do on less developed countries. Money enters the latter almost entirely in the form of loans from Japanese banks and in one way or another ends up financing mainly the activities of Japanese direct investors and traders. The result is a further consolidation of the power of Japanese capital in the less developed countries and a weakening of the power of both local capital and local labour. In the advanced countries, however, since finance enters in the form of both bank lending and indirect investment, Japanese money flows towards all the leading-edge productive and servicing activities that characterise the advanced countries. It not simply confronts and attracts power relations which are equal to its own, but helps to weave the web that increasingly ties together all the leading-edge activities of the advanced powers as a whole. It thus stimulates and strengthens local capital in the advanced country, just as it undermines and weakens the power of local capital in the less developed country.

FINANCE FOR THE RICH

Money-Go-Round the World

Because sheer size is the distinctive feature of indirect investment, which is driven by quests to have ever greater quantities of surplus distributed back to it, the largest centres of world capitalism (the US, Europe and Japan) continue to dominate the global money-go-round. Up until the mid-1980s, the LDCs were virtually excluded from the calculations of international *zaiteku,* and even since then only a few countries have received limited attention. Most of the money going to LDCs is still associated with one or other form of aid and enters via loans from governments, private banks and international institutions. However, towards the late 1980s, in response to the high rates of accumulation resulting mainly from the boom in foreign investment, as well as to the de-regulation of financial controls due to pressures from the foreign investors, indirect investment in a number of Southeast Asian countries has increased rapidly.

Figure 6.1 shows the changing flows of all securities investments among the three regions of the advanced capitalist world, as well as stock investments in Asia, in the three key years of 1987, 1991 and 1993. The breakdown within the boxes is according to balance of payments categories, indicating the balance on the current account (which broadly reflects the trade balance) and the two capital accounts, that is, long-term and short-term. Long-term capital comprises most of the indirect investments referred to above, including long-term lending by banks, as well as finance for direct investment. The rates of accumulation and patterns of trade among the advanced countries account for the magnitudes and directions of the flows.

Although the enormity of the amounts might suggest that the costs and benefits are not equal, the process is characterised by constant changes which even out in the long run and which reveal the process as one from which all – the advanced countries – benefit. However, in the short and

Figure 6.1   Securities investments and financial flows among advanced powers, 1987–93 ($billion)

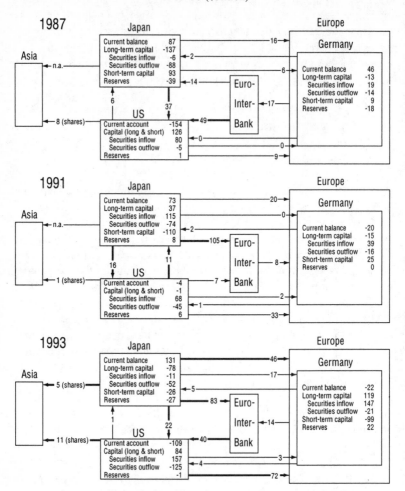

Source: *Nihon Ginkō Geppō*, May 1994, p. 37.

medium term, the chronic trade and investment imbalances among them tend to produce imbalances in the flows of finance as well, the one compensating for the other: when the US cannot pay by means of its exports for all the goods it imports and must somehow borrow the difference, money flows into it in a disproportionate way. However, in the long run imperialist powers can restore trade balances, even at some price as we have seen, and the financial flows tend to cancel one another out as well. Much in the way that large banks and powerful industrial corporations strengthen one another through the links they forge by means of credit, so too does the flow of finance from one advanced country to another strengthen both sides by reinforcing their relationship: only they have the productive power which can both generate and find productive uses for the huge amounts of money involved. Finance is for the rich in today's world order, and Japanese money that flows into the US stimulates the productive power needed to restore the balance, all so that the rich can get richer. The role of the poor in all this is to create wealth, not appropriate it.

Since so much of the productive power of the advanced countries has also been located within the less developed countries through FDI and its links with appropriate financial and commercial networks, much of the finance that flows back and forth between advanced countries represents wealth that was actually created in the less developed world in the first place. What the directions of these flows simply do is determine the relative shares of the different advanced countries in the overall globally-created surplus. As was explained in Chapter 1, the way this takes place is through the price mechanism for the whole range of goods and services, including financial services, which are traded globally.

During the latter half of the 1980s, as typified by the year 1987, booms and current account surpluses in Japan and Europe steered the flow of finance towards the US, whose higher interest rates signalled the higher yields it offered and whose fiscal and trading deficits constituted its need. At the same time, in response to the quickening pace of global financial deregulation, international banks from all the advanced countries massively increased their lending, not least for real estate purchases in the US, UK and Canada. By 1990 the net cross-border financial flows due to the lending of international banks had soared to $465 billion.

The transitional period around 1991 resulted from the onset of recession in Japan and Europe, which triggered a large increase in bad debts and a world-wide credit crunch: for example, in the period December 1985 to June 1990, the real estate bad debts of US commercial banks zoomed from $17.8 billion to $43.3 billion, that is, from about a third of their total bad debts of $51 billion to over a half of the new total of $81.9 billion. In response, net cross-border financial flows due to the lending of international banks plummeted to a paltry $85 billion in 1991. It was chiefly this credit crunch which choked off worldwide FDI in the early 1990s (Nihon bōeki shinkōkai, 1993a, pp. 16–7).

The other main mechanism through which recessions in the advanced countries re-directed the flows of finance was a shift in the trade balances of the three leading powers. In the latter half of the 1980s, the trade surpluses of Japan and Germany steered finance mainly from Japan and Europe towards the deficit-ridden US. However, after 1990 the US current account went into the black due to an improvement in its trade balance, but its capital account went into the red because investment from overseas plummeted in response to mounting recessions in Europe and Japan. Thus money flowed out of the US in 1991. Japan's trade surplus, which had simultaneously been falling, went into the red in the first quarter of 1991, the value of the yen having dropped to almost 160 to the dollar in April 1990. Following the collapse of the Tokyo Stock Exchange on 2 April (one day late!) in 1990, land and stock prices continued to fall throughout the rest of the year, leading to a large outflow of long-term capital that year of $43.6 billion. Although the resulting credit crunch led to heavy selling in 1991 by Japanese investors of their overseas securities, rising income from Japan's overseas bonds, in response to the cheaper yen, attracted a substantial inflow of foreign capital and pushed the long-term capital account into the black by $37.6 billion. For the first time in many years, the flows between Japan and the US more or less balanced each other, and both were in a more similar position to steer their surplus funds towards a more needy Europe, especially Germany, which following its reunification became a major recipient of foreign capital movements. The pattern in 1991 thus differed markedly from those of the late 1980s. There were even hopes that the structural causes of the trade friction between the US and Japan had been eliminated and that greater harmony could prevail among the leading advanced powers (Nihon bōeki shinkōkai, 1993a, pp. 17–9; *Nihon ginkō geppō*, May 1994, pp. 36 ff.; *NW*, 8 March 1993, p. 15; 21 June 1993, p. 15; 30 August 1993, p. 12).

Subsequent balance of payments changes, however, especially the return in 1993 of Japan's chronic trade surplus with the US, began to restore some of the uneven directions of the streams of finance that characterised the late 1980s. Money flowed from Japan to the US, and from Japan and the US into Europe. Although recessions in both Japan and Europe precluded a revival of world-wide FDI in the proportions of the 1980s, the main global flows were broadly similar to those of the 1980s, with three notable exceptions: Asia – for the first time ever – also became an important recipient of global financial inflows, money went into rather than out of Europe and the US became both the single largest source and target of world-wide securities investments (Nihon bōeki shinkōkai, 1993a, pp. 15–9, 1994, pp. 7–8).

The main source of the finance that went into the US was Japan and derived from the latter's trade surplus, while the main targets of US securities investors were Europe (especially Germany), Asia (including Japan) and Latin America. US indirect investments abroad almost trebled from their 1991 level of $45 billion to $125 billion, which was more than double the Japanese total that year. But the US was also the largest recipient of security investments in 1993, with a total of $157 billion entering the country in comparison to an inflow of only $68 billion in 1991. It was closely followed by Germany, which absorbed $147 billion that year compared to $39 billion in 1991. The pattern that emerged in 1993 was thus for the US and Japan to be the main sources of the currents, which all pointed in the direction of the US, Germany and Asia. Short-term capital flows have continued to be dominated by the Euro–Interbank markets, to which Japan is now the largest contributor. However, with the scale of the US economy once again reflecting itself in the field in which sheer size is all that matters, Japan's weight in global finance has fallen from the heights it occupied in the late 1980s (*Nihon ginkō geppō*, May 1994, pp. 36 ff.).

The increase in US overseas securities investments has largely resulted from long-term global financial liberalisation, which has led more American investors to move into mutual funds, whose share of the total US foreign stock purchases soared from 10 per cent to 50 per cent during the course of 1993, the amounts rising from some half a billion dollars in January 1992 to over seven billion dollars by December the following year. These high-earning funds had previously focused on the domestic market, but in the context of low US short-term interest rates and high share prices, they shifted into foreign stocks. Table 6.1 shows how rapidly stock purchases increased in 1993, not just in traditional markets in Europe, but also in newer markets such as Asia, Canada and Latin America. The prolonged recession in Japan and, compared to the US, the relatively high PERs (share price to earnings ratios) for Japanese shares, sharply reduced investments in that country, even though those by long-term pension funds began to increase again in 1993. The sheer mass of US indirect investment in the freer world order of the 1990s is able to ensure that American investors get the same highest globally-available yields regardless of the state of the domestic economy. US investments in overseas bonds have soared even more rapidly since 1991, with the focus and growth rate in Europe far outstripping the similar European-focus of US stock investments and with an even greater decline in Japanese bonds than the decline of interest in the Japanese sharemarket (*Ibid*, pp. 38 ff.).

The patterned movements of global finance that have been emerging in the 1990s reflect a combination of old and new developments: the sheer size of the main capital markets (particularly the US), the dismantling of protective barriers, discrepancies in the yields of different products in

Table 6.1 US Overseas securities investments, by region, 1991–93

| | Shares | | | | | | Bonds | | | | | |
| | 1991 | | 1992 | | 1993 | | 1991 | | 1992 | | 1993* | |
	$ bil.	%	$ bil.	%	$ bil.	%	$ bil.	%	$ bil.	%	$ bil.	%
Japan	13.9	43.6	4.4	13.6	6.2	9.1	-2.1	-14.1	-0.2	-1.2	-2.9	-4.3
Europe	14.7	46.1	18.1	56.0	31.5	46.5	19.1	128.2	19.3	111.6	62.8	93.5
UK	8.3	26.0	11.5	35.6	16.5	24.3	n.a	n.a.	n.a.	n.a.	n.a.	n.a.
Germany	1.5	4.7	0.8	2.5	2.7	4.0	n.a	n.a.	n.a.	n.a.	n.a.	n.a.
Canada	-0.4	-1.3	-0.3	-0.9	5.1	7.5	7.8	52.3	6.9	39.9	14.0	20.8
Asia	1.5	4.7	4.4	13.6	10.8	15.9	n.a	n.a.	n.a.	n.a.	n.a.	n.a.
Latin Am.	2.6	8.2	5.0	15.5	12.3	18.1	n.a	n.a.	n.a.	n.a.	n.a.	n.a.
TOTAL*	31.9	100.0	32.3	100.0	67.8	100.0	14.9	100.0	17.3	100.0	67.2	100.0

* Bonds in 1993 cover the period January to September. TOTAL includes other.
Source: Nihon ginkō geppō, May 1994, pp. 39–40.

Table 6.2   Size and yields of the world's main share and bond markets, 1992–93

	Market Size in 1992 ($ billion)				Changes in Share (%) & Bond (% points) Yields			
	Shares	Index	Bonds	Index	1992	1993	1992	1993
US (New York)	3 878	100	2 044	100	10.6	13.3	–0.26	–1.19
Japan (Tokyo)	2 321	60	1 278	63	–26.4	2.9	–0.87	–1.48
UK (London)	934	24	608	30	15.2	19.3	–1.42	–1.95
Germany (Frankfurt)	321	8	993	49	–2.1	46.7	–0.9	–1.50
France (Paris)	329	9	579	28	5.0	47.1	–0.53	–2.37
Hong Kong	172	4	0.5	0	28.3	115.7	–	–
Singapore	50	1	101	5	2.3	59.1	–	–

Source: *Nihon ginkō geppō*, May 1994, pp. 38–9.

different advanced countries, the ups and downs of the latter's respective trade cycles and trade balances and the gradually increasing weight of some Asian markets. However, one of the effects of the growing scale of global financial flows is increasing synchronisation of the advanced countries' trade cycles, so that for the first time since World War Two all of the leading ones could, around the mid-1990s, be in some or other stage of upswing. The result would not just be unprecedented prosperity for their upper classes, but also an unprecedented concentration of their economic might and influence over the less developed world. Table 6.2 shows the size of the main share and bond markets as well as their respective yields in 1992–93, confirming the dominance of the advanced countries, especially the US, as well as the signs of their impending coordinated boom. It also shows the rapidly growing share markets of Asia – the hub of the world's surplus creation – particularly in locations without financial restrictions such as Singapore and Hong Kong, as well as the absence of proper bond markets in the region. Since Asia borrows heavily from the advanced countries for its productive activity and since lending is an almost one way street leading from the international banks, it is not surprising that markets for lending money are so one-sided.

Japan's Indirect Investments

Japan's large current account surplus in 1993, which the high yen boosted through the so-called J-curve to a record $131.4 billion, produced a record net outflow of capital: the long-term amount more than doubled from

$28.5 billion in 1992 to $78.3 billion, although the short-term amount fell from $78.6 billion to $52.9 billion. A full 80 per cent of the former consisted of securities investments, which, in contrast to the slump in FDI flows and loans that year, ballooned from $26.2 billion to $62.7 billion. Whether or not there are opportunities to expand the direct surplus-extracting investments or the unproductive ones which support these, the money-go-round continues to distribute to investors the quantities of surplus they have come to expect. Table 6.3 shows these movements on a balance of payments basis over the period 1984–93. The outflow of long-term capital began in the early 1980s as Japan's trade balance went into the black, and it peaked just before the high yen recession and then gradually eased off in response to the declining trade surplus, even turning to a net inflow of $37.1 billion in 1991. However, the sudden escalation of the trade surplus that year reasserted the trend towards the long-term outflow. The preferred form of overseas *zaiteku* has been the purchase of foreign bonds rather than shares, and long-term rather than short-term investments.

When Japanese capital has borrowed abroad, usually to get access to cheaper money, its favoured method, except in the crisis year of 1991, has been to enter into short-term rather than long-term contracts. Financial deregulation in three major areas in the 1980s (interest rates, type of business allowed and the international use of the yen) have all encouraged Japanese companies to reduce their borrowings from Japanese banks, to borrow more in overseas markets and to increase their direct financing, for example, through entering the corporate bond market. So long as government regulations kept interest rates in Japan at artificially low levels, heavy borrowing from *keiretsu* banks was a good short-term as well as a good long-term strategy, but as interest rates have been allowed to rise, cheaper sources of short-term finance have been sought out, often in international markets. Many Japanese investors were also happy to put their money into these markets, where they earned higher yields than were offered by Japanese banks. The result is that the less regulated foreign money markets became mediators between Japanese investors and borrowers. However, a significant move away from the pattern of the 1980s (in which Japan borrowed short-term but lent long-term) seems to have taken place as a result of the current recession as Japanese companies curtail their borrowing. Since 1991, increases in both short-term and long-term *lending* have accompanied each other, and the smaller long-term outflows (due to recession) that characterised the 1980s have been compensated by large short-term outflows in the 1990s. Another reason for this trend has been a change in Japan from the 1980s obsession with 'income gain', which focused on interest-rate differentials and the

Table 6.3   Japan's balance of payments, 1984–93 ($ billion)

	1984	1987	1988	1989	1990	1991	1992	1993
Current account	35.0	87.0	79.6	57.2	35.8	72.9	117.6	131.4
Trade balance	44.3	96.4	95.0	76.9	63.5	103.0	132.3	141.5
Long-term capital	-49.7	-136.5	-130.9	-89.2	-43.6	37.1	-28.5	-78.3
Foreign capital inflow	7.1	-3.7	19.0	102.9	77.2	158.5	29.5	-4.7
Japanese capital outflow	-56.8	-132.8	-149.9	-192.1	-120.8	-121.4	-58.0	-73.6
a) Securities (net)	-23.6	-93.8	-66.7	-28.0	-5.0	41.0	-26.2	-62.7
Foreign capital inflow	7.2	-6.0	20.3	85.1	34.6	115.3	8.1	-11.0
Japanese capital outflow	-30.8	-87.8	-86.9	-113.2	-39.8	-74.3	-34.3	-51.6
i) Shares								
Foreign capital inflow	-3.6	-42.8	6.8	7.0	-13.3	46.8	8.7	20.0
Japanese capital outflow	-0.1	-16.9	-3.0	-17.9	-6.3	-3.6	3.0	-15.3
ii) Bonds								
Foreign capital inflow	3.5	6.7	-21.6	2.4	17.0	21.2	-8.2-	-0.2
Japanese capital outflow	-26.8	-72.9	-85.8	-94.1	-29.0	-68.2	-35.6	-29.9
iii) External bonds								
Foreign capital inflow	7.4	30.1	35.1	75.7	30.9	47.3	7.6	-30.8
Outflow (yen bonds)	4.0	2.0	1.9	-1.2	-4.5	-2.5	-1.7	-6.4
b) Outward FDI	-6.0	-19.5	-34.2	-44.1	-48.0	-30.7	-17.2	-13.7
Inward FDI	0.0	1.2	-0.5	-1.1	1.8	1.4	2.7	0.1
c) Loans extended (outflow)	-11.9	-16.2	-15.2	-22.5	-22.2	-13.1	-7.6	-8.2
Borrowing abroad (inflow)	-0.1	-0.1	-0.1	17.8	39.1	38.1	15.9	4.3
Short-term capital flows	10.9	53.4	48.5	54.1	28.7	-102.2	-78.6	-52.9
a) Net short-term flows	-4.3	23.9	19.5	20.8	21.5	-25.8	-7.0	-14.5
b) Monetary movements	15.2	29.5	29.0	33.3	7.2	-76.4	-71.6	-38.4
of which official	-2.4	-42.3	-15.5	24.7	20.9	17.1	1.4	-23.5
Foreign exchange banks	17.6	71.8	44.5	8.6	-13.6	-93.5	-73.0	-15.0

Note: negative signs (−) mean the outward flows exceeded the inward flows.

Source: Nihon ginkō geppō, May 1994, pp. 32–4; Ōkurashō, 1993b, pp. 40–5; *Kokusai shūshi tōkei geppō,* Mar. 1994, pp. 59–74.

long-term accumulation of portfolios, to the more recent emphasis on 'capital gain' and greater attention to short-term trading following the decline in interest-rate differentials. Even the banks have been moving in this direction. (Düser, 1990, pp. 17, 36; *NW*, 15 November 1993, p. 16).

It was previously noted that, although FDI flows have continued to fall with the deepening of the current recession, money has been available for raising overseas indirect investments in securities. This shows how in recession times, FDI tends increasingly to set aside all but the essential surplus-creating projects. Chapter 4 demonstrated that much of the FDI that took place during the years of the bubble economy was in the finance industry and had less to do with surplus creation than with quantitative surplus appropriation, very much like indirect investments. All kinds of assets, including giant corporations, were also purchased in the expectation simply of making capital gains. However, when recession strikes, these kinds of investments are no less essential, but the harsher climate makes it more important to entrust the task to professional fund managers. Their more careful targeting of a variety of portfolios for the sake of generating money rather than goods steers them to the securities markets rather than the M&A markets. They thus rarely acquire more than the 10 per cent of stock required to classify an undertaking as a direct rather than a portfolio investment. Table 6.4 shows their geographical location in the period 1985–93.

The institutions which play the largest roles in securities markets in Japan are the banks (city banks, long-term credit banks and trust banks), especially in government bond dealing, and the securities houses, which dominate public bond dealing. The banks originally entered this traditionally forbidden realm from outside Japan by setting up overseas subsidiaries that were beyond the reach of the Japanese authorities. However, although Japanese banks and securities companies now compete with one another in the securities market, there are also *keiretsu* relations among them. For example, the big four securities houses all have connections with a major city bank: Nomura Securities with Daiwa Bank, Daiwa Securities with Sumitomo Bank, Nikko Securities with Mitsubishi Bank, and Yamaichi Securities with Fuji Bank and the Industrial Bank of Japan. But the major banks also control most of the smaller securities houses, for example, the Industrial Bank of Japan controls Wako, New Japan, Okasan and Toyo. And the large securities houses also have ownership connections with the smaller ones. For example, among Nomura's fifteen affiliates are Kokusai, Sanyo and Ichiyoshi, while Nikko's eleven affiliates include Tokyo and Toyo (Düser, 1990, p. 85; *NW*, 3 May 1993, p. 12).

Table 6.4   Japan's securities investments, by country, 1985–1993 ($ billion and %)

	1985		1987		1988		1989		1990		1991		1992		1993	
	$ bil.	%	$ bil.	%	$ bil.	%	$ bil.	%	$ bil.	%	$ bil.	%	$ bil.	%	$ bil.	%
US	31.3	56	37.4	41	36.2	41	26.5	23	−16.1	−41	15.6	21	8.8	27	21.9	50
UK	6.2	11	8.7	10	10.7	12	11.1	10	0.2	5	14.5	20	17.1	53	16.8	39
Germany	0.4	1	5.6	6	6.0	7	4.5	4	−2.0	−5	0.3	0	8.1	25	17.4	40
France	0	0	1.0	1	0.6	1	3.9	3	5.6	14	3.3	5	2.5	8	10.0	23
Luxembourg	11.7	21	27.2	30	25.4	28	48.1	42	32.4	82	21.4	29	−2.8	−9	−18.0	−41
Switzerland	0.5	1	0.4	0	0.9	1	1.2	1	1.9	4.8	1.2	2	0.7	2	2.0	5
Australia	1.0	2	2.4	3	1.8	2	1.5	1	−1.1	−3	2.6	4	−1.7	−5	−4.4	−10
Canada	2.2	4	2.5	3	1.4	2	4.8	4	0.9	2	1.1	1	1.6	5	−5.8	−13
Other	2.2	4	4.9	5	5.1	6	11.8	10	15.7	40	12.9	18	−1.9	−6	3.8	8

Source: Nihon ginkō geppō, May 1994, p. 42.

Other major *zaiteku* players include Japan's giant manufacturing and trading companies, which regularly put their surplus funds into securities. From time to time, some of these companies actually receive more of their total profits from this source than from their specialised activities. For example, during the high yen recession of 1986–87, companies like Toyota, Nissan, Matsushita, Sharp and Sony were only preserved from large losses by their massive *zaiteku* operations (Steven, 1990, p. 33).

Three main patterns to Japan's indirect investments are emerging in the 1990s. First, they have continued their traditional focus on the other two centres of advanced capitalism, that is, the US and Europe. But within Europe, Germany and France, rather than Luxembourg, now join the UK as the main targets, indicating the greater importance of links with the region's industrial heartland than simply the absence of regulations, which is all Luxembourg had to offer (*NW*, 8 March 1993, p. 4).

Second, there is the overall decline in the weight of Japanese securities investments relative to those of the US, simply because in an area where sheer size is the measure of weight, the world's largest capitalist country would sooner or later carry the most weight, a relationship that had been temporarily distorted by Japan's bubble economy. By the end of 1993, the market value of the Tokyo Stock Exchange stood at $2.9 trillion, compared to $4.5 trillion for New York and $1.2 trillion for London. This final trend is also related to the previously-mentioned move towards greater short-term as opposed to long-term trading. Because of the large foreign-exchange losses incurred by Japanese institutional investors during the 1980s, they have purchased fewer foreign securities in the 1990s. Their foreign securities grew rapidly in relation to their total assets in the 1980s, but these ratios have now stabilised around the 10 per cent levels of the mid-1980s (*Nihon ginkō geppō*, May 1994, p. 44; *NW*, 25 April 1994, p. 16).

Trickle Up from the Poor

Finally, there is the rapidly growing interest in Asian share markets by Japanese institutional investors, although this does not mean that Asia is in the process of joining the advanced capitalist world. Rather, it signifies the increasing power of the advanced countries to prise open the last of the barriers which LDCs had hoped might promote their independent development, that is, government regulation of their financial sectors. Apart from the effect of growing deregulation, participation in Asian share markets is motivated by a desire to *securitise* monies that had previously been lent via the banks Following the Latin American debt crisis of the mid-1980s,

Japanese investors wanted to ensure that their monies were safe and went into sound profit-earning projects. By the end of September 1993, Nomura estimated that 57 Japanese trust funds with assets of $3.7 billion had been set up that specialise in Asian stock markets. As an official of the Investment Trusts Association explained, 'Japanese share prices have stagnated, the European economy is in a slump and the recovery in the US economy is slow. Therefore investment trust firms choose Asian markets' (*NW*, 8 October 1993, p. 12). The largest of those markets at that time were Hong Kong, Malaysia and Thailand, with market capitalisations of about $220 billion, 11 billion and 6 billion dollars respectively. Although small in comparison to Tokyo's $2900 billion, their yields were high. Nomura's index for Asian markets (including the above three plus Singapore and Indonesia) more than tripled in the period 1985–93, while the Nikkei index rose by only 50 per cent (28 June 1993, p. 18; 2 August 1993, p. 24; 1; 2 November 1993, p. 21; 28 March 1994).

In early 1994 another new trend began to appear in Japan: the disposal of bonds due to foreign exchange losses resulting from the higher yen, especially in relation to the Australian and Canadian dollars, and due to rising long-term interest rates in the US and Europe. The other side of the trend was a sudden increase in overseas investment in Japanese stocks and bonds, and so a reversal in the direction of the global financial flows that characterised 1993. Such are the fortunes of the money-go-round (*NW*, 11 April 1994, p. 4).

Japan's Net Overseas Assets

Due to increasing financial liberalisation and internationalisation (such as the growth of Euro-markets and the establishment of Tokyo offshore markets), the 1980s saw a phenomenal growth in Japan's overseas assets and liabilities, and the country's large trade surpluses have resulted in net capital outflows which built up an enormous stock of net overseas assets. From a mere $10.9 billion in 1980, the total soared to a whopping $513.6 billion by the end of 1992. In the meantime, US trade deficits had resulted in capital inflows which cut that country's overseas assets to a net liability of $521.3 billion. These staggering statistics somewhat overstate the real picture, because the amounts record what was originally paid for the assets rather than their current market values. Since US assets have been held for a much longer time than Japanese assets, their book value understates their real value by much more than does the book value of Japan's more recently acquired assets. Nonetheless, Japanese capital clearly has a significant power to appropriate wealth from abroad, which throughout the

1980s has compared favourably with that of the US and in the 1990s significantly exceeded it. Table 6.5 shows that Japan's net income from overseas investment has grown very rapidly since the mid-1980s: from $6.8 billion in 1985 to $41.4 billion in 1993. It would have added massively to Japan's invisible payments surplus had expenditures on travel and shipping not spiralled simultaneously.

A breakdown of Japan's total overseas assets and liabilities as of December 1992 is provided in Table 6.6. The most important items are long-term private-sector direct and indirect investments, and short-term private monetary movements. Loans, both private and official, constitute a relatively small proportion of Japan's net overseas assets, since overseas borrowing does not lag very much behind overseas lending. So apart from FDI, Japan's key overseas assets comprise securities investments, that is, bonds and shares.

Japan's major securities companies have had subsidiaries in the advanced countries for many years. For example, the big four (Nomura, Nikko, Daiwa and Yamaichi) established themselves in New York in the 1950s and 1960s, and they were joined by another thirteen smaller firms (e.g. New Japan, Kankaku, Sanyo, Wako, Okasan, Kokusai, Yamatane, Cosmo, Tokyo) in the 1970s and 1980s. The move to Europe took place about ten years later, the big four entering at least one of London, Frankfurt, Amsterdam, Zurich, or Paris in the 1970s and then the others in the 1980s. Twenty-six lesser firms have since followed them, the smallest ones only in the late 1980s and early 1990s. The pattern in Asia has been different, with waves into particular countries occurring either when they first de-regulated their financial sectors or when their capitalist development began to generate significant capital markets. The big four entered Hong Kong and Singapore in the late 1960s or early 1970s for the first reason, and Seoul in the early 1980s in response to the economic transformation of South Korea. The move into Taiwan was delayed by the collapse of Japan's bubble economy and by government regulations in Taiwan, but by the middle of 1993 the big four had all set up representative offices in the country after having closed down units in Europe, the US and Australia. ASEAN countries have had to wait till the late 1980s or early 1990s for the big four to make any kind of move. Apart from these leviathans, only a handful of smaller firms have ventured into Asia beyond Hong Kong and in some cases Singapore. Outside the three central zones, Japan's securities companies are conspicuous by their absence, with only the big four in Australia, Nomura and Daiwa in São Paulo and the big four and three others in Bahrain (*Shūkan kinyū zaisei jijō*, 9 August 1993, pp. 114–9; *NW*, 2 August 1993, p. 16).

Table 6.5   Wealth appropriation overseas by the leading advanced countries*

Net Overseas Assets	1982	1985	1987	1988	1989	1990	1991	1992	1993
Japan	24.7	129.8	240.7	291.7	293.2	328.1	383.1	513.6	–
US	–	–	–	–183.7	–312.3	–294.8	–364.9	–521.3	–
Germany	–	–	–	209.7	269.8	357.9	343.4	333.9	–
Net Overseas Investment Income									
Japan	1.7	6.8	16.7	21.0	23.4	23.2	26.7	36.2	41.4
Direct investments	1.0	1.7	2.0	1.7	2.3	2.6	4.3	5.9	6.5
Other Investment Income	0.7	5.1	14.7	19.3	21.1	20.6	22.4	30.3	34.9
US	–	–	7.7	12.6	14.8	20.3	13.0	6.2	–

* Gaps indicated the unavailability of comparable data.

Source: Ōkurashō, 1993b, pp. 21–2, 88–89; *Kokusai shūshi tōkei geppō*, March 1994, p. 29.

Table 6.6   Japan's accumulated overseas assets and liabilities,
December 1992 ($ million)

	Assets	Liabilities	Net Assets
Long-term Assets	1 315 551	658 469	657 082
Private	1 132 193	578 826	553 367
Direct investment	248 058	15 511	232 547
Deferred exports	44 569	23	44 546
Loans	143 411	119 679	23 732
Securities investments	655 491	431 422	224 069
Other	40 664	12 191	28 473
Official	183 358	79 643	103 715
Deferred exports	1 404	0	1 404
Loans	88 261	79 643	8 618
Other	93 693	0	93 693
Short-term	719 687	863 150	−143 150
Private	646 897	807 208	−159311
Monetary movements	599 888	384 677	215 211
Other	47 009	122 531	−75 522
Official	72 790	55 942	16 848
Monetary movements	72 789	46 648	26 141
Other	1	9 294	−9 293
TOTAL	2 035 238	1 521 619	513 619

Source: Ōkurashō, 1993b, p. 19.

Although there is growing activity in Asia, portfolio investment continues to be a specialty of the advanced capitalist world, because its distinctive qualitative feature is its purely quantitative power, on the one hand to finance the enormous requirements of which the advanced countries alone are capable, and on the other to deliver proportionate quantities of surplus in return. The availability of and need for these quantities of finance in the advanced countries stems from the nature of 'international capital'. The relationship between technologically advanced productive power and the 'magical' power of credit, the one reinforcing the other because big lenders need reliable customers and because leading-edge technology requires heavy borrowing, is a feature of advanced capitalism. Portfolio investment by fund managers is one form in which this finance is continually steered towards the most productive industrial undertakings, whose profitability continues to expand the funds available for further direction into profitable outlets.

When portfolio investments move from one advanced country to another, far from resulting in a crippling power of the lenders over the producers, the flow of finance functions to stimulate the already efficient producers to even greater efficiency, much in the way that direct investment and trade among advanced countries stimulate rather than destroy competitive power. For example, Figure 6.1 showed that during the latter half of the 1980s, Japan's casino economy absorbed a large proportion of the surplus distributed to the advanced countries because US capital had sent into too many unproductive foreign activities (such as overseas military expenditure) too much of the surplus that had previously gone its way. At the time, Japanese investors needed to find *reliable* external outlets for vast quantities of money for which profitable domestic outlets had dried up, and only the US qualified in terms of both scale and reliability. On the other hand, so great was the need of the massive US economy to borrow overseas that only the enormous Japanese surplus could meet the demand. But this borrowing from Japan by the already productively (and therefore financially and commercially) powerful US capital did not translate into control over investment strategies in the US, however much some Japanese businessmen might have wished it did. Rather, it made available to US producers funds which they could use to sharpen their productive power even further.

The reason why such massive lending by Japan to the US stimulated independent productive power is that all the relationships of full-fledged 'international capital' already exist in the US, in particular close links between technologically-advanced industry and large-scale finance. While the US might have needed a greater *quantity* of finance, its own networks already controlled vastly greater quantities and were thus immune to any control which might have been intended by Japanese lenders. The increase in the amount of finance their existing strength was able to attract thus enhanced the independent power of the US, in two main ways. First, the American networks were able to direct the finance into the activities they deemed would launch another general upward cycle, and second, in order to attract the amount of money which it required, US capital had to tighten up some of the slack in the whole range of productive and unproductive activities which the previous boom had left in its wake. Such massive lending to a less developed country would have had neither of these effects. First, with limited ability to rely on its own capital markets and independent financial strength, the weight of foreign money and the networks through which it enters would broadly determine the uses to which it is put. In a less developed country this would steer the money to the limited range of industries which do possess some productive power, usually because they are dominated by foreign capital in the first place. Secondly, the 'slack' that a powerful external lender can require a borrower to remove as a condition of the loan can include a large number of very important activities in a less developed country, such as a quality system of university education. The World Bank has repeatedly refused loans to African countries which 'waste' money on tertiary education. An advanced country, however, can sustain vast 'unproductive' activities like these without undermining its capacity to deliver high yields to its lenders.

The power of FDI, trade and finance to enhance the mutual strength of advanced countries is related to the role each plays in relation to the others in these countries. Capital in its homogeneous, purely quantitative, form of money has a power which is both a cause and an effect of its transformation into productive capital. Money is power because it can generate surplus in the productive place, but it wields power when it steers itself away from less productive into more productive avenues. International capital's financial power is thus part and parcel of the networks which facilitate the movement of capital through each of its various forms: from money (purely quantitative) to the production of qualitatively-different surplus-bearing goods, which are then marketed to yield increased quantities of money. Unless one sees financial flows among the advanced countries in the context of FDI and trade among the same advanced countries, the *distinctiveness* of Third World debt, namely, that it always invokes the possibility of some kind of crisis, is lost.

Bank Loans

One of the effects of current world-wide financial de-regulation is to erode the distinctions among different financial institutions, so that insurance companies start providing credit for the housing market, stockbrokers provide commercial credit and commercial banks deal in securities. Nevertheless, even though institutional barriers become blurred, a fundamental distinction remains between the traditional role of banking, that is, *creating* credit by lending more money than is actually deposited in them, and that of fund managing which is simply 'lending' the money of clients to the highest and safest bidder. To a qualitatively greater degree than is involved in securities investments (which themselves 'securitise' the money 'lent' to their sellers), the power to *create* or *grant* credit rests or falls with the reliability of those who *receive* the credit, because a bank can only afford to lend amounts in excess of its deposits so long as depositors do not simultaneously withdraw their money and so long as borrowers continue to service their loans (Hall, 1992).

Such happy relationships have generally surrounded the activities of Japanese companies and banks in the advanced countries. The FDI projects which need bank finance have been able to get it from any one of a number of sources: through the *keiretsu* connections in Japan of the parent company making the investment, the local overseas branch of the Japanese bank connected to the parent company, or simply from one or other of the local foreign banks. The latter is a real option for Japanese subsidiaries in an advanced country, because the reliability and power of the local banking sector stems from links to its own advanced productive sector, and the willingness of local banks to lend to Japanese subsidiaries stems from the knowledge that these are as reliable as domestic firms. Each side has its own independent source of power which, when they meet, does not translate into dominance by either, but in mutual strengthening. In practice, however, Japanese companies have hitherto been more conservative than this, and have on the whole preferred to borrow from local branches of their own banks or via the networks of their parent companies in Japan.

This raises the distinction between what Düser (1990, p. 13) calls 'international banking', or the cross-border transactions of Japanese banks, and 'multinational banking', which comprises the business of institutions which have themselves moved abroad. The first involves the flow of money from Japan to foreign countries, the second the relocation overseas of an institution which can then raise local money to support its own lending in that country.

International Banking

If the medium- and long-term overseas lending of all private institutions in Japan is included, the same trend we have repeatedly encountered emerges once again: increasing weight of the advanced countries and Asia and a decline in the importance of all other regions, as revealed by Table 6.7, which is based on data from the Ministry of Finance. Japanese banks and other lenders are interested only in a flourishing capitalism that can be relied on to return their money together with an appropriate yield. The huge Latin American demand for syndicated loans in the 1970s and early 1980s led to a belief that capitalism in that region fitted the bill, but by the latter half of the 1980s forces associated with underdevelopment translated the accumulated loans into a severe debt crisis. Japan held about 15 per cent of Latin American debt in the mid-1980s (compared to 40 per cent by US), and has since been radically reducing its lending to that part of the world. It has been assisted by the US-inspired 'structural adjustment' programme, which has also led to the conversion into bonds of large debts to Japan: $9.3 billion by Mexico and $2.7 billion by Venezuela in 1990 and $3.5 billion by Argentina in 1993 (Ōkurashō data). The move towards *securitisation* by all the advanced countries, which is replacing bank lending to LDCs with the purchase of securities, is a direct consequence of the Latin American debt crisis. However, Brazil and Argentina still account for large proportions of Japan's lending to debtor countries, with all of the top seventeen banks still having large outstanding loans to both countries. By March 1993, the medium- and long-term loan balances of Japanese banks to their top ten borrowers in the less developed world were, in billions of dollars: Hong Kong (19.7), China (9.4), Indonesia (8.2), Brazil (7.5), Thailand (4.7), Argentina (4.4), India (4.1), South Korea (4.0), Liberia (3.1), Singapore (2.6), Malaysia (2.2), Algeria (2.0) and Mexico (1.7). The prominence of China (and Hong Kong which 'services' China), where Japanese banks have left their European (with loans of $1.4 billion) and US (with loans of only $ 700 million) rivals far behind, recalls the sudden prominence of China in Japan's current wave of foreign investment and in Japan's recent trade (*NW*, 6 September 1993, p. 17; 7 June 1993, p. 17).

Since Japanese financial institutions have, due to the collapse of the bubble economy, also been curtailing their lending to all parts of the world except Asia, their total outstanding loans fell by $33 billion in the brief period 1991–93. The result is that by the end of 1993 the three key zones of US, Europe and Asia absorbed over 80 per cent of their accumulated overseas lending, up from 62.6 per cent in 1988.

The most pronounced change that is currently taking place, need one say, is once again towards Asia. By the third quarter of 1992 a full 70 per cent of all loans extended by the banks of the advanced countries to the less developed countries went to Asia. The figure for Japanese banks was 90 per cent. Officials in the Bank of Japan placed the balance of lending by Japanese *banks* (as opposed to that of all financial institutions) to Asia at about $70 billion as of June 1992, which amounted to a whopping 40 per cent of their total of $170 billion in overseas loans. According to the same sources, lending to Europe and the US combined accounted for only 31 per cent of the total. The Ministry of Finance data on bank lending was more conservative, but almost as startling: in the fiscal years 1990–93 Asia's share of the total soared from 19 to 25 per cent, North America's remained constant at 40 per cent, while Europe's fell from 32 to 27 per cent. Asia was expected to surpass Europe within a year. Rates of return on risk assets after deduction of expenses were reported to have been between 15 and 40 per cent higher in Asia in the early 1990s than in the US or Europe (*NW*, 22 March 1993, p. 17; 5 July 1993, p. 17; 18 April 1994, p. 13).

Much of the lending to Asia continues to go to large-scale infrastructural projects which usually involve a wide range of Japanese companies,

Table 6.7   Accumulated overseas loans of Japan's private financial institutions, 1988–93

	1988		1989		1990		1991		1992		1993*	
	$ bil.	%	$ bil.	%	$ bil.	%	$ bil.	%	$ bil.	%	$ bil.	%
OECD Countries	155.0	54.9	202.9	60.2	244.3	67.8	255.6	67.3	249.6	66.6	226.1	64.9
North America	70.7	25.0	99.7	29.6	128.4	35.6	131.9	34.6	132.6	35.4	126.1	35.4
Western Europe	68.1	24.1	85.4	25.3	99.6	27.6	108.8	28.6	103.7	27.7	93.7	26.3
Oceania*	17.5	6.2	19.4	5.8	17.9	5.0	17.7	4.6	15.1	4.0	15.0	4.2
LDCs	92.9	32.9	99.1	29.4	88.1	24.4	97.0	25.5	98.6	26.3	97.6	28.0
Asia	38.2	13.5	45.1	13.4	48.7	13.5	55.8	14.6	54.7	14.6	57.3	16.1
Latin America	45.5	16.1	44.7	13.3	31.2	8.7	31.6	8.3	33.6	9.0	30.1	8.5
Africa	7.0	2.5	6.4	1.9	5.5	1.5	5.5	1.4	5.5	1.5	5.6	1.6
Middle East	0.9	0.3	1.2	0.4	1.2	0.3	2.2	0.6	2.9	0.8	2.9	0.8
Russia/East Europe	15.5	5.5	15.8	4.7	11.4	3.2	9.8	2.6	8.9	2.4	7.6	2.1
International Institutions	19.1	6.8	19.1	5.7	16.7	4.6	17.7	4.7	17.5	4.7	17.6	4.9
TOTAL	282.5	100	336.9	100	360.5	100	381.1	100	374.6	100	348.2	100

*The 1993 regional totals are as of September 1993, while the OECD and LDC sub-totals and the grand total are as of December. Since most lending to 'Oceania' is to Australia and New Zealand, the region is included under OECD.
Source: Data supplied by Ōkurashō.

reinforcing the same tight links between production, marketing and finance that characterise government lending to Asia. For similar reasons, as will be demonstrated in the discussion on Japan's ODA, private bank lending to Asia is qualitatively very different from the lending to Europe and North America. Coming through the same networks as FDI and trade, indeed as the conveyor-belt of a lot of the investment and trade, it adds to the overall accumulation of power that enables Japanese capital to carve out and consolidate a highly integrated zone strategy within the region. Among the recent lending destined to serve this purpose in varying degrees are syndicated loans for a $2 billion liquefied natural gas plant in Malaysia and a $1.3 billion and a $1.5 billion oil refinery in Thailand. After having frozen project finance to the Philippines since 1983, a government-led consortium of Japanese banks together with Mitsubishi Corporation provided a loan in 1993 for a project to improve electricity supplies in that country, which had degenerated to the point of choking off foreign investment. The reason for re-commencing the lending to this risky country was that MITI's long-term trade insurance would cover 90 per cent of the loans and because Mitsubishi Corporation would export to the project most of the required equipment (*NW*, 17 May 1993, p. 17; 12 July 1993, p. 19; 26 July 1993, p. 17; 6 September 1993, p. 17).

Japan's biggest overseas lenders have been the leading *keiretsu* banks: Dai-ichi Kangyo, Sumitomo, Fuji, Mitsubishi, Sanwa, Tokai and Sakura. In the 1970s, the main boost to their international lending came from opportunities in the Euromarket and in the US, both of which continued to accelerate in the 1980s, although much of their lending in the 1980s has also been in relation to world-wide Japanese FDI and trade (notably in California), as well as in the form of syndicated loans to LDCs. The Bank of Tokyo, due to the special status of foreign exchange bank granted to it in 1954, has been the largest lender to debtor countries, but also the one to cut this debt most radically: from ¥671.3 billion in March 1988 to ¥262.6 billion in March 1994 (Ōkurashō, 1994b, various issues for each of the banks concerned).

Apart from the change in the geography of the lending by Japanese banks, the 1980s have also seen a growing shift, which has been accelerated by the current recession, from lending which involves the flow of money from Japan to lending through overseas branches which raise their own finance from their domestic markets, that is, a shift from international banking to multi-national banking. Since the geographical locations selected by Japanese banks for their overseas establishments have paralleled the focus of their overseas lending, their FDI and their trade, they have further consolidated the networks which assist their mutually-reinforcing activities. Lending to LDCs is being more rigorously related to profit making than it was in the past, both through its tighter focus on appropriate parts of the world, such as Asia, and through the growing on-the-spot networks that link it with investment and trade (Ajia taiheiyō shiryō sentā, 1993, p. 21).

Multinational Banking

Japanese banks have been slower than other institutions in establishing themselves abroad. During the early stages of internationalisation, which centred heavily on trade, their functions of providing finance were often performed by the *sōgō shōsha*, those multi-functional behemoths which specialised in network building, beginning with trade but then expanding into every other capitalist activity. Often the *sōgō shōsha* would bring syndicates together which included the banks, especially for investment in infrastructural projects relating to trade in raw materials.

Gradually, however, overseas branches were needed to nurture the growing international business of the banks, from financing FDI projects to participating in the securities markets of Europe and the US. By June 1993, an impressive combination of offshoots of Japanese banks had established themselves overseas (Table 6.8), again mainly in the advanced countries and LDC tax havens, but recently also in a number of Asian countries outside Hong Kong and Singapore, whose liberal environments have attracted Japanese financial institutions since the 1970s. Recently favoured locations in Asia include China, Taiwan, South Korea, Malaysia, Thailand, Indonesia and Vietnam. The general pattern has been similar to that of the securities companies previously discussed, that is, for Japanese banks first to establish themselves in the centres of surplus distribution and trade in the advanced countries, then to seek out tax havens wherever they might be, and finally to follow waves of direct investments, usually after about a ten-year lag, in order to consolidate zone strategies with all-round capability.

The triple engine of this internationalisation process has been recession (beginning with the 1970s oil shocks but accelerating with each subsequent downswing), de-regulation (which took off in the 1980s) and the need to link lending more directly to money making (securitisation). Three types of local presence have resulted. First, there are *representative offices*, which can really only generate business for the parent bank and which are thus more suited to international than to multi-national banking. Second, *branches* are the parent banks' local agents in foreign countries and are most able to deal with corporate customers in major

Table 6.8   Japanese banks' overseas establishments, by country, June 1993

	Banks	Branches	Subsidiaries	Rep. Office	Total
North America		137	93	48	278
US	55	137	83	38	258
Canada	10	–	10	10	20
Europe		82	113	76	271
UK	28	28	33	22	83
Germany	14	15	19	24	58
Switzerland	22	–	22	4	26
Belgium	18	6	13	2	21
France	10	10	2	4	16
Spain	9	13	–	2	15
Italy	8	8	4	2	14
Holland	7	0	7	4	11
Luxembourg	7	–	9	–	9
Other	5	2	4	12	18
Asia		108	88	148	344
Hong Kong	40	39	47	29	115
China	9	14	–	55	69
Singapore	21	21	27	5	53
Indonesia	11	1	13	15	29
South Korea	13	15	–	9	24
Thailand	6	5	1	12	18
Malaysia	2	3	–	12	15
India	3	5	–	4	9
Philippines	1	1	–	5	6
Taiwan	2	3	–	1	4
Other	1	1	–	1	2
Latin America		8	19	45	72
Brazil	14	–	16	16	32
Panama	5	4	2	1	7
Argentina	1	1	–	5	6
Other	3	3	1	23	27
Australia	19	–	19	27	46
Middle East	3	1	2	18	21
Africa	–	–	–	2	2
Other (eg. Cayman Islands)	19	19	28	–	47
TOTAL	61	355	362	365	1 082

Source: *Shūkan kinyū zaisei jijō*, 9 August 1993, p. 68.

cities, particularly MNCs of both Japanese and non-Japanese origin. Finally, *subsidiaries* are locally incorporated institutions which participate in the whole range of banking and securities business allowed under local legislation. They are often joint ventures with local interests, and thus indicate the full maturity of multi-national banking. Customers extend well beyond MNCs to smaller firms and even include households and individuals.

Subsidiaries tend to be concentrated in the advanced countries and LDC tax havens, where massive amounts of surplus that are created all over the world tend to be distributed to managers of large quantities of money. However, although some banks began to set up subsidiaries in Asia many years ago, most of the ventures were in investment banking and leasing or in the tax havens of Hong Kong and Singapore. The only exception was Indonesia, where all the big *keiretsu* banks established joint ventures in commercial banking around 1989–90. Nevertheless, the rush to match direct investment and trading capabilities in Asia with comparable banking facilities is an even more recent phenomenon than that. Before elaborating the details, the main features of multi-national banking in the advanced countries need to be outlined (*Shūkan kinyū zaisei jijō,* 9 August 1993, pp. 102–7).

Advanced Countries

All the above generalisations have exceptions; for example, the large all-round presence of Japanese banks in Germany, which lacks a financial centre comparable to London, is intended more to service Japanese investors and traders than to participate in *zaiteku* or to seek out local customers, while in the UK fund management remains the predominant motive in spite of Japan's massive investment and trade with that country. Because most advanced countries have served both functions, especially since the waves of FDI into them in the 1980s, there is always a combination of the two purposes anyway. Only Luxembourg and Switzerland have a strong Japanese presence simply in order to participate in Euro-market dealing. For the same reason, the presence of Japan's trust banks is almost entirely confined to the world's financial centres and tax havens (Düser, 1990, pp. 111–1).

The Bank of Tokyo still has the largest branch network of all, with a total of 44 overseas branches, 43 subsidiaries and eighteen representative offices. Its nearest rival is Sakura Bank, with 24 branches, 39 subsidiaries and 20 representative offices. All *keiretsu* banks have been rapidly increasing their overseas presence, with the establishment of large numbers of subsidiaries in the late 1980s and early 1990s, and an increase in the average number of branches possessed by each from 13 to 20 in the period March 1988 to June 1993. But with the exception of California, the only part of the world where they function as fully integrated local banks, they still tend to operate largely from the main financial centres of the advanced countries and the LDC tax havens, with little real contact with local customers. So long as their chief functions were to service Japanese direct investors and traders as well as the odd local MNC, this strategy might have been sufficient. In order to appropriate substantial local sources of finance and have them nourish expansions in the productive and commercial operations of their own *keiretsu* members, they require many more local customers than they have hitherto been able to attract (*Shūkan kinyū zaisei jijō*, 9 August 1993, pp. 94–6; Düser, 1990, p. 8).

The quick way to obtain access to such local networks is through finding well-placed local partners, for example, through the acquisition by Sumitomo of a 12.5 per cent stake in America's Goldman Sachs in 1986 or the Bank of Tokyo's buying *into* Britain's Touche Remnant in 1984 and its buying that company *out* in 1989 (Düser, 1990, pp. 97, 122). The slower way is gradually to expand their customers beyond the needs of local Japanese firms, which are generally not sufficient on their own to support an independent banking subsidiary. Unfortunately not many studies have documented the degree to which this shift has actually taken place. In the UK, which has the most established Japanese banking presence in the world, the list is quite long and ranges from wholesale distribution companies, through the financial services sector to building societies, water supply, government services and construction projects like the Euro-tunnel. In Europe's largest capitalist country, Germany, even by the end of the 1980s some 60 per cent of the customers of Japanese banks were still Japanese traders and investors. Since German corporations have their own close relationships with particular German banks, much like the situation in Japan, it has been difficult for Japanese banks to break into the corporate market. Only about 5 per cent of big German companies were estimated to have close ties with Japanese banks in 1989 (Düser, 1990, pp. 121–2).

The path to multi-nationalisation has thus not been uniform or followed the patterns of other advanced countries: while the first steps in internationalisation were taken in order to serve Japan's overseas trade and investments, the next major steps came from the existence of profit-making opportunities overseas which had no relation to these *keiretsu* supporting activities, such as syndicated loans, Eurobonds and Californian retail markets (Düser, 1990, p. 135). However, with increasing replacement of syndicated loans with 'securitised' loans, some of the territory of banks has been taken over by *zaiteku* operators, who much more specifically target the advanced countries. It might therefore be difficult for Japanese banks to move very far beyond their present concentration on Japanese clients involved in trade and investment, especially in the advanced countries where their competitors are more than equal to them, even though they in no way threaten their existence.

The growing presence of Japanese banks also poses few threats to the advanced countries. Düser (1990, p. 167) concluded that they should be welcomed into the European Community because they help make Europe more competitive, by stimulating European banks to greater efficiency, by helping Europe improve its access to the Japanese market and by ensuring capital flows into Europe. Financial flows to and from the advanced countries, whether in the form of bank loans or through dealing in securities, function to strengthen both sides. Financing the rich ensures the expansion of the finance because it helps make the rich even richer. Not so financial flows to the less developed countries, whose overall weakness requires that they receive 'aid'.

Asia Zone

In one of the few available studies on the funding of Japanese FDI, Tokunaga (1992b, p. 156) pointed out that 'FDI is not in principle a method for Japanese firms to transfer money over national borders. It is instead a method for securing the ownership of firms . . . in order to maintain . . . competitive advantage.' He found that in both the advanced and the less developed countries, although small firms get most of their funds via the parent in Japan, large firms rely more heavily on raising their finance locally, typically through local branches or subsidiaries of Japanese banks. However, data from a 1984 MITI survey (*ibid*, pp. 164 ff.) revealed some interesting regional differences between the degrees of borrowing from local Japanese banks. While about 20 per cent of loans by manufacturing subsidiaries in Asia, Europe and the US were from the investors in Japan, leaving about 80 per cent to be raised locally in all three regions, different proportions of these locally raised funds came via local Japanese banks: 36 per cent in ASEAN, 26 per cent in Asia as a whole, 44 per cent in the US and 85 per cent in Europe. Japanese manufacturers in the advanced countries, where their productive power cannot attract finance away from their equally powerful competitors, apparently need their own banking networks to ensure that they get the finance they need. However, in less developed countries, Tokunaga found that they are able to borrow from non-Japanese financial institutions simply on the basis of their own reputations and networks, in which Japanese banks play an equally important though less visible part. In ASEAN countries such as

Thailand, for example, where Japanese banks do not have a strong presence, it is common for Japanese companies to borrow from local banks on the basis of guarantees provided either by the parent company in Japan or by the branches of Japanese banks in Hong Kong or Singapore. So great is the productive power of Japanese manufacturing companies, and so extensive are their supporting financial and commercial networks in the region, that they can raise money on the basis of their reputations alone, that is, the knowledge that they are backed by these networks and are safe havens for any monies invested in them. The result is an ironic twist in the direction in which finance flows: once again from local institutions in less developed countries towards Japanese companies.

Japanese companies prefer to raise money locally in LDCs because they can thereby avoid foreign exchange losses, because 'loans or credits are extended to highly trustworthy Japanese subsidiaries or those guaranteed by Japanese banks or the parent companies almost at interbank rates,' and because they can take advantage of the concessional low-interest finance made available by a number of governments, such as Malaysia and Thailand, to promote exports (*ibid*, p. 166). Although Japanese companies are also beginning to raise finance in the emerging local bond markets in Asia, these are usually too small to function as viable alternatives to the banks as they sometimes can in the advanced countries. A possibly more useful development is the addition of financial functions to the regional headquarters (International Procurement Office, IPO) which many companies have established in Singapore. These include raising investment funds for the use of subsidiaries in the region, so that Singapore is increasingly becoming the nexus of the Japanese network system in Asia. As Tokunaga (*ibid*, p. 187) noted, 'The expanding regional intracompany production, distribution, settlement, and financing networks have thus made Singapore the most important regional financial center, including foreign exchange activities.'

None of this, however, means that more cannot be achieved with the addition of a greater banking presence in Asia. On the contrary, that is exactly what the banks are increasingly attempting to do. In the first six months of 1993, the Ministry of Finance received nineteen applications to open branches in East and Southeast Asia: eight in Malaysia, six in Thailand, three in Hong Kong and two in China. Vietnam has since been a favourite location, especially because US and European banks were quicker in establishing themselves there and because numerous infrastructural projects are waiting to be exploited by the full range of Japanese investors and traders. Banking can be a very profitable business in Asia, not simply because the weakness of local banks continually exposes them and their customers to 'bad-loan crises', thus making reliable Japanese banks all the more attractive. It is also profitable because finance that is carefully directed to the right surplus-creating channels can enhance the fortunes of the entire group of companies involved. In India for example, ordinary deposit rates of around 5 per cent and short-term lending rates of around 15 per cent have been generating 10 per cent profit margins (*NW*, 28 June 1993, p. 27; 6 September 1993, p. 24; 6 December 1993, p. 20; 18 April 1994, p. 13; 8 August 1994, p. 18).

The *Nikkei Weekly* (22 November 1993, p. 21) recently noted how the 'city banks are rushing to open branches in Southeast Asia', because the rapid escalation of investment in the region is 'boosting the demand for locally-denominated loans . . . for capital investment and operating funds'. The paper went on to explain how important it was for companies that aimed at the domestic market to have reliable sources of local finance, since having localised their production and then also increasingly their marketing, fully successful zone strategies depended also on localising their financial operations as well and linking all three together.

If the full connotation of the word 'finance' is not simply money but control over the avenues into which the money flows, then finance does not go into the less developed world in any great quantities. This is not because productive power in LDCs is low – on the contrary it is exceptionally high in regions like Asia because it is organised by international capital – but because LDCs lack their *own comprehensive* networks to appropriate for themselves this productive power and hence to put the finance into the service of their own development. Their own weak banking networks parallel the weakness of their productive and commercial networks, and the absence of effective links among these magnifies the problem and allows international capital to intervene at any stage to appropriate for itself any emerging strength that might appear: productive, commercial or financial. If finance only flows into LDCs in order to flow out again in even larger quantities, it does not really enter the countries in any meaningful sense.

If finance therefore flows out of rather than into LDCs, what about 'aid'? Surely when deliberate attempts are made to turn the flow the other way, some level of success should be achieved. The problem, however, is that the rich only give 'aid' if it functions like finance, that is, remains firmly in the hands of international capital and earns yields which are comparable to those received in the advanced countries.

'AID' FOR LDCS

The word aid already connotes the essential power difference involved in all flows of money from the advanced to the less developed countries. And it is this power difference which turns 'aid' on its head, from what is ostensibly intended to be a form of financial assistance in order to reduce inequality, into another mechanism which reinforces and widens that inequality. The reason is the presence in the advanced donor countries and absence in the receiving LDCs of the relationships we have stressed throughout this study that tie financial power to technological-industrial and commercial power. Money has no power at all, as we have seen, unless it is continually transformed into and out of productive capital, and in an increasingly de-regulated world this means productive capital with global competitive power. It is the characteristic feature of less developed countries to have very few such globally-competitive industries, with most that fall into this category relating either to 'rent-earning' raw materials, or to industries created and controlled by foreign capital.

In the borderless world which international capital keeps trying to force onto LDCs, although not onto itself, 'aid' cannot but reinforce existing patterns of inequality. Unless it flows into the already competitive sectors of countries with some existing cutting-edge, it is dissipated in projects that cannot survive the competition from imports or foreign investment. Aid thus flows to the already strong, but not to the too strong. Very little aid goes to Africa because Africa has been so weakened by its colonial past that few opportunities exist for the aid to function productively and multiply like finance. In the absence of relationships with leading-edge productive and commercial power, money simply disappears. But aid does not go to those who possess their own productive and commercial net-works – they get finance – only to those capable of eliciting the magical power of money to augment itself, not on the basis of their own productive and commercial networks, but those of the donor. Because aid actually tends to function in relation to the donor's investment and trading net-works, it ends up not as aid at all, but simply another form of finance, an adjunct of international capital's power to dominate and exploit the less developed world.

Global View of Aid

There is thus always an ambiguity about aid and the quantities involved, but the ambiguity is not very different from the dilemmas facing LDCs in relation to foreign trade and investment. Although both of the latter have destructive effects on those local industries that are not themselves world leaders, the choice is usually to have investment and trade either in these industries or no investment and trade whatsoever. Aid is simply part of the same set of relationships: while it comes through and reinforces existing networks, the choice is between the development of existing strengths or no development at all. The result has been a general belief among LDCs that the more aid that flows to them from the advanced countries the better. Because there is little opportunity to affect the qualitative uses or effects of the flows, quantity has come to be seen as the measure which ranks the advanced countries as donors. The only qualification on pure quantity is that the monies come via government channels and fall into a loose set of official categories – grants and loans – which confer on them the grand title of Official Development Assistance (ODA). Table 6.9 shows the ranking of the leading advanced countries on this measure from 1975–92. By 1988, Japan had moved into the top position, which it briefly lost back to the US in 1990 but has since recovered.

It is generally recognised in Japan that government loans and grants are indistinguishable from non-government financial flows in almost all respects other than name, especially when their effects on the recipients are considered. In an apparent recognition of this and in an attempt to put the stamp of benevolence on all their transactions with LDCs, both capital and the state prefer the broader term *keizai kyōryoku* (economic cooperation), which covers every transaction with LDCs that is expressed in terms of money from Japan. Table 6.10 itemises them over the period 1970–92: the largest non-official amounts are the direct and indirect investments already discussed. Compared to other DAC (Development Assistance Committee) countries, Japan's ODA comprises a similar share of national income, but because of Japan's much larger private flows since the mid-1980s, Japan's total 'economic cooperation' has gone well above that of other DAC countries. Another significant component of that total is the official finance granted for private FDI projects, an amount which in 1990 soared to $4.2 billion or 22 per cent of the total. The term 'cooperation' is thus not much more than a euphemism for the essential profit-making motives behind Japan's investment and trade with LDCs. These activities, which have been more than adequately commented on, will no longer be of concern.

Japan's ODA

In attempts to encourage donor countries into policies that benefited the recipients rather than themselves, aid has commonly been divided into a

Table 6.9 Net ODA flows of DAC countries, 1981–92 ($ billion and %)

	1975	1985	1986	1987	1988	1989	1990	1991	1992
Japan									
ODA flows ($ billion)	–	3.80	5.63	7.45	9.13	8.97	9.07	10.95	11.15
Share of all DAC ODA flows	8.4	12.9	15.4	17.9	19.0	19.1	16.7	19.3	18.2
Share of all DAC total flows	7.1	13.8	26.2	25.3	25.6	28.6	27.3	–	–
US									
ODA flows ($billion)	–	9.40	9.56	8.95	10.14	7.68	10.19	9.40	10.76
Share of all DAC ODA flows	29.5	32.0	26.1	21.5	21.1	16.4	18.7	16.6	17.5
Share of all DAC total flows*	43.4	2.2	22.2	14.8	20.9	19.4	14.5	–	–
France									
ODA flows ($ billion)	–	4.00	5.11	6.53	5.46	5.84	7.19	7.39	8.29
Share of all DAC ODA flows	15.4	13.6	13.9	15.7	11.6	12.8	13.6	13.0	13.5
Share of all DAC total flows	9.8	10.6	11.2	9.7	6.9	6.7	8.8	–	–
Germany									
ODA flows ($ billion)	–	2.94	3.83	4.39	4.73	4.95	6.32	6.89	7.57
Share of all DAC ODA flows	12.4	10.0	10.5	10.6	9.8	10.6	11.6	12.2	12.3
Share of all DAC total flows	12.3	6.8	9.6	9.9	14.1	14.4	19.8	–	–
UK									
ODA flows ($billion)	–	1.53	1.74	1.87	2.65	2.59	2.64	3.20	3.20
Share of all DAC ODA flows	6.4	5.2	4.7	4.4	5.5	5.5	4.9	5.6	6.2
Share of all DAC total flows	5.8	5.2	4.7	4.5	5.1	4.0	–6.2	–	–
Italy									
ODA flows ($billion)	–	1.10	2.40	2.62	3.19	3.61	3.40	3.35	3.78
Canada ODA flows ($billion)	–	1.63	1.70	1.89	2.35	2.32	2.47	2.58	2.52
Other ODA flows ($billion)	–	5.03	6.69	7.83	9.38	9.78	11.68	12.92	14 152

*Refers to total of ODA plus other (private) flows to LDCs by all DAC countries.
Source: Tsūshō sangyōshō, 1993c, pp. 39–44 (supplement) 72

Table 6.10   Japan's 'economic cooperation', 1970–92 ($ million spent)

	1970	1975	1980	1987	1988	1989	1990	1991	1992
Government ODA	458	1 148	3 353	7 342	9 134	8 965	9 222	11 034	11 330
as a per cent of national income	0.23	0.24	0.32	0.31	0.32	0.31	0.31	0.32	0.30
average per cent of DAC countries	–	–	0.38	0.35	0.36	0.34	0.33	0.33	–
Bilateral aid	372	850	2 010	5 135	6 422	6 779	6 940	8 870	8 482
Grant-aid	121	202	702	2 108	2 908	3 037	3 019	3 395	3 862
Cash grants	100	115	375	1 154	1 549	1 556	1 374	1 525	1 733
Technical aid	22	87	327	954	1 359	1 481	1 645	1 870	2 130
Yen loans (non-grant aid)	250	649	1 308	3 027	3 514	3 741	3 920	5 475	4 620
To multi-lateral organisations	87	297	1 343	2 207	2 712	2 186	2 282	2 163	2 848
Other Official Flows	694	1 369	1 478	1 808	–639	1 544	3 470	2 699	–
Export credits (over 1 year)	350	339	823	–2 047	–1 839	–1 245	–1 028	–510	–
Direct investment finance	143	1 016	767	287	1 410	1 892	4 209	3 155	–
To multi-lateral organisations	201	15	–112	–47	–211	897	290	54	–
Private Flows	669	363	1 958	14 723	12 822	13 502	6 262	11 142	–
Export credits	387	83	74	1 081	219	687	–14	602	–
Direct investment	262	223	906	7 421	8 190	11 290	8 144	5 003	–
Other bilateral securities	4	40	660	4 357	2 830	1 289	–2 581	6 227	–
To multi-lateral organisations	18	7	318	1 865	1 583	236	711	–690	–
Grants by voluntary organisations	3	10	26	92	107	122	103	168	–
TOTAL	1 824	2 890	6 815	20 349	21 423	24 133	19 057	25 043	–
as a per cent of national income	0.92	0.59	0.66	0.85	0.75	0.84	0.64	0.74	–
average per cent of DAC countries			1.06	0.55	0.63	0.61	0.44	–	

Source: Tsūshō sangyōshū, 1993c, pp. 21, 25.

number of categories, such as grant-aid (or donations) versus loans, and aid which is untied versus aid which is tied (typically to the purchase of Japanese goods). Loans are also assessed according to an international measure of their 'softness' in terms of interest rates and repayment periods, know as their 'grant element': a purely commercial loan has a grant element of zero per cent. The higher the grant element of the loans and the greater their untied proportion, the more it is hoped LDCs can escape the power networks through which the advanced countries channel their 'aid' and convert it into their own 'finance'. Although there is probably some relationship between the terms on which aid is granted and the independent development that results from it, the channels through which the advanced countries wield power extend well beyond these legal categories.

Nevertheless, Japan does not rank very highly even on these formal measures of altruism: nineteenth among DAC countries on the first and third measures (grant aid versus loans and the softness of the loans). Table 6.11 shows that its grant aid (comprising cash grants and technical aid) is below 40 per cent of the total in comparison to a nearly 80 per cent average – it is 100 per cent for the Scandinavian countries – and that Japan's loans are considerably 'harder' than the DAC average.

However, on the second measure, the official degree to which bilateral aid (both grant-aid and loans) is 'untied' to the purchase of Japanese goods and services, Japan's ranking is higher than that of other DAC countries. In 1990 it was 82.1 per cent compared to a DAC average of 60.6 per cent (69.5 per cent for the US, 47.1 per cent for France, 33.8 per cent for Germany, 16.6 per cent for Italy and 38.8 per cent for Canada) (Tsūshō sangyōshō, 1993c, pp. 31–2). This high figure results from a number of

Table 6.11   Grant aid and grant element of DAC countries' ODA, 1983–91 (%)

	1983	1984	1985	1986	1987	1988	1989	1990	1991
Grant Aid as per cent of Total ODA									
DAC average	79.7	76.8	80.8	84.3	84.3	73.3	78.5	78.5	–
Japan	55.2	48.2	47.4	60.7	47.3	36.1	52.4	39.3	38.1
Grant Element of Loans									
DAC average	91.2	90.0	91.4	93.2	93.2	88.9	91.5	93.3	89.8
Japan	79.5	74.2	73.5	81.7	75.5	72.5	81.0	77.1	73.8

Source: Tsūshō sangyōshō, 1993c, p. 30.

factors. First, it has risen considerably over the years in response to criticism of its failure to measure up with the DAC average in the past, particularly before 1975, when tied loans to LDCs first began to be phased out. Second, in view of the very high proportion of Japan's ODA that comprises loans, which, for reasons still to be explained, require less formal tying than does grant-aid in order to ensure that they benefit the donor, the impressiveness of the official level of untied aid from Japan dwindles somewhat. Japan's aid can present itself as untied only because most of it comes in the form of loans, which can be left untied in theory only because they are so easy to tie in practice. This *de facto* tying of yen loans, through the way that Japanese companies always seem to win contracts in relation to projects financed by them, requires explanation.

Grant-Aid: Mechanism for Tying Yen Loans

Even the Foreign Ministry admits that Japanese companies have won the majority of orders from projects financed by yen loans, but it claims that the proportion has fallen in recent years, from 68 per cent in 1985 to 27 per cent in 1990 and 35 per cent in 1992 (Gaimushō keizai kyōryokukyoku, 1993a, p. 107). While it also notes that the share received by LDC companies has risen from 24 per cent to 52 per cent, it fails to identify how many of these local firms are really *LDC-based* and how many of them are joint-ventures with Japanese companies. As Edward Lincoln points out (1993, p. 125), 'Many projects that involve "indigenous" contractors are joint ventures effectively controlled by Japanese interests. These ventures' imports of equipment from Japan that are resold to the project count as local procurement.'

Most studies of Japan's foreign aid agree on the mechanism through which so-called untied loans are actually tied directly or indirectly to the procurement of Japanese goods. Normally the process begins with the main form of Japan's grant-aid and the institution through which it is channelled, that is, the 'technical cooperation' funnelled through JICA (Japan International Cooperation Agency). Technical aid, which has exceeded cash grants since 1990, largely comprises payment of the wide range of technical personnel employed in relation to Japan's developmental projects. According to JICA, the purpose of technical aid is to raise the level of technology, skill and knowledge in developing countries, firstly by inviting technicians from them to Japan for training, secondly by dispatching Japanese experts to help raise local skill levels and to participate in planning and finally by supplying necessary materials. The three purposes come together in what is called project-type technical cooperation, which involves planning, designing and implementing developmental projects. These are particularly attractive to Japanese companies, since they can draw in other forms of ODA as well. The more visible ones, such as hospitals, can serve public relations functions, while others, such as roads and ports, can improve the general business infrastructure for Japanese businesses. Cash grants are often deliberately directed towards the more costly projects, which in practice also end up attracting finance from yen loans and involve considerable participation from Japanese companies. These latter projects may not always be consciously linked up to wider corporate interests or, even if they are, accompanied by any ungenerous intentions. But in situations of tight networking among a wide range of on-the-spot companies and officials, the conscious intentions of individuals do not matter very much.

The process usually begins with the identification of a project by a Japanese subsidiary in an LDC, typically one of those multi-functional giants the *sōgō shōsha*, which has a finger in almost every pie and is well placed to find something pivotal to the way the country is developing, especially when that development is being spearheaded by Japanese capital. The *sōgō shōsha* then communicates the need for the project to the local government, which in turn applies to the Japanese government for aid to promote it. The first and most critical form this promotion takes is provision of technical aid in the shape of feasibility studies, surveys, engineering consultation, design and planning, all of which result in project specifications that are most suited to Japanese technology and even to specific Japanese firms. Although the development consulting firms attempt to present themselves as neutral, much of the information they require comes from local Japanese companies, often via the networks of the *sōgō shōsha*. However, in most cases the officials and private contractors involved in putting together the project's technical requirements genuinely believe in the superiority of their product, so that when international tenders go out for contracts relating to its construction, it is honestly believed that the best job would be done by Japanese companies or subsidiaries. But since technology refers to a 'way of doing' something in the broadest sense, and not just to machinery, materials or abstract knowledge, attempts to transfer Japanese technology naturally involve transferring the institutional forms through which the Japanese do things. Japanese companies are naturally best equipped to carry out projects requiring Japanese technology, and the government is happy for yen loans to go to projects which have been so thoroughly scrutinised and rigorously put together. There is nothing sinister about this, perhaps because the process is regulated by such tremendously powerful forces, which are not usually noticed by the individuals working under them. The result is that Japanese contractors become involved, not simply when grant aid, which is tied, is used to finance the projects, but even when there is open international bidding for contracts to be financed by 'untied' yen loans. Robert Orr recently described the process in the *Nikkei Weekly* (4 October 1993, p. 6):

> This has less to do with any regulatory restrictions and more to do with the 'network' of trading companies and other interested firms. . . The network lends itself to a profound lack of transparency in the bidding process. . . It seems that frequently bids are virtually won before they are 'officially' let.

Japanese companies benefit from this 'project-type technical cooperation' at both ends: during the stages of planning and construction they get access to lucrative profit-making contracts through what amount to government subsidies. The editors of *Ampo*, who have observed Japanese aid more thoroughly and over a longer time than anyone else, wrote (Vol. 21, No. 4, 1990, p. 5):

> The overwhelming majority of aid projects are carried out on the ground by private enterprises who are seeking profits. Within Japan, construction companies make bridges and tunnels, subsidized by the government, and the international version of this is foreign assistance. Foreign governments are like Japanese local governments receiving subsidies from central governments. . . . It is foolish to imagine there is no competition for concessions or no race for the billions of yen in aid contracts. For private companies, aid is good business.

The other end, the use of the project once completed, is also one which serves Japanese capital particularly well. This can also be looked at through the analogy of foreign governments acting like local governments, which recalls the argument in Chapter 1 that aid serves to extend the 'reach' of the advanced state over the LDC in the current world order, from which direct imperial rule has almost entirely disappeared. From this point of view, the most important problem facing Japanese capital in LDCs is the absence of infrastructure (roads, ports, power, communications systems, etc.) to support their activities. No Japanese company can on its own afford to build these, and no 'local' government has the tax base or fiscal leeway to help very much. The only solution is intervention by the 'central' government, but in the new world order the appropriate method is what was called *social investment aid*, which performs the same function as the direct intervention under classical imperialism.

The overwhelming weight of social investment aid in Japan's total ODA is partly revealed by the degree to which the recipients of aid correspond to Japan's trade and investment partners in the less developed world. Because trade and investment require infrastructure, there is a tendency for countries to be selected for their future potential and to receive massive social investment aid, and then, as the infrastructural projects come on stream, to become important trading partners and hosts to private investments. In the 1960s and 1970s what are now the Asian NICs were targeted in this way, in the 1980s the ASEAN countries were the most favoured, while in the 1990s it is the new targets of low-cost investment: China, Vietnam and South Asia (*FEER*, 22 April 1993, pp. 68–72; *NW*, 25 October 1993, p. 2; 22 November 1993, p. 28; 21 March 1994, p. 9). Throughout, the overwhelming focus has been on Asia. Table 6.12 shows these tendencies in the period 1980–92.

Table 6.13 provides a more explicit indication of the predominance of social investment aid, which comprises not just what is called economic

Table 6.12   Recipients* of Japan's bilateral aid, by shares received in 1980–92

	1980	1985	1986	1987	1988	1989	1990	1991	1992
Asia Total	70.6	67.7	64.8	65.1	62.8	62.5	59.3	51.0	65.1
Indonesia	17.9	6.3	–	13.5	15.3	16.9	12.5	12.5	16.0
China	–	15.2	12.9	10.5	10.5	10.5	10.4	6.6	12.4
Philippines	4.8	9.4	11.4	9.2	8.3	6.0	9.3	–	12.2
Thailand	9.7	10.3	6.8	5.7	5.6	7.2	6.0	4.6	–
Bangladesh	11.0	4.8	6.4	6.4	5.3	5.3	5.4	–	–
Malaysia	3.3	4.9	–	5.3	–	–	5.4	–	–
Burma	7.8	6.0	6.3	–	–	–	–	–	–
India	–	–	5.9	5.8	–	3.8	–	10.5	5.0
Pakistan	–	–	4.8	–	4.7	–	–	–	–
Vietnam	–	–	–	–	–	–	–	–	3.3
Africa	18.9	15.0	15.4	13.4	18.8	17.8	15.4	10.5	12.2
Latin America	6.0	8.8	8.2	8.0	6.2	8.3	8.1	9.5	9.1
Middle East	2.5	1.7	2.4	3.3	2.4	2.0	1.5	7.4	2.0

*Only major recipients are specified. Hence gaps in particular years do not mean that no aid was received by the countries concerned in those years, only that the share was very small.
Source: Tsūshō sangyōshō, 1993c, 1993, p. 26.

Table 6.13   Purposes of Japan's bilateral aid (promised), 1988–92 (%)

	1988	1989	1990	1991	1992
Economic Infrastructure	39.4	31.7	31.5	40.6	27.3
Transport	12.4	14.0	19.0	20.5	10.5
Energy	13.2	6.3	5.3	14.8	9.7
Other	13.8	11.4	7.2	5.3	7.1
Productive sector	19.3	16.9	17.1	17.4	27.0
Programme aid	24.1	32.1	31.0	28.9	27.0
Structural adjustment loans	0.3	7.2	3.2	9.4	7.7
Commodity loans	5.3	10.2	15.6	10.4	3.1
Debt relief programmes	2.7	3.6	4.3	2.7	6.8
Other	15.8	11.1	7.9	6.4	9.4
Social infrastructure & services	16.0	17.5	19.7	12.3	17.6
Other	1.1	1.8	0.7	0.9	1.1

Source: Tsūshō sangyōshō, 1993c, pp. 28–9.

infrastructure, but also much of what is listed as productive sector and even programme aid. Productive sector aid also comprises what was called *private investment aid* in Chapter 1, that is, aid for projects which also contribute to the productivity of capital, but not in the LDC itself, as does economic infrastructure. Rather, the beneficiaries from the end use of the projects are particular private companies in Japan, for example, the importers of shrimps from Asian shrimp farms which have received aid classified as for the 'productive sector'. Only what is referred to as social infrastructure and services tends to fall outside the category of *social capital aid*, that is, aid which directly or indirectly contributes to the profit-making of Japanese companies. But in so far as it helps cheapen the cost of labour or to raise its efficiency it *indirectly* contributes to profit making and is thus also part of *social capital aid*. The Japanese are not known to contribute much in the way of what was called *social expenses aid*, which has no purpose other than to win cooperation from the local people and their government.

If only yen loans are considered, the proportion of aid going into economic infrastructure (transport, communications and power) is even higher than the average of around a third indicated by Table 6.13: it was 57.2 per cent in 1981–85 and 44.3 per cent in 1991. The contrast with other DAC countries was very great in the 1970s, but in recent years infrastructural aid as a proportion of total aid has risen sharply for most DAC countries apart

Table 6.14   Japan's growing shares of Asian ODA, 1980–88

		US	Japan	Europe	Other Int. Org.	World %	Total $ mil.
Malaysia	1980	0.6	50.9	23.5	12.8	12.2	100	160
	1988	0.0	57.3	16.4	20.2	6.2	100	225
Indonesia	1980	13.2	38.5	32.1	7.4	8.9	100	1 108
	1988	4.0	58.5	24.4	6.7	6.4	100	2 162
Thailand	1980	3.9	45.4	20.1	6.7	23.9	100	433
	1988	3.5	65.5	13.7	7.8	9.4	100	666
Philippines	1980	16.5	34.1	16.4	4.6	28.4	100	321
	1988	13.7	65.4	8.2	5.6	7.0	100	1 020
China	1980	0.0	6.5	27.1	0.0	66.4	100	66
	1988	0.0	32.9	25.2	3.7	38.2	100	2 051
Latin America	1980	13.7	3.8	49.7	1.9	30.9	100	3 497
	1988	24.2	8.0	42.1	3.7	22.1	100	5 601
LDCs	1980	12.8	6.1	32.7	27.0	21.3	100	37 714
	1988	14.7	15.0	37.3	9.5	23.6	100	50 968

Source: Nagata, 1992, p. 36.

from the US. For example, in the period 1975/76 to 1989/90 Germany's rose from 17.7 to 26.7 per cent and Britain's from 3.4 to 23.5 per cent, while America's crept up from 2.3 to 3.3 per cent and Japan's fell from 36.6 to 31.9 per cent (Tsūshō sangyōshō, 1993c, pp. 84–5).

Since Japan's non-grant aid focuses so heavily on economic infrastructure and since this non-grant aid from Japan comprises such a high proportion of the total non-grant aid provided by DAC countries (57.2 per cent in 1991), Japan has left its mark on the infrastructure of a number of countries, especially in the ASEAN region. A typical example is the high proportion of electric power generation plant provided by Japan: 31 per cent in Indonesia, 20 per cent in Thailand, 51 per cent in peninsula Malaysia and 50 per cent in Nepal. Japan has also furnished 54 per cent of Kenya's telephone exchange equipment; and over 4000 kilometres of railroad in China. Many of the experts dispatched by JICA are on leave from their corporations; for example, an NTT employee who was sent to Kenya subsequently returned to NTT to the position of responsibility for sales to LDCs. Table 6.14 shows how during the 1980s the main Asian recipients of Japanese aid became overwhelmingly dependent on Japan for their ODA (Tsūshō sangyōshō, 1993c, pp. 87–8; Lincoln, 1993, p. 124).

Financial Aid

What is called 'financial aid', which falls into the two categories of grants
and loans, is thus very different from the financial flows that move among
the advanced countries. Far from promoting independent productive
power and control over each of the moments in the circuit of capital, it
produces growing dependence on its 'donors' by redirecting local activity
into the networks of international capital, thus ensuring its function as
'finance' for their trade and investment. Table 6.15 shows that yen loans,
which are almost entirely spent on projects and commodities, typically
constitute well over 80 per cent of Japan's financial aid, and that the single

Table 6.15   Government financial aid, by purpose, 1988–92

	1988	1989	1990	1991	*1992	Total
Grant Aid	214.1	214.4	201.7	200.8	196.3	3 050.2
Reparations	–	–	–	–	–	356.6
Quasi-reparations	–	–	–	–		174.6
General grant aid	101.0	113.4	97.6	91.2	102.2	1 310.3
Fisheries grant aid	12.5	11.4	7.6	8.5	6.3	124.1
KR# food aid	15.0	11.2	11.8	12.1	13.4	267.5
Increased food production (IFP)	47.0	32.5	27.2	28.3	26.7	442.1
Aid for cultural activities	2.2	1.6	2.5	3.0	1.3	23.5
Non-project grant aid	16.4	26.1	24.0	29.2	18.7	133.6
Exchange rate fund	–	–	–	–	–	13.4
Debt relief	11.9	14.6	19.5	22.2	22.8	154.4
Disaster relief	8.2	3.2	11.1	5.8	4.5	61.9
Small grants	–	0.3	0.3	0.5	0.4	1.5
Non-Grant aid (Yen loans)	1 108.5	1 010.5	1 070.5	979.3	1 047.1	13 702.4
Quasi-reparations	–	–	–	–	–	70.7
Project loans	876.0	746.1	715.1	603.1	632.7	9 818.1
Commodity loans	185.1	236.6	287.9	344.6	153.4	2 708.3
Debt relief						
re-finance	–	–	–	–	–	49.0
reschedule	47.4	27.8	67.5	31.7	260.9	675.0
Deferred payment exports	–	–	–	–	–	381.3
TOTAL	1 322.5	1 224.9	1 272.2	1 180.1	1 243.3	16 752.6

*April –December
#Food Aid, which was first negotiated during the Kennedy Round (1964–67), is known
as KR Food Aid.

Source: Tsūshō sangyōshō, 1993c, p. 197.

Table 6.16   Japan's total yen loans as of December 1992, by region and purpose (¥ billion)

	Quasi-Reparations	Project	Commodity	Debt Relief	Food	Total
East Asia	70.7	5 844.1	1 033.4	193.9	288.0	7 430.1
South Asia	–	2 061.5	968.1	147.0	57.4	3 233.9
Middle East	–	313.6	108.6	3.8	–	426.1
Africa (North of Sahara)	–	378.0	143.5	228.7	–	750.1
Africa (South of Sahara)	–	388.5	158.8	60.9	35.0	643.2
Central America	–	260.3	62.9	21.6	–	344.8
South America	–	381.6	86.4	57.9	1.0	526.9
Oceania	–	43.0	9.5	–	–	52.5
Europe	–	147.4	137.1	10.2	–	294.8
Total	70.7	9 818.1	2 708.3	723.9	381.3	13 702.4

Source: Tsūshō sangyōshō, 1993c, p. 208.

largest category of grants are general grants, which also comprise monies going to Japan's ubiquitous projects. A spokesperson for the Ministry of Finance in 1991 made the purpose of Japan's aid very clear when he said it was 'a magnet for private capital. . . . Japan will increasingly use its aid . . . as seed money to attract Japanese manufacturers or other industrial concerns with an attractive investment environment' (quoted in Lincoln, 1993, p. 124). As of March 1993, the outstanding balance of the OECF (Overseas Economic Cooperation Fund), the vehicle of Japan's non-grant aid, was $58.7 billion, about one-third of the amount owing to the World Bank and almost three times the outstanding balance of the Asian Development Bank (Tsūshō sangyōshō, 1993c, p. 89). Table 6.16 confirms once again the massive concentration of this money into *social capital aid* in Asia.

CONCLUSION

Japan's fifth medium-term five-year goal (1993–97) promises to offer aid to the value of $70–75 billion, to increase the annual amounts by 7–9 per cent, to raise the percentage of ODA to GNP from its level of 0.3 per cent in 1992, to expand the share of grant aid and aid for basic human needs as well as for research, to broaden the categories of aid that can be given and to deepen Japan's links with NGOs (non-governmental organisations) (Tsūshō sangyōshō, 1993c, pp. 32–3). However, the possibility of a qualitative change from the current focus on social capital aid is extremely remote. One of the remarkable features of the wide range of studies on Japan's aid, from the more left-leaning research of the Pacific Asia Resources Centre (publisher of *Ampo*) to the mainstream work of Ensign (1992) and Orr (1991), or even the apologetic publications of the Japanese government itself, is that no doubt whatsoever is left over the patterns and purposes of Japan's aid, or even the role of private sector networks in bringing aid into harmony with trade and investment.

What I have tried to emphasise in this chapter are the reasons for the different consequences that financial flows from Japan to the advanced countries have from the consequences of such flows into the less developed countries of Asia. In both cases the monies are channelled by institutions which have multiple linkages with the institutions responsible for the Japanese trade and investment that accompany them. What makes the difference is not any feature of the Japanese networks or linkages among the three pivotal elements of Japan's 'international capital', but the networks of power among the local capitalists it confronts in the two parts of the world. In the advanced countries, Japanese capital faces comparable networks of power, ones which can just as easily siphon finance from Japan into activities which reinforce their own strength. The result is an increase in the myriads of cross-cutting links and networks that bind advanced capitalism from the three pivotal zones into an increasingly single force. However, the only self-expanding activities into which private or government money can flow in the less developed countries of Asia are ones that are linked to and therefore controlled by Japanese productive and commercial power, or that of other advanced countries. Regardless of the specific intentions of Japanese aid officials, aid to less developed countries functions as finance for Japanese capital.

7 Conclusion: Patterned Underdevelopment in the New World Order

What characterises the new imperialism is networks of power, not just between production, marketing and finance within particular advanced countries but also networks linking the latter to one another. The result is that they increasingly operate as a single system of power, even though the conflicts which divide them are never fully transcended by their common purposes vis-à-vis the less developed countries. I have thus hitherto refrained from attributing the unevenness of capitalist development in Southeast Asia or anywhere else to Japanese FDI, trade or finance, because the significant thing about any one of these is its relations with the others. Underdevelopment and its typical manifestations are the overall outcomes of this power structure, and not of any one or more of its functional elements or geographical centres. It was therefore not possible to look at what I call patterned underdevelopment until each part of that system, at least as they come from and extend into Japan, had been examined. Even though capitalist development in Asia has been more successful than in Africa, the Middle East, Oceania or even Latin America, some of the most telling examples of this phenomenon are to be found within the Asian region, in the very countries targeted by Japanese investment, trade and finance.

The term patterned underdevelopment refers to a combination of political economic tendencies which are connected to one another and constitute the *whole situation* of underdevelopment. Broadly speaking, getting into that situation is a consequence of *not having* the networks linking production, marketing and finance that constitute the unique power of capital in the advanced countries. When a country lacks its own 'international capital' and must ally with networks from abroad, its development is characterised by a number of tendencies that are driven by the requirements of these networks. Not all tendencies are equally strong or equally present in all cases, but they nonetheless do go together to form a package of 'under-developments'.

At least six such connected tendencies can be identified: uneven development due to the colonial legacy of reliance on raw materials or low-cost

246

labour, the dominance by foreign capital of industries requiring high-tech plant and equipment, heavy reliance on overseas markets to generate economic growth, persistent balance of payments deficits, mounting overseas debt and periodic degeneration into social and political crisis. Rather than attempt to document the degrees to which these phenomena exist in LDCs, let alone those in Asia, I concentrate on showing why Japan's global investments, trade and finance, far from eroding the patterns of underdevelopment from the past, are extending them throughout the world, not least into the advanced countries themselves, including Japan.

COLONIAL LEGACY OF UNEVEN DEVELOPMENT

The Asian countries in which Japanese capital first became interested after the war were either those whose large raw material supplies had been the main attraction behind their original colonisation, or the ones which subsequently separated from these countries, mainly because of the Cold War, but which continued to maintain close links with them. Among the latter are Hong Kong and Singapore, that is, the city-state NICs which lost all direct access to the raw materials in their previous hinterlands of China and Malaya, and so which had to exploit their locations by making *trade* and cheap labour the pivots of their developmental efforts. Asian countries can therefore be classified into three groups according to their colonial legacies, which are still reflected in their industrial structures.

The first group comprise the US-backed 'halves' of the countries which were divided during the early years of the Cold War, such as Taiwan and South Korea, which in varying degrees revealed three main tendencies. The first resulted from the loss of their raw material hinterlands to the (mainly communist) other halves, leaving them with the need to specialise in services and labour-intensive manufacturing. Second, these countries were all especially vulnerable to penetration by their previous colonisers and the advanced powers on which their existence as anti-communist bastions depended most heavily. Finally, the industrial structures of all of them changed significantly since independence, largely because of the very rapid growth of their labour-intensive manufacturing and service industries in response to their 're-colonisation'. The main structural changes have either been introduced from the outside, for example, by Japan into Taiwan and Singapore, or resulted from special factors, such as the unique brand of nationalism which shifted the terms of the alliance between South Korean capital and international capital significantly in the former's favour. This group of countries became the modern Asian NICs, which are the least underdeveloped – but they are possibly the most *unevenly* developed – because they are most fully the creations of international capital. Among these divided countries only South Vietnam stagnated, because having been ravaged by war and Cold War for more than half a century, it was until recently shunned by foreign capital.

The second group of countries comprise the vast raw-material-rich hinterlands of classical colonialism, although much of this part of Asia, which includes China, Laos, Burma and Cambodia, was also at various times ravaged by war, Cold War and communism, and thus tended to stagnate for similar reasons to Vietnam. For a long time the demands made on these countries by international capital underwent few changes, apart from increasing the quantities of raw materials, but during the past decade their vast populations have also begun to offer attractive opportunities to reduce the costs of labour-intensive manufacturing and even to provide markets. With the final end of the Cold War, however, the lowest wages which resulted from the greatest degrees of stagnation are emerging as one of the main lures for foreign business, particularly in Vietnam, which also has large supplies of unexploited raw materials.

The final group of countries are the mainly South Asian regions originally colonised less for their potential raw material supplies than for access to the products of their traditional industries and for their capacity to serve as markets. India is the classic example. This legacy has continued in so far as international capital has revealed little interest in establishing new productive industries in countries where it has few existing activities from which to branch out or networks to serve them. However, since South Asia still possesses enormous potential as a market, its cheap labour is beginning to attract a lot of attention, particularly from Japan and the Asian NICs.

What all three groups of countries have in common is their *uneven* development, that is, their continued reliance on a narrow range of industries to propel their growth and generate their wealth. The particular industries might change, for example, to larger shares of manufacturing in GNP, but within these manufacturing industries new gaps emerge to express the underdevelopment, which is essentially constituted by the technological gap that remains between the branches of manufacturing less developed countries specialise in and those dominated by the advanced countries. Table 7.1 suggests that even when the technological content of LDC exports rises, so does that of the advanced countries, even though the blunt two-point quantitative indicator which is used does not capture the real distance covered by the continuous technological leaps achieved by the leading industries of the advanced countries. When this lead is occasionally believed to come under some kind of threat, the advanced countries cry out for greater protection of their 'intellectual property rights'. One of the roles being found for the World Trade Organisation is to do just that, and one of the purposes behind bringing China into it is to prevent China from appropriating control of technologies which might be 'transferred'.

The reasons for the continued uneven development of Asia lie in the enduring operation of the same production networks from the advanced countries, with all their characteristic links to commercial and financial centres of power, that originally shaped the industrial structures of what were once 'classical' colonies. It is natural that with changes in their own industrial structures, what the advanced countries now require from their 'neo-colonies' has also changed, broadly from raw materials to labour-intensive branches of manufacturing. It is also natural that the R&D content of these new industries in their neo-colonies should rise along with the technological improvements that international capital introduces in all industries, including labour-intensive ones, wherever it operates. The changing global divisions of labour are thus the outcome of the persistent technological superiority of the advanced countries in the industries with the *highest* R&D content. Control of technology is the key to the power they have to carve out their own niches of development in Asia through the competitive power of their goods, either their exports or those locally produced by their overseas subsidiaries. That they leave gaps of underdevelopment alongside their most successful developments results from their very nature, which is to appropriate for themselves any sign of local productive power and to destroy any sign of weakness. Their FDI, trading and financial networks thus constitute the excavators which gouge out the

Table 7.1   R&D content of selected Asian countries' exports, 1975–87

	1975 High/Medium	Low	1980 High/Medium	Low	1987 High/Medium	Low
Indonesia	2.0	10.3	2.9	10.5	6.9	24.2
Malaysia	24.6	31.4	22.3	24.4	30.7	28.3
Philippines	5.3	53.3	8.6	46.2	20.9	33.4
Singapore	28.0	54.2	36.0	44.1	54.3	33.1
Thailand	8.2	43.2	19.2	38.2	20.2	50.9
South Korea	21.6	67.5	28.8	64.9	43.4	52.6
Japan	53.9	44.0	69.7	28.4	82.9	15.6

Source: Tsūshō sangyōshō, 1993d, p. 38.

industrial voids that the LDCs are compelled to leave for the advanced countries themselves to fill, voids that leave room for the *lower* – not necessarily *low* by some fixed standard – R&D-intensive developments assigned to them.

The leading-edge technology monopolised by the developed countries is itself the product of the same networks which maintain their own more *even* development, networks which constantly link advantages in any one industry to advantages in others and allow an across-the board accumulation of technological advances. In this way uneven development functions to reinforce the one-sided technical growth which is also the fundamental cause of uneven development. The cement in this vicious circle comprises the networks which extend each and every breakthrough in scientific knowledge or its application from one evenly developed industry to another and from one advanced country to the others. The result is that when Japanese companies or any others that are linked up with international capital enter Asia, they are able to marshal technical resources of truly global proportions. Since the crucible of this technological knife-edge is first and foremost foreign direct investment, the second element of patterned underdevelopment is the leading role of foreign investment in LDC capitalism.

FOREIGN INVESTMENT DOMINATED

Foreign direct investment constitutes the front line of international capital's onslaught on the less developed world, not simply because dominance in the production place, the chief locus of technology, is the key to overall dominance, but because it is an activity in which cooperation among the advanced powers is the greatest. Their agreement at almost every level of foreign investment policy throughout the world presents a marked contrast to the continual bickering and jockeying for advantage that characterises their global trading policies. An example of the difference is the greater agreement the World Trade Organisation is able to achieve among them over such matters as TRIMs (Trade-Related Investment Measures) or TRIPs (Trade-Related Aspects of Intellectual Property Rights) than over things like 'unfair trade policies'. Both of the former are primarily designed to protect the common interests of the advanced countries against attempts by the LDCs to restrict foreign investment or to appropriate for themselves the technologies which spearhead foreign investment (Industrial Structure Council, 1994, pp. 119–29, 268–9)

Especially since the FDI-boom of the 1980s, economic growth throughout Asia has been driven more and more by investment as opposed to consumption, and investment by foreign as opposed to local capital. With the notable exception of Singapore, which has a long and consistent history of favouring foreign investment, much of Asia had in the 1960s and even 1970s relied largely on consumption demand to stimulate growth and on investment by local capital to meet this demand, in an attempt to industrialise by means of import substitution (ISI). It was a strategy that relied heavily on the power of local networks to draw on and combine all the productive, commercial and financial resources of the country in order to promote a more even development than what was inherited from the colonial past. The weakness of these local networks, relative to those of the advanced powers that consciously conspired to replace ISI with an industrialisation strategy that put international capital back into the driver's seat, became apparent in the 1980s when one after another Asian country came to favour export-led growth (ELG).

Since the only industries that can survive in global markets are ones which can compete with the world's leading producers, that is, with the advanced countries, such industries have to rely on international capital for their competitive edge. ELG, which we soon see also has important market and trading implications, was largely a euphemism for investment-led growth and foreign-capital-led growth. ISI depended too much on local consumption, which, through the resulting need to keep up local wage levels, robbed the less developed world of its central attraction. It is no accident that the two countries which shifted most dramatically in the 1980s from consumption-led to investment-led growth, Malaysia and Thailand, have also received the greatest increases in foreign investment, especially from Japan. The Thai share of total registered capital in the country fell from 71.7 per cent in the period 1960–85 to 64.7 per cent in 1986–92, with Japan accounting for a full 46.6 per cent of the foreign share in the latter period (Tsunekawa, 1994, p. 131). At no time in 1988–92 did local investors account for more than a quarter of applications filed at the Board of Investment (*NW*, 15 August 1994, p. 18).

In spite of having the lowest wages in the region, the Philippines and to a lesser extent Indonesia have been much slower in replacing consumption with investment and local manufacturing with foreign-controlled manufacturing. The differences owe a lot to the degree of nationalist political organisation and struggle in the different ASEAN countries. For example, even the Philippines managed to attract considerable FDI during the 1989–90 boom following the restoration of 'confidence' in the Aquino regime: among Board of Investment approved investments during those years, only 53 per cent was by local companies, and a full 12 per cent came from Japan. With the collapse of the boom, however, FDI in the Philippines fell from $783 million in 1991 to a mere $294 million the next year, with Japanese capital among the main foreign investors to look for safer waters. But being slower than Thailand in attracting large waves of manufacturing FDI has not prevented countries like the Philippines and Indonesia from making up for lost ground. Both recorded massive increases in FDI in the first half of 1994: a 550 per cent jump in the Philippines to $960 million and a whopping $7.1 billion in Indonesia that almost exceeded the previous year's total (Tsūshō sangyōshō, 1993d, p. 7, 13; Yoshino, 1992, p. 185; *NW*, 15 August 94, p. 18).

The stagnation of countries like the Philippines reveals that in a world cornered by international capital there is only one thing worse than being flooded by foreign investment, and that is not being flooded by foreign investment, because stagnation is the inevitable result of possessing the power neither to insulate local industry from the machinations of international capital nor to compete with it. The Philippines had no alternative to making extra efforts, for example, by tackling electricity shortages, to bring on the extra FDI it received in 1994.

The red carpet Singapore has long laid out for foreign investors might, in such a context, be viewed as much as a submission to a power it could not check as an opportunistic welcome to forces which both fed it and fed on it. Table 7.2 provides one measure of the alliance between that country's rulers and foreign investors. If one recognises that control in technology-intensive industries can be achieved through very small levels of foreign ownership – in fact it can even at times be achieved without any such ownership at all – then the minimal role of local capital is all the more striking, accounting for only 15 per cent of production and a mere 8 per cent of direct exports.

Table 7.2   Foreign control of Singapore's manufacturing industry in 1990 (S$ million)

	Firms	Employees	Production	Direct Exports
100% local capital	2 508	102 000	10 769.1	3 665.3
less than 50% foreign capital	329	42 300	6 446.6	3 025.4
over 50% foreign capital	245	35 400	9 853.1	5 877.3
100% foreign capital	621	171 800	44 263.8	34 431.6
TOTAL	3 703	351 700	71 333.2	46 999.5

Source: Nihon bōeki shinkōkai, 1993b, p. 40.

The absence in LDCs of local networks sufficient to the task is most clearly revealed by the nature of the networks which do operate. They reveal the same unevenness that characterises the overall 'underdevelopments' of the countries in which they operate. With the significant exception of South Korea, none of the numerous business groups which dominate local capitalist organisation and activity in Asia has any kind of technological-industrial base. In those rare cases where industrial corporations are central to a group's activities, such as the Astra or Gobel groups in Indonesia, the local firm is more of a 'receptacle' for the operation of foreign capital, in this case Toyota and Matsushita respectively (Yoshihara, 1988; Steven, 1990, pp. 217–8, 220).

The local networks are thus largely confined to the kinds of industries which characterised their colonial development – trade, real estate, raw materials and light industry – and which fell into local hands during the transition from direct colonial rule to political independence. Control of the newer high-tech industries does not come through government fiat, but requires networks based on the kind of even capital accumulation denied to the countries of Asia. Even the exceptional case of South Korea reveals an overall uneven development and a corresponding absence of key industrial technologies within its *chaebol* (business groups). For example, in spite of valiant attempts by the big four – Hyundai, Samsung, Daewoo and Goldstar – to bridge the gap, they remain as dependent as ever on Japanese and US technology for their strength in the car and electronic industries, their R&D expenditures comprising only minute proportions of those of their competitors in the advanced countries. Along with the rest of Asia, including such long stalwart opponents of foreign investment as China and India, South Korea has been forced to relax its regulations to allow greater foreign participation in domestic industry and therefore control over it. The importance of this foreign control lies in the way it reinforces the networks of international capital and weakens those of local capital, thereby allowing other elements of capitalist 'underdevelopment', including the local networks through which they are carried out, also to be steered more towards the interests of international capital. The most critical of these are the market linkages which express themselves in patterns of trade.

EXPORT-LED GROWTH

If the replacement of consumer-led growth with investment-led growth was one effect of the shift from local to foreign investment, then another was a restructuring of markets from domestic to overseas. The replacement of the local networks, which linked local production with local marketing, with foreign networks which broke those links meant that the new structures of production would be connected to new patterns of marketing, to be determined by international capital's own internal requirements. Since the latter operates on both global and regional scales, there were strong tendencies to replace the domestic sales of local producers with the export markets of foreign capital. Much as capital in Japan had found in exports a way round the limits on domestic markets which low-cost production imposes, so does international capital resort to exports whenever similar limits get placed on local markets in countries whose low wages or abundant raw materials make them attractive environments for production. By the 1990s, economic growth in ASEAN had in almost all cases come to depend even more on export demand than on investment demand, with the few exceptions all showing strong tendencies in the same direction (Tsūshō sangyōshō, 1993d, p. 7). It was shown in Chapter 5 that these tendencies are strongest among Japanese subsidiaries operating in ASEAN countries. In the years 1980–92, exports as a percentage of GDP soared from 15.4 to 32.1 per cent in Indonesia, 50.8 to 87.7 per cent in Malaysia, 21.4 to 38.6 per cent in Thailand (to 1991), and 25.4 to 31.8 per cent in the Philippines. The fall from 165.2 to 137.8 per cent in Singapore hardly affected ELG in that country (Aoki, 1994, p. 109). In South Korea the climb began earlier, from around 10 per cent in the late 1950s to some 60 per cent in the late 1980s (Mizuhashi, 1994, p. 62).

In 1989 almost 70 per cent of the total manufacturing production of Japanese subsidiaries in Malaysia was in electrical and transport machinery, and over 70 per cent of this was exported (Aoki, 1992, p. 75). Malaysia was transformed almost overnight by Japanese and American electrical companies from a predominantly raw materials exporting country to one whose leading export product was microchips (Sekiguchi, 1992, p. 164). In Thailand, manufactured exports jumped from 2 per cent of total exports in 1960 to 50 per cent in 1985 and 75 per cent in 1990, predominantly due to escalating FDI in manufacturing (Tsunekawa, 1992, p. 213). In the period 1986–90, Japan dominated the FDI scene in that country, contributing between 40–50 per cent of the total in most years (Aoki, 1992, p. 65), while the export ratio of its projects rose from 71 per cent for those approved in 1986 to 93 per cent for the ones in 1990 (Tsunekawa, 1994, p. 221).

Indonesia, which has now fully abandoned ISI in favour of export-led growth, saw a rapid increase in the export-orientation of Japanese companies in the country: in 1987 only 35 per cent of companies setting up in the manufacturing industry were classified as export-oriented (ones which expect to export over 65 per cent of output), whereas by 1990 the proportion had soared to 80 per cent (Watanabe, 1992, p. 144). The composition of Indonesia's exports has not surprisingly reflected the patterns of FDI in the country: in 1981–90 non-oil and -gas exports grew from 18 per cent to 57 per cent of the total, with textiles leaping from 3 per cent to 20 per cent of the same total and plywood from 4 per cent to 19 per cent (Watanabe, 1992, p. 148).

The redirection of markets into exports and the structure of trade towards intra-industry trade within the Asian region has been widely heralded as a sign of growing Asian independence (Tsūshō sangyōshō, 1993d, p. 171), but its real meaning lies more in the opposite direction. The only Asia-wide networks through which this trade is being coordinated are the functional *keiretsu* structures of Japanese capital and the more personal contacts among Chinese capitalists that extend into very few industrial channels. Severing links between production and marketing within particular countries cannot therefore generate independent strength on a regional level when the only all-round power networks in the region belong to international capital, especially from Japan and to a lesser extent the US. Without understanding the way international capital links the whole range of its operations into a package of mutually supporting activities, developments such as increasing shares of manufacturing in GDP and of manufacturing exports in total exports (Table 7.3), or even increasing

Table 7.3   ASEAN and NICs manufactured exports as shares of total exports, 1965–89

	1965	*1989*
NICs		
Hong Kong	87	96
South Korea	59	93
Singapore	35	73
Taiwan	35	73
ASEAN		
Indonesia	4	32
Malaysia	6	44
Philippines	6	62
Thailand	4	54

Source: Kohama, 1992, p. 10.

intra-regional trade within most branches of manufacturing, can all give the misleading impression of growing Asian autonomy.

The erosion of Asian autonomy, at least in the case of ASEAN countries, is suggested by the loss of market diversity (that is, the falling share of 'other' markets in Table 7.4) and by the even more rapid increases in trade with the advanced countries, especially in the 1980s when FDI and export-led growth got into high gear, and especially in the higher-tech industries which are supposed to bring greater independence. Table 7.4 suggests that the export-led growth initiated by foreign capital in the region could be sending Asia's exports into the same advanced countries (or their NIC satellites) from which the investments came, thereby consolidating the networks of international capital rather than those fostering Asian independence. The networks of US capital in the computer industry are a potent example.

The changing patterns of ASEAN trade also draw attention to the way trade friction among the advanced countries has been displaced into Asia and is increasingly being acted out on this region's stage. Not simply is

Table 7.4   Changing markets of ASEAN manufactured exports, 1970–90

Manufacturing	*Intra-ASEAN*	*NICs*	*China*	*Japan*	*US*	*EU*	*Other*	*Total*
1970	12.6	5.2	0.0	10.8	29.5	15.5	26.4	100.0
1980	21.4	6.5	1.0	10.4	19.2	20.9	20.5	100.0
1990	18.3	9.0	1.3	11.0	24.8	18.7	17.0	100.0
Textiles								
1970	14.8	4.6	0.0	2.5	19.7	8.6	49.9	100.0
1980	11.2	6.1	0.6	4.4	17.6	30.3	29.9	100.0
1990	11.2	3.4	0.2	5.1	28.0	26.9	25.3	100.0
Electrical machinery								
1970	9.7	11.6	0.0	0.5	37.9	10.9	29.4	100.0
1980	22.2	7.6	0.6	2.9	36.7	16.7	13.3	100.0
1990	19.7	10.2	0.4	6.1	31.3	19.7	12.6	100.0
Computers								
1970	42.8	3.8	0.0	0.6	0.1	0.3	52.5	100.0
1980	18.5	16.4	0.0	2.5	25.0	28.0	9.5	100.0
1990	2.4	7.2	0.2	3.3	51.5	22.8	12.7	100.0
Motor vehicles								
1970	31.5	3.7	0.0	0.2	2.3	1.2	61.1	100.0
1980	64.5	10.6	0.0	1.9	2.6	4.5	15.8	100.0
1990	33.6	8.3	1.9	4.5	5.1	5.2	41.4	100.0

Source: Tsūshō sangyōshō, 1993d, 1993, p. 171.

export-led growth depriving Asian capital of the opportunity to build mutually supportive relationships between production and marketing, but it is making the less developed world once again pay for the problems of the advanced countries. Since this latter issue is one of trade balances, it is best illustrated in relation to the fourth element of patterned underdevelopment, namely, the tendency towards persistent balance of payments deficits.

BALANCE OF PAYMENTS DEFICITS

It might appear strange that such devotion to export industries should have a tendency to worsen rather than to improve the balance of payments performance of LDCs. However, the problem lies in the growing propensity to import resulting from the requirement that an already weak industrial base should become competitive in world markets or face extinction. Uneven development is thus reproduced and deepened by the destructive effects on infant industries of competition from foreign capital, in world markets and in the domestic market via imports or the goods produced locally by foreign companies. The trend is thus for the range of products to fall that local companies can make, especially the more technology-intensive ones in which the advanced countries specialise. And since these are the very goods that are most needed by the growing export industries – plant, equipment and sophisticated components – export-led growth has a way of accelerating their importation at rates which push the balance of payments over the abyss. In 1981–92, the share of components in Japan's electrical machinery exports climbed from 41 to 55 per cent, while in transport machinery it almost doubled from 9 to 17 per cent (Uchida, 1994b, p. 40).

A typical case is Thailand, whose boom in the late 1980s was spearheaded by foreign capital, much of which comprised the small subcontracting firms that make parts for Thailand's assembly industries: motor vehicles, electrical appliances and electronic goods. Their structure is pyramid-shaped, and they draw in more imports from their apex in Japan than they are capable of exporting. We have already seen how the rising prices of Japan's 'high value-added' goods have lifted the general price level of Japan's exports, as well as how the *exchange* between the capital-intensive goods made by expensive Japanese labour and the labour-intensive goods made by cheap Asian labour is essentially *unequal*. The rapidly increasing volumes of Asian exports needed to pay for given volumes of Asian imports, all at prices which make the balance of trade seem to go the other way, constitutes a classical case of the *unequal exchange* discussed in Chapter 1. The regular revaluations of the yen only exacerbate the inequality of the trade, since they multiply the quantities of LDC goods that are needed to pay for the same quantities of Japanese goods. Even the myth of South Korea's growing independence is suddenly shattered by its rising trade deficits with Japan, as the *Nikkei Weekly* (2 August 1993, p. 24) pointed out: 'The chronic trade deficit with Japan exposes South Korean industry's failure to wean itself from high technology Japanese components.'

The linkages between production and marketing in LDCs therefore function to reinforce the power of international capital, which wrenches local linkages apart and transforms the directions of trade just as thoroughly as it transforms the nature of production, by appropriating both into its own networks and leaving in its wake a 'patterned underdevelopment' in which local capital can play only a limited part. Most of the surplus that is created by the narrow ranges of industries that survive is either accumulated in order to generate more wealth for its foreign owners or is 'unequally traded' away into the advanced countries. A fairly sure indicator of the extent to which this process occurs is the size of the balance of payments deficits which have accompanied accelerating foreign investment and export-led growth.

Table 7.5 illustrates how the FDI boom of the late 1980s, especially in the high-tech machinery industries, was associated with worsening

Table 7.5   ASEAN and NICs trade balances, by year and region ($ million.)

By Year		1988	1989	1990	1991
ASEAN	Trade balance	4 658	–730	–9 935	–12 071
	Raw materials	21 059	19 703	19 546	19 170
	Industrial goods	–21 872	–19 882	–29 092	–30 559
	machinery	–12 978	–16 565	–24 009	–26 104
NICs	Trade balance	14 594	11 017	–527	–5 161

By Region (1991)	Total	Japan	US	EU
ASEAN	–12 071	–6 334	3 033	–2 220
NICS	–5 161	–38 541	23 874	3 462

Source: Nihon bōeki shinkōkai 1993b, p. 39; Yamamoto, 1994, pp. 190, 201; ASEAN Centre, 1993, p. 21.

balance of payments in both the ASEAN countries and the NICs. The trade surplus the former used to enjoy from its raw material exports was eaten away mainly by the growing quantities of capital and intermediate goods needed by Japanese factories in the region. The NICs, which had always specialised in selected branches of machinery, plunged into record levels of deficit with Japan, and although they had traditionally covered these by stepping up exports to the US, this has become more difficult. The US has its own deficit with Japan to deal with and has been intensifying its resistance to the re-routeing of that deficit via Asia (Figure 7.1).

The tendencies in LDCs towards trade deficits only benefit the advanced capitalist countries to the extent that the shortfalls can somehow be paid for, that is, that they remain *potential* rather than *actual*, otherwise the deficits amount to gifts from the advanced countries. And so this contribution to patterned underdevelopment must function as a disciplinary force, to give even more encouragement to the foreign-owned export industries and to help force the LDCs to restrict their own consumption, and so their own wages and living standards, by restricting imports to goods which serve the export industries.

Hence, Japan's surplus with East Asia can function as a solution to the structural limits on Japan's own domestic market only so long as East Asia can somehow cover its deficit. Hitherto this has been done by running corresponding trade surpluses with the US, whose looser 'system' of corporate and state networks than Japan's has been less able to protect its

Figure 7.1 Re-routeing Japan's surplus to the US via East Asia, 1991 ($ billion)

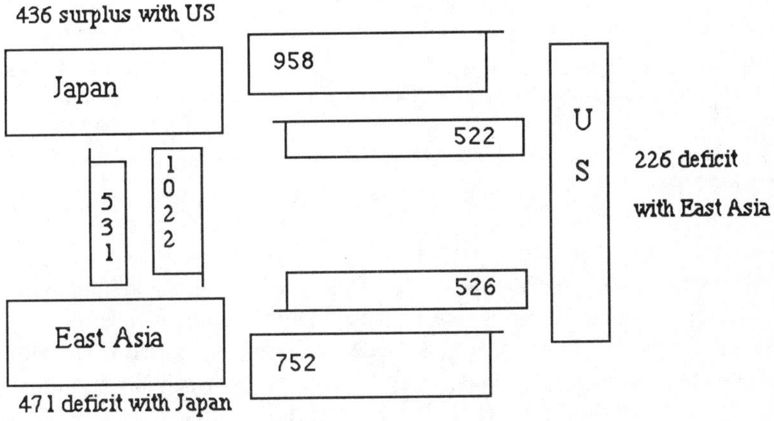

436 surplus with US

Japan

958

522

U
S

226 deficit
with East Asia

5
3
1

1
0
2
2

526

East Asia

752

471 deficit with Japan

Source: Uchida, 1994b, p. 40.

domestic market from the 're-imports' from its own subsidiaries in Asia or the exports of its rival's. Since the time when the US could cover the shortfall simply by issuing paper dollars ended with the demise of the previous world order, the world's leading imperialist power has resorted to more of the wide range of protective measures that are still available to it, including re-organising its technological and industrial base, expanding its alliances with other advanced powers, bending the rules – which are largely of its making anyway – of organisations like the World Trade Organisation, and the good old-fashioned bullying tactics it still seems able to get away with.

Whenever the US manages, by whatever means and via whatever avenue, to send some of Japan's surplus back to where it came from, the consequences in Japan are felt in the form of recessions triggered by deficiencies in demand. However, so closely related are the fortunes of international capital that all the advanced countries are adversely affected by recessions in any one of them. Solutions other than sending recessionary pressures back and forth among one another are therefore constantly being sought. One of these is to move even more of Japan's productive power out of the country, leaving only what the domestic market has the power to absorb, a 'solution' that means greater hollowing out of Japanese industry and increasing levels of unemployment. However, Japan is hardly likely to opt for bringing this element of patterned underdevelopment right onto its own doorstep, even though, as we shall presently see, it might not be given the option. The other alternative is for Asia simultaneously to absorb growing shares of Japan's surplus and diminishing shares of the US deficit, thus allowing the friction among the advanced powers to give way to their common interests in relation to the less developed countries. But there is only one very temporary way for such an alternative to work, only one way for Asia to cover its mounting deficits with both advanced capitalist regions – all three if Europe joins in – and that is by means of borrowing.

DEBT CRISES

LDCs face never-ending pressures to borrow from overseas to cover their trade deficits, but like the deficit itself, borrowing is only a short term 'solution' to the problem of patterned underdevelopment, in this case balance of payments crises. Unless the debt can be serviced and eventually eliminated, the lenders end up paying for the deficit, which is no solution at all from their point of view. We have seen how following the Latin American debt crisis of the 1980s, which drummed this lesson home with added urgency, the networks of international capital have preferred to steer their lending in LDCs directly towards *securitised* productive activities rather than leave governments to squander the monies on imports.

We have also seen how credit, when it is granted to appropriate surplus-generating activities, functions almost magically to mobilise capital into never-ending self-expansion. And international capital, through its elaborate networks in LDCs which link the provision of this credit to its own foreign investment projects and 'export-led' markets, once again wrests this magical power from local financial institutions. It can then appropriate for itself the totality of the mutually-reinforcing outcomes: profitable production, effective marketing and safe lending. The real debt crisis for the less developed world is not when it defaults on its debt – that is a crisis for the lenders of the advanced capitalist world – but when it does not default, for that means the full-circle of control by international capital has closed in. It means that international lenders have succeeded in limiting their credit to 'successful' projects, which are normally the ones whose production and marketing they also control. High levels of debt that are being successfully serviced are thus a sign of high levels of control by international capital, and that means very narrow limits on borrowing for unproductive activities, such as covering trade deficits.

However, in so far as some debt to cover the trade imbalances of LDCs is tolerated, this is only when the remaining productive debt is being fully serviced and the expectation is that the trade imbalances are no more than temporary. Whenever this expectation seems to have been misplaced, overseas lenders, whether private banks or international institutions such as the World Bank, tighten the conditions of their loans to include specific measures to rectify the trade deficits. Raising the proportion of such unproductive debt always brings with it a threat that credit will dry up unless the weight is shifted back in favour of productive debt. Hence borrowing to cover persistent trade deficits is once again a solution only when it is *not actualised*, that is, when there is no persistent borrowing.

The contrast between the overseas debt of Thailand and the Philippines illustrates the difference between what can now be called the productive and the unproductive debt crises to which LDCs are prone and which constitute this fifth element in their patterned underdevelopment. Thailand's 'productive debt' crisis is one of growing foreign control resulting from the way international capital increasingly usurps each moment in the turnover of the total social capital, from the provision of credit, through the production process and finally to marketing. During the FDI boom of 1988–91, Thailand's total accumulated overseas debt almost doubled from $17.9 billion to $33.1 billion, the proportion of private debt more than doubling from 29.6 to 62.2 per cent of the total (Toritani, 1994, p. 307). The willingness of private financial institutions to increase their lending so rapidly is an indicator of the productive uses to which the credit was being put and the surplus-appropriating power they gained from it.

The 'unproductive debt' crisis of the Philippines, however, has resulted from the only thing which, in the current world order, can be worse than such growing foreign control, and that thing is abandonment by foreign capital altogether because it cannot achieve the control it requires. At least from the point of view of overseas lenders, if not the Filipino people, too much past overseas debt was incurred to pay for trade deficits and other unproductive expenses, such as military methods of social control – itself one of the tendencies of patterned underdevelopment. Since this kind of debt does not help generate the wealth needed to service it, international capital becomes increasingly reluctant to provide it, so that the mounting debt crisis in this case is a growing *inability* to borrow. In 1985–92, a period two years longer than the one in which Thailand doubled its overseas borrowing, the overseas debt of the Philippines rose by a mere $4.7 billion from $26.3 billion to $30.9 billion, over half of the increase coming from Japan in the form of ODA. The largely unproductive debt in 1985, which equalled a full 81.7 per cent of the country's GNP, was already so crushing that the Philippines was hard pressed to attract any productive debt whatsoever. Japan's private banks simply refused to lend to the Philippines (Itō, 1994, p. 180, 188).

Either way, the contribution of debt crises to patterned underdevelopment is the added leverage they allow international capital to get over LDCs through its control over credit – by granting it in one case and withholding it in the other – and therefore over all that flows from the power of credit and back into it. However, a wizardry that no amount of borrowing can achieve is the total elimination by this means of balance of payments deficits. Uneven development of whatever kind, whether between Japan's productive power in consumer goods and the capacity of its domestic market to purchase them, or the many forms into which this unevenness is displaced internationally, comes at a price for someone, somewhere, and that typically is unemployment, wage squeeze and the militarisation of politics, or more broadly, repeated social and political crises.

SOCIAL AND POLITICAL CRISES

Although the political-economic effects of international capital's control of productive, marketing and financial networks in less developed countries needed to be looked at individually in their specific forms, the social and political effects can be discussed under a single heading, because joblessness, low wages and military oppression constitute a much more familiar package and because it is well beyond the scope of this study to document the detailed manifestations of these latter contributions to patterned underdevelopment. I wish rather to focus on the changing geographical locations of the worst forms of crisis that are emerging under the new world order.

It has been repeatedly argued that international capital from the advanced countries has come to achieve its purposes more through networks of relationships than through military might. Imperialist military power, whether to conquer colonies under classical colonialism, or to keep neo-colonies safe from communism during the period of super-power rivalry, functioned to intensify the geographical concentrations of the social crises resulting from international capital's global exploitations. This was why US imperialism, which even after World War Two continued to function much more directly through military power than its rivals, was so much more thoroughly associated with the misery of entire populations than was Japanese or European imperialism, which more quickly learned to rely on their productive, marketing and financial networks. They were thus more able to forge functional alliances with local elites and incorporate them into their own networks. Since military conflicts tend to force whole populations into rigidly opposing camps by polarising the countries concerned, and since the purpose of most wars during the period of super-power rivalry was to keep the one side open to capitalist penetration by the other, military power sharpened the division of the world into rich and poor *countries*, with not too much blurring through differences within countries. Past world orders thus gave a geographical pattern to the social crises brought on by capitalist imperialism which closely paralleled the boundaries of nation states.

What has been changing in recent years is not that military power is no longer used to keep the world open to imperialist exploitation, but that when this power is exercised from without it is wielded through the international institutions that the advanced powers jointly control. Military power is of course also still wielded, as it was in the period of super-power rivalry, through the militarisation of politics within the most exploited territories. The use of the military as a political weapon against the lower classes has generally resulted from an alliance between the advanced powers and the elites of the countries concerned, which have no other way to maintain their 'comparative advantage' of possessing low-paid disciplined labour forces. But it was the external force employed by particular powers which contributed most to the high polarisation of human misery into different types of nation states.

Now that networks of relationships have become the main instrument through which advanced powers dominate the LDCs as well as conduct their rivalries with one another, the geographical concentrations of the human costs of imperialism have become much more diffuse. Within the advanced countries in particular, growing segments of the populations experience social and political crisis as a normal part of everyday life, largely because the increasing degrees of mutual penetration by one another's networks reinforce their own tendencies towards uneven development. The strategic alliances they need to conclude with one another enable them to muster exceptional strength at particular times and places, and this accelerates the ups and downs of their accumulation patterns. Silicon Valley in the US or Toyota City in Japan are examples of extreme concentrations of technological industrial power resulting from the operation of national and international networks, and they function to hollow out cavities within the advanced countries them- selves. They do this not just through their capacity to destroy competi- tors within their own borders, a strength which is enhanced by the links that they have with the powerhouses of other advanced countries, but also through the gaps they leave behind when they journey abroad. All the tendencies that are associated with patterned underdevelopment can therefore appear within the advanced countries, not least the social and political costs.

The United States and Europe have long revealed sizeable pockets of permanent depression even in the midst of their most prosperous times, largely because of their high levels of internationalisation. Although Japan's journey towards the same fate has been a bit slower and a bit more indirect, there are signs that the pace is quickening and that Japanese capital cannot escape the mounting pressures, particularly from rival powers but also from within its own ranks, to allow the same degrees of uneven development within its territory which other advanced powers have long had to tolerate in theirs. In a world order no longer threatened by wars among the advanced countries, the Japanese state also has less need to preserve the nationalism that served it so well on its journey to this status. Both capital and labour within Japan can with greater assurance be exposed to the competitive power of foreign capital, since some hollowing out of Japanese industry and some permanent unemployment to match the permanence of Japan's insecure and low-paid workforce poses fewer threats to the nation's survival than it once did. If that means no more than growing alienation and misery for the minority of the population that gets caught up in Japan's own patterned underdevelopment, then the price for capital is not necessarily too high.

What would be too high a price are trade disputes with the US that degenerate into levels of recession that affect capital as a whole and for long periods, such as the current recession. A more permanent state of depression for a minority of the population, something that has been tolerated in the US and Europe for a long time now, is, from the point of view of Japanese capital, a form of uneven development that can be tolerated so long as it helps reduce the existing one of uneven growth that cuts deep into capital's own lifeblood every few years.

There are growing signs that such a choice is being consciously made. For example, a survey in September 1994 by *Nihon Keizai Shinbun*, Japan's largest business daily, revealed that an across-the-board expansion of production and employment abroad is, possibly for the first time, being carefully coordinated with cuts in production and employment at home. According to the survey, employment abroad was expected to rise at a rate of 10 per cent a year until the end of the decade, production at twice that rate also until the end of the decade (resulting in a total increase of 150 per cent over 1993) and capital investment by the same amount at least in the immediate future. However, within Japan employment was expected to fall by well over 1 per cent in the next two years, production to remain flat (with a total rise of only 10 per cent in 1993–2000) and equipment investment to shrink. The ratios of domestic-to-overseas production of some companies, such as Akai, were expected to be reversed as soon as 1995, while the procurements of components abroad would surge by 54 per cent in 1994 and 30 per cent in 1995. Never before had any survey revealed such a conscious recognition that further overseas expansion would require measured reductions in domestic growth (*NW*, 5 September 1994, p. 10.).

Not that even high rates of domestic growth had ever protected the entire population from the loss of jobs or the insecurity of non-living wages, which are rampant in the Japanese system. If unemployment were officially measured in ways similar to those of other advanced countries, Japan's record would not stand up today any more than it did during the 1970s and 1980s (see page 42 above). Because of the large numbers of part-time, temporary, casual and day labourers in Japan, none of whom can be officially regarded as unemployed, and because of the futility of registering as unemployed in a system that offers little assistance to the jobless, especially females, the current official level of some 3 per cent grossly distorts the seriousness of the problem. In fact the mountain of unemployment and especially under-employment in Japan is the main source of the very wide wage differentials that exist among unskilled and semi-skilled workers in Japan's labour market, differentials that allow employers to slash wages simply by altering the composition of their workforces. By no stretch of the imagination can one therefore say that Japanese capitalism has the best record of 'full employment' amongst the advanced countries. Even during the boom of the late 1980s when complaints were rife over labour short-ages, what was meant were shortages of vulnerable, flexible, low-paid workers who constitute Japan's reserve army of labour. Thus what even higher unemployment means for Japan is mainly higher official levels due to the greater difficulties people will have of finding even temporary jobs and so larger numbers of long-term unemployed.

In spite of the higher domestic cost, it appears that the only solution to the long-standing contradiction between Japanese capital's enormous pro-ductive power and its limited domestic market is no longer to export the manifestations of the problem – the surplus goods to high-wage America and Europe – but to export the fundamental cause – the productive power itself, in the hope that suitable markets can also be found. In so far as zone strategies are designed to find the balance between production and market-ing outside Japan which could never be struck within the country, they too are part of the new directions which Japanese capital is exploring. Since production within Japan is apparently to be limited to what the domestic market can absorb, new dimensions of unemployment will result from the new levels of production. These might, from capital's point of view, even have the desirable effect of further reducing wages, which even though low in terms of the living standards they can support, are high in dollar terms due to the rise of the yen.

If there is an increasingly conscious decision among Japanese capitalists to produce abroad *instead of* at home, as opposed to their 1980s policy of *as well as* at home, then this is an effect of the long but unsuccessful quest to find overseas markets commensurate with Japan's domestic productive power. But it is also a consequence of the way this lack of success rebounded back onto Japan in the form of a rising yen which transformed the country from a low-cost to a high-cost production place. In the 1980s it was hoped that expanding production both at home and abroad could be combined through industrial restructuring. The mass consumer-goods industries were to be relocated and enlarged overseas, leaving a gap for an expansion of the new higher value-added industries at home. However, while the restructuring might have alleviated some of the unemployment resulting from the first movement, it did nothing to help the market absorb the increased production stemming from the second. Although some noises in favour of a 'solution' along these lines can still be heard today, it seems to be recognised that the restructuring of the late 1980s simply raised the value of the surplus goods which the Japanese market could not absorb. What was needed within Japan was not the production of different goods, but of fewer goods. Internationalisation is thus now being driven more equally by both engines: cheaper production sites abroad to *replace* some of the dearer domestic ones *and* strategically-located production sites with easy access to the necessary markets. But these engines are not necessarily pulling in the same direction because the different zone strategies are not fully coherent even within themselves, let alone in relation to one another.

The success of the Asia-zone strategy depends totally on whether Asia can balance its own trade, and so long as the region is made to absorb goods which can no longer be sold in the US or Europe, Asia's deficit with Japan has to be cleared in the very markets to which Japan itself can no longer gain easy access. The North American-zone strategy involves tackling the US market increasingly from within by producing in that country as much as possible of what has to be sold there, but then the market shares won by these 'local producers' will make it harder not easier for Asia to clear its deficits with Japan through running surpluses with the US, especially since the latter has become quite aggressive towards Asian countries which engage in 'unbalanced' trade. The Asian and North American strategies are thus unlikely to function with very much success at the same time. And since Europe is continuing to strengthen its regional trading networks against penetration from the outside, Japanese capital's strategy in that zone depends even more heavily than it does in the US on local production, but Japanese producers in Europe are less well established than they are in any other zone.

The outcome is hardly likely to be a trouble-free ride in any of the three main zones, either for Japanese capital or for the peoples of the various regions. And although the Japanese state can function as a communications centre in Japan and help coordinate national solutions for diverse *keiretsu* interests, it has neither the experience nor the network abroad to put together an international solution that makes the different zone strategies cohere. However, the social and political effects of this incongruity between what is planned for Asia and what can be got away with in the advanced countries will be as unequal as the uneven development and power differences that led to the contradictory strategies in the first place.

Japanese FDI, trade and finance in Asia all tend either to replace their local counterparts or to incorporate them through unequal alliances. They also tend to displace more workers through the 'inefficient' local activities they destroy than the workers they hire, and they can swiftly expand and contract their operations in any one place in response to workers' demands. This is because no one place is much more than a cog in a very large wheel and because poverty is so rife in the region that few workers can press their demands with much resolution anyway. Very little of the same could be said of Japanese businesses in the advanced countries, where they are as often as not petitioners looking for what they themselves do not have and cannot get from the less developed countries: technology, alliances with equals or superiors, access to comparable networks, finance in the real sense of the word and markets of truly mass proportions. To allow more of the social and political costs of the uneven development of Japanese capitalism to fall on people within its own borders does not therefore eliminate the costs of its operations abroad, or the different degrees to which it can displace these costs onto the advanced and the less developed countries.

NEW WORLD ORDER

The new world order is not as predictable a place as were its predecessors, since reliance on networks has the paradoxical effect of both strengthening the power of imperialism and of opening up gaps in its armoury. It strengthens this power because military force is always a two-edged sword, indicating as much a loss of control as a method of securing it, while the new *functional* networks create more incentives to cooperate which combine carrots and sticks. Whatever the mix, the new world order tends to give almost everyone at least something to lose, the size of this something simply increasing with the quality of the interlocking networks that exist in the different advanced countries and with the bargaining power that outsiders bring when they conclude alliances with them. This is why in today's world one finds so many enigmatic truths like, 'the only thing worse than foreign investment from an advanced to a less developed country (or trade or debt) is the absence of such foreign investment (or trade or debt).' The web of power is so great that unless it can be fully thrown off, being part of it seems preferable to being beyond its reach.

The gaps opened up by the reduced use of arms – notwithstanding the difficulty the US has to adjust to the new reality – to maintain the current world order stem from the gradual disappearance of a single command point for the system as a whole. In the period of classical colonialism each imperialist state had its own such command point, while in the post-war period of super-power rivalry, the US assumed that role throughout the entire world. Now, much as the Japanese system itself, for all its strengths and weaknesses, functions domestically 'without anyone in charge' through its *keiretsu* networks (Van Wolferen, 1989), the international system is holding out the same apparently anomalous possibilities. Thus, although it is harder for present-day LDCs to appropriate the resources needed to bridge the wider technological gaps that separate them from the advanced countries, there is no self-conscious centre guarding the multitudinous impersonal networks from the occasional takeover. South Korean nationalism is the most impressive example of how alternative networks can be constructed, and even though large technological gaps remain, its experience reveals possibilities that did not exist to the same degree under classical colonialism or even under super-power rivalry.

But the new world order also seems to be more difficult to confront, by both bourgeois nationalism in the less developed world and by those who still believe that capitalism of any flavour is a repressive social system. Bourgeois nationalism is more hard pressed today than it was before or just after World War Two, because it is now harder to exploit some rivalry among the big powers and bring one or other of them over to the side of any form of independence. Again the case of South Korea and what it could get away with from the US contrasts with the limits placed on bourgeois nationalism in Iraq.

NOT THE LAST WORD

The fate of socialism under the new world order is equally perplexed. The possibility of making transitions in specific countries through the use of state power as was previously attempted by the communist movement is more remote than before, not because the communist state was too powerful for the well being of its citizens – although that was the case – but because it was too weak to deal with the power of imperialism, not least the new imperialism and its more subtle methods of operation through networking. But for the same reason it is now easier to build cross-border political movements and to begin to place checks on the very essence of capitalism's international strength: the ability to displace problems from one part of the world to another. Networks among those who have borne most of the social and political costs of the new imperialism have proliferated in just a few years throughout Asia, including Japan, even though they have hitherto focused on putting an end to particular abuses, such as the three Ps (poverty, prostitution and patriarchy) faced by Asian women or human rights violations and the absence of trade union rights faced by most Asian populations. These cross-national issue-based struggles might have less dramatic effects than Bolshevik revolutions, but their wheels grind more firmly for the very reason that they grind more slowly from the bottom up. Formulating and implementing its new three-zone strategy has been the main task Japanese capital has set itself as it enters the new world order. How to resist such a challenge or at least minimise its impact through formulating a different vision is thus one of the key issues facing the peoples of Asia.

References

JAPANESE SOURCES

Journals

Jietoro sensā [JETRO Sensor]
Kaigai tōshi kenkyūjohō [Review of the Research Institute of Overseas Investment]
Keizai [Economics]
Kokusai shūshi tōkei geppō [Balance of Payments Monthly]
Nihon ginkō geppō [Monthly Bulletin of the Bank of Japan]
Sapio [Sapio]
Sekai [World]
Shūkan tōyō keizai tōkei geppō [Monthly Statistical Report of the Oriental Economist]
Shūkan kinyū zaisei jijō [Kinzai Weekly]

Books and Articles

AJIA TAIHEIYŌ SHIRYŌ SENTĀ (1993) *Nihon keizai kokusho: IMF/Segin/GATT ni yoru sekai shihai no kōzō to Nihon* [Black Paper on the Japanese Economy: Japan and the Structure of World Rule under the IMF, the World Bank and GATT] (Tokyo: Ajia taiheiyō shiryō sentā, 1993).

ANAZAWA, MAKOTO (1992) 'Nikkei takokuseki kigyō to seichyō no toraian-guru' [Japan's Muti-national Corporations and the Growth Triangle], in Kohama (ed) (1992a).

AOKI, TAKESHI (1992) 'Nihon no chokusetsu tōshi to netowāku keisei' [Japan's Foreign Investment and Network Formation] in Kohama (ed) (1992a).

AOKI, TAKESHI (1993) *Yushutsu shikō kōgyōka senryaku: Marēshia ni miru sono hikari to kage* [The Strategy of Export-led Industrialisation: Looking at the Bright and Dark Sides of Malaysia] (Tokyo: Nihon bōeki shinkōkai, 1993).

AOKI, TAKESHI (1994) 'ASEAN ikinai bungyō kōzō no genjō to mondaiten' [The Present Structure of the Internal Division of Labour within the ASEAN Region and its Problems], in Itoga (ed) (1994).

CHŪSHŌ KIGYŌCHŌ [Small and Medium Enterprise Agency] (1993/94) *Heisei 5/6 nenkan chūshō kigyōchō hakusho* [1993/94 White Paper on Small and Medium Enterprises] (Tokyo: Ōkurashō insatsukyoku, 1993/94).

GAIMUSHŌ KEIZAI KYŌRYOKUKYOKU [Economic Cooperation Bureau of the Ministry of Finance] (1993a) *Wagakuni no seifu kaihatsu enjo* [Japan's Official Development Assistance], jōkan [Volume 1] (Tokyo: Kokusai shinshutsu kyōkai, 1993).

GAIMUSHŌ KEIZAI KYŌRYOKUKYOKU (1993b) *Wagakuni no seifu kaihatsu enjo*, gekan: kunibetsu enjo [Volume 2: Aid by Country] (Tokyo: Kokusai shin-shutsu kyōkai, 1993).

271

GURŪPU KIKI [Group Kiki] (1993) *Dōshite yūcho ga ikenai no* [Why are Postal Savings not Allowed] (Tokyo: Kiki shuppan, 1993).

HANAMI, TADASHI.(ed) (1993) *Anata no tonaribito: gaikokujin rōdōsha* [Your Neighbours: Foreign Workers] (Tokyo: Tōyō keizai shinposha, 1993).

HŌMUSHŌ NYŪKOKU KANRIKYOKU [Immigration Bureau of the Ministry of Justice] 'Heisei 4 nen ni okeru nyūkanhō ihan jiken ni tsuite' [Concerning Incidents of Violation against the Immigration Laws in 1992], May 1993.

HŌMUSHŌ NYŪKOKU KANRIKYOKU (1994) 'Heisei 5 nen ni okeru gaikokujin oyobi Nihonjin no shutsunyūkoku tōkei ni tsuite, [Concerning Statistics on the Entry and Departure of Foreigners and Japanese into Japan], April 1994.

HORAGUCHI, HARUO (1992) *Nihon kigyō no kaigai chokusetsu tōshi: Ajia en no shihshutsu to tettai* [Japanese Companies' Foreign Direct Investment: Entry into and Withdrawal from Asia] (Tokyo: Tokyo daigaku shuppankai, 1992)

ISHII, MASASHI (1992) *Nihon kigyō no kaigai jigyō tenkai* [Development of Overseas Business by Japanese Companies] (Tokyo: Chūō keizaisha, 1992).

ITŌ RYŌICHI (1994) 'Fuiripin – teimei dasshutsu wa kanō ka' [Can the Philippines Escape from the Gloom that Hangs over it?], in Watanabe (ed) (1994).

ITOGA, SHIGERU (ed) (1994) *Ugokidasu ASEAN keizaiken: 2008nen e no tenbō* [ASEAN Economic Zone on the Move: Prospects for the Year 2008] (Tokyo Ajia keizai shuppankai, 1994).

IYOTANI, TOSHIO (1994) 'Nihon no gaikokujin rōdōsha seisaku no tenkan ni mukete' [Towards Changing Japan's Policy on Foreign Workers], *Sekai,* No. 596, June, 1994.

KAGAKU GIJUTSUCHŌ [Science and Technology Agency] (1994) *Heisei 5 nenkan kagaku gijutsu hakusho* [1993 White Paper on Science and Technology] (Tokyo: Ōkurashō insatsukyoku, 1994).

KAJITA, TAKAMICHI (1994) *Gaikokujin rōdōsha to Nihon* [Japan and Foreign Workers] (Tokyo: Nihon yūsō shuppan kyōkai, 1994).

KEIZAI (1991a) Sōtokushū [General Special Issue], 'Nihon kigyō kaigai tenkan no jittai' [The Turn Abroad by Japanese Companies], No. 331 (November, 1991).

KEIZAI (1991b) Tokushū [Special Issue], 'Dō naru Tōajia keizaien' [What Will Happen to the East Asian Economic Region], No. 332 (December 1991).

KEIZAI KIKAKUCHŌ [Economic Planning Agency] (1993a) *Heisei 5 nenkan sekai keizai hakusho* [1993 White Paper on the World Economy] (Tokyo: Ōkurashō insatsukyoku, 1993).

KEIZAI KIKAKUCHŌ (1993b) *Heisei 5 nenkan keizai hakusho* [1993 White Paper on the Economy] (Tokyo: Ōkurashō insatsukyoku, 1993).

KEIZAI KIKAKUCHŌ CHŌSAKYOKU [Research Bureau of the Economic Planning Agency] (1993) *Heisei 6 nenkan Nihon keizai no genkyō* [The Condition of the Japanese Economy, 1994] (Tokyo: Ōkurashō insatsukyoku, 1993).

KEIZAI KIKAKUCHŌ SŌGŌ KEIKAKUKYOKU [General Planning Bureau of the Economic Planning Agency] (1993) *Kinyū jiyūka to kinyū shisutemu no anteisei* [Financial Liberalisation and the Stability of the Financial System] (Tokyo: Ōkurashō insatsukyoku, 1993).

KOHAMA, HIROHISA (ed) (1992a) *Chokusetsu tōshi to kōgyōka: Nihon, NIES, ASEAN* [Direct Investment and Industrialisation: Japan, NIES and ASEAN] (Tokyo: Nihon bōeki shinkōkai, 1992).

KOHAMA, HIROHISA (1992b) 'ASEAN shokoku e no chokusetsu tōshi to kōgyōka: yōyaku to ketsuron' [Industrialisation and Direct Investment in ASEAN Countries: Summary and Conclusions], in Kohama (ed) (1992a).

KOJIMA IKUO (1992) *Gaishikei kigyō no keiretsu to seiryoku chizu* [Maps of the Networks and Power of Foreign Companies] (Tokyo: Nihon jitsugyō shuppansha, 1992).

KOKUSAI KYŌRYOKU JIGYŌDAN [Japan International Cooperation Agency] (1993) *Kokusai kyōryoku jigyōdan nenpō: 1993* [Annual Report of the Japan International Cooperation Agency, 1993] (Tokyo: Kokusai kyōryoku jigyōdan, 1993).

KOMAI, HIROSHI (1994) 'Zainichi Iranjin e no chōsa kekka o fumaete' [An Argument Based on the Results of the Study on Iranians in Japan], *Sekai*, No. 596, June 1994.

KUWAHARA, YASUO (1993) 'Gaikokujin rōdōsha mondai no seiji keizaigaku' [The Political Economy of the Problem of Foreign Workers], in Hanami (ed) (1993).

MIYAZAKI, ISAMU (1994) Dokuhon shirīzu [Reader Series] *Sekai keizai dokuhon* [Reader on the World Economy] (Tokyo: Tōyō keizai shinposha, 1994).

MIZUHASHI, YŪSUKEA (1994) 'Taiwan – "Taiwan keiken" to wa nani ka' [Taiwan: What is the 'Taiwan Experience'] in Watanabe (ed) (1994).

NAGATA, MASAHIRO (1992) 'Chokusetsu tōshi kara mita Ajia taiheiyō no keizai, bōeki no hatten' [Economic Development and Trade in Asia and the Pacific from the Point of View of Direct Investment], in Kohama (ed) (1992a).

NIHON BŌEKI SHINKŌKAI [JETRO] (1993a/94a) *1993/94 Jietoro hakusho, tōshihen: Sekai to Nihon no kaigai chokusetsu tōshi* [1993/94 JETRO White Paper, Investment: The World and Japan's Foreign Direct Investment] (Tokyo: Nihon bōeki shinkōkai, 1993/94).

NIHON BŌEKI SHINKŌKAI(1993b) *1994 Jietoro hakusho, bōekihen: Sekai to Nihon no bōeki* [1994 JETRO White Paper, Trade: The World and Japan's Trade] (Tokyo: Nihon bōeki shinkōkai, 1993).

NIHON KEIZAI SHINBUNSHA (ed) (1994) Nikkei bunko 662 [Nikkei Bunko No. 662] *Vijiuaru Nihon sangyō* [A Visual Picture of Japanese Industry] (Tokyo: Nihon keizai shinbunsha, 1994).

NYŪKAN KYŌKAI [Japan Immigration Association] (1992) *Shutsunyūkoku kanri kihon keikaku* [Basic Plan for Immigration Control] (Tokyo: Nyūkan kyōkai, 1992).

NYŪKAN KYŌKAI (1993) *Zairyū gaikokujin tōkei* [Statistics on Foreign Residents] (Tokyo: Nyūkan kyōkai, 1993).

ŌKURASHŌ [Ministry of Finance] (1991a/93a) *Zaisei kinyū tōkei geppō: tainaigai minkan tōshi tokushū* [Monthly Bulletin of Monetary and Financial Statistics: Special Issue on Inward and Outward Private Overseas Investment], No. 476/500, December 1991/93 (Tokyo: Ōkurashō insatsukyoku, 1991/93).

ŌKURASHŌ (1993b) *Zaisei kinyū tōkei geppō: kokusai shūshi tokushū* [Monthly Bulletin of Monetary and Financial Statistics: Special Issue on Balance of Payments], No. 496, August 1993 (Tokyo: Ōkurashō insatsukyoku, 1993).

ŌKURASHŌ (1994a) 'Heisei 5 nendo ni okeru taigai oyobi tainai chokusetsu tōshi jōkyō' [1993 Internal and External Foreign Direct Investments], 3 June 1994.

ŌKURASHŌ (1994b) *Yūka shōken hōkokusho* [Reports on Share Values].

274   *References*

OSABE, SHIGEYASU, TANAKA, TOMOYOSHI, KOKUBO, YASUYUKI, ONADA, AKIHIRO and SASAI, YASUHIKO (eds) (1994) *Kakudai yōroppa no shōten* [A Focus on an Expanded Europe] (Tokyo: Nihon bōeki shinkōkai, 1994).

ŌSONO, TOMOKAZU (1992) *Hitome de wakaru kigyō keiretsu to gyōkai chizu* [Industrial Maps for Understanding Corporate Groups at a Glance] (Tokyo: Nihon jitsugyō shuppansha, 1992).

RŌDŌ DAIJIN KANBŌ KOKUSAI RŌDŌKA [International Labour Section of the Secretariat of the Ministry of Labour] (1994) *Heisei 6 nenkan kaigai rōdō hakusho: NIES, ASEAN shokoku no keizai hatten to chingin henka* [1994 White Paper on Foreign Labour: Economic Development and Wage Changes in all the NIES and ASEAN Countries] (Tokyo: Nihon rōdō kenkyū to kikō, 1994).

SAPIO (1994), 'Ajia kara mita Nippon no shōtai' [Japan's Character as Seen from Asia], 23 June 1994.

SEKIGUCHI, JUNKO (1992) 'Nihon, Ajia NIES no tai Marēshia tōshi to kōgyōka [Industrialisation and Japanese and Asian NIES Investment in Malaysia,' in Kohama (ed) (1992a).

SHŪKAN TŌYŌ KEIZAI (1993a/94a) Rinji zōkan/data bank [Special Issue/Data Bank] *Kaigai shinshutsu kigyō sōran, kaishabetsu hen* [Japanese Multinationals: Facts and Figures, by Company] (Tokyo: Tōyō keizai shinposha, 1993/94).

SHŪKAN TŌYŌ KEIZAI (1993b/94b), Rinji zōkan/data bank [Special Issue/Data Bank] *Kaigai shinshutsu kigyō sōran, kunibetsu hen* [Japanese Multinationals: Facts and Figures, by Country] (Tokyo: Tōyō keizai shinposha, 1993/94).

SUZUTA, ATSUYUKI (1993) Shinsho: gyōkai no jōshiki [Latest: Common Sense on the World of Industry] *Yoku wakaru ginkō gyōkai* [An Easy Understanding of the Banking World] (Tokyo: Nihon jitsugyō shuppansha, 1993).

TAKEUCHI, HIROSHI, MACHIDA, YŌJI and KISCHI, AKIRA (1987) *Endaka Jukyō: gekihen sehu Nihon Keizai shinchizu* [The High Yen Recession: The Rapidly Changing New Economic Math of Japan] (Tokyo: Yūhikake Livret).

TANAKA, HIROSHI (1992) 'Kaigai chokusetsu tōshi to bōeki' [Foreign Direct Investment and Trade], *Kaigai tōshi kenkyujohō*, Vol. 18, No. 9 (September, 1992).

TANAKA, TAKUO (ed) (1994) *Ajia taiheiyō no chiiki kyōryoku* [Regional Cooperation in Asia and the Pacific] (Tokyo: Chūō keizaisha, 1994)

TANIURA, TAKAO (1990) Ajia kōgyōka shirīzu, 10 [Asia Industrialisation Series, No. 10] *Ajia kōgyōka to gijutsu iten* [Asian Industrialisation and Technology Transfer] (Tokyo: Ajia keizai kenkyūjo, 1990).

TEJIMA, SHIGEKI ET AL (1994) '1993 nendo kaigai chokusetsu tōshi ankēto chōsa kekka hōkoku, [Report on the 1993 Survey of Foreign Direct Investment], *Kaigai tōshi kenkyujohō*, Vol. 20, No. 1 (January, 1994).

TORITANI, KAZUO (1994) 'En no kokusaika no genjō to genkai' [The Status and Limits of the Yen's Internationalisation], in Uchida (ed) (1994a).

TSUCHIYA, HARUHITO (1994) *Maruchi medeia nyūmon* [An Introduction to Multi-Media] (Tokyo: Nihon jitsugyō shuppansha, 1994).

TSUNEKAWA, JUN (1994) 'Tai – Ajia no raisubōru kara kōgyōkoku e' [Thailand: From Asia's Rice-Bowl to Industrialised Country], in Watanabe (ed) (1994).

TSŪSHŌ SANGYŌSHŌ [Ministry of International Trade and Industry] (1993a/94a) *Heisei 5/6 nenkan tsūshō hakusho* [1993/94 White Paper on Trade and Industry] (Tokyo: Ōkurashō insatsukyoku, 1993).

TSŪSHŌ SANGYŌSHŌ (1993b/94b) *Heisei 5/6 nenkan tsūshō hakusho: kakuron* [Details of the 1993/94 White Paper on Trade and Industry] (Tokyo: Ōkurashō insatsukyoku, 1993/94).

TSŪSHŌ SANGYŌSHŌ (1993c) *Heisei 5 nenkan keizai kyōryoku no genjō to mondaiten* [Economic Cooperation and its Problems, 1993] (Tokyo: Tsūshō sangyō chōsakai, 1993).

TSŪSHŌ SANGYŌSHŌ (1993d) *ASEAN sangyō kōdoka vijiyon* [Prospects and Challenges for the Upgrading of Industries in the ASEAN Region] (Tokyo: Tsūshō sangyō chōsakai, 1993).

TSŪSHŌ SANGYŌSHŌ SANGYŌ SEISAKUKYOKU KOKUSAI KIGYŌKA [International Company Division of of the Policy Bureau of the Ministry of International Trade and Industry] (1990a/93a) *Dai 18–19/22 kai wagakuni kigyō no kaigai jigyō katsudō* [Overseas Business Activities of Our Country's Firms, Nos 18–19, 22] (Tokyo: Ōkurashō insatsukyoku, 1990/1993).

TSŪSHŌ SANGYŌSHŌ SANGYŌ SEISAKUKYOKU KOKUSAI KIGYŌKA (1993b) *Dai 26 kai Gaishikei kigyō no dōkō* [Trends among Foreign Firms, No. 26] (Tokyo: Ōkurashō insatsukyoku, 1993).

UCHIDA, KATSUTOSHI (ed) (1994a) *Kokusaika no naka no Nihon keizai* [Japan's Economy in the Midst of Internationalisation] (Kyoto: Minerva shobō, 1994).

UCHIDA, KATSUTOSHI (1994b) 'Nihon keizai no hatten to kokusaika' [The Development and Internationalisation of the Japanese Economy], in Uchida (ed) (1994a).

UMETANI, SHUNICHIRŌ (1993) 'Fuhō shūrō gaikokujin no jittai' [The Situation of Illegal Foreign Workers], in Hanami (ed) (1993).

URATA, SHŪJIRŌ (1992) 'Nihon no chokusetsu tōshi to Ajia no bōeki' [Japan's Foreign Investment and Asia's trade], in Kohama (ed) (1992a).

UZAWA, TOSHITAKA (1994) *Shinsho: gyōkai no jōshiki* [New: Common Sense on the World of Industry] *Yoku wakaru jidōsha gyōkai* [An Easy Understanding of the Auto World] (Tokyo: Nihon jitsugyō shuppansha, 1994).

WATANABE, MACHIKO (1992) 'Nihon Ajia NIES no tai Indoneshia tōshi to kōgyōka' [Industrialisation and Japanese and Asian NIES Investment in Indonesia], in Kohama (ed) (1992a).

WATANABE, TOSHIO (ed) (1994) *Dokuhon shirīzu* [Reader Series] *Ajia keizai dokuhon* [Reader on the Asian Economies] (Tokyo: Tōyō keizai shinposha, 1994).

YAMAMOTO, KAZUTO (1994) 'Kokusai bungyō taisei no hatten to hembō' [The Development and Transfiguration of the Structure of the International Division of Labour], in Uchida (ed) (1994a).

YAMAZAKI, KYŌHEI, KOBAYASHI, NOBUO, SHIMAZU, SADAO and ISHIKAWA, KŌICHI (eds) (1993) *ASEAN kōgyōka to shinjigen* [New Dimensions of ASEAN Industrialisation] (Tokyo: Nihon bōeki shinkōkai, 1993).

YASUHARA, NORIKAZU, TAKADA, SHIGEKI, NISHIMURA, KIMIE, and OGAWA, YOKO, 'Kinen no wagakuni no seihin yunyū dōkō' [Recent Tendencies of Japan's Manufacturing Imports], *Kaigai tōshi kenkyūjohō*, Vol. 20, No. 4 (April, 1994).

YOSHINO, FUMIO (1992) 'Fuiripin no keizai hatten to gaishi seisaku' [Economic Development of the Philippines and the Policy of Foreign Capital], in Kohama (ed) (1992a).

ENGLISH SOURCES

ABEGGLEN, JAMES C. (1994) *Sea Change: Pacific Asia as the New World Industrial Centre* (New York: The Free Press, 1994).

AMPO (1990) Special Issue, 'Japanese Official Destruction and Alienation,' Vol. 21, No. 4 (1990).

AMPO (1993) Special Issue, 'Black Paper on the Economic Superpower,' Vol. 24, No. 4 (1993).

ASEAN CENTRE (1993) *ASEAN-Japan Statistical Pocketbook* (Tokyo: ASEAN Centre, 1993).

BURTON, FRED and SAELENS, FREDDY (1994) 'International Alliances as a Strategic Tool of Japanese Electronic Companies,' in *Japanese Multinationals: Strategies and Management in the Global Kaisha*, ed. by Nigel Campbell and Fred Burton (London and New York: Routledge, 1994).

CLARKE, SIMON (1990) 'The Marxist Theory of Overaccumulation and Crisis,' *Science and Society*, Vol. 54, No. 4 (Winter 1990–1991).

CLARKE, SIMON (ed) (1991) *The State Delute* (New York: st. Martin's Piess).

DE VOS, GEORGE A. and WACATSUMA, HIROSHI(ed) (1966) *Japan's Invisible Race: Centre in Creative and Personality* (Berheley: University of California Press).

DÜSER, THORSTEN J. (1990) *International Strategies of Japanese Banks: The European Perspective* (New York: St Martin's Press, 1990).

EMMANUEL, ARGHIRI (1972) *Unequal Exchange: A Study of the Imperialism of Trade* (London: New Left Books, 1972).

ENSIGN, MARGEE (1992) *Doing Good or Doing Well: Japan's Foreign Aid Program* (New York: Columbia University Press, 1992).

GIBSON, KATHERINE AND GRAHAM, JULIE (1986) 'Situating Migrants in Theory: The Case of Filipino Migrant Contract Construction Workers,' *Capital and Class,* 29 (Summer 1986).

HALL, MIKE (1992) 'On the Creation of Money and the Accumulation of Bank-Capital,' *Capital and Class*, 48 (Autumn 1992).

HANAZAKI, MASAHARU (1990) 'Deepening Economic Linkages in the Pacific Basin Region: Trade, Foreign Direct Investment, and Technology,' Japan Development Bank Research Report, No. 20, September 1990.

HARVEY, DAVID (1982) *The Limits to Capital* (Oxford: Basil Blackwell, 1982).

HATADE, AKIRA (1992) 'Trainees in Japan,' *Ampo,* Vol. 23, No. 4 (1992).

INDUSTRIAL STRUCTURE COUNCIL JAPAN (1994) *1994 Report on Unfair Trade Policies by Major Trading Partners: Trade Policies and WTO* (Tokyo: Research Institute of International Trade and Industry Publications Department, 1994).

HACHISUKA, KAZUYO (1992) 'Projections of Japan's Trade Surplus in 1995: Analysis of Japan's Trade Structure in the '80s,' Japan Development Bank Research Report, No. 26, February, 1992.

ICHIE, MASAHIKO (1993) 'Economic Zones and East Asia: Prospects for Economic Activity Orientated Market Integration,' Japan Development Bank Research Report, No. 37, December, 1993.

JESSOP, BOB (1990) *State Theory: Putting the Capitalist State in its Place* (Oxford: Basil Blackwell, 1990).

JOURNAL OF JAPANESE TRADE AND INDUSTRY (1994), 'The Japanese Economy, 1994,' No. 3 (June) 1994.

KATŌ, TETSURŌ (1994) 'The Political Economy of Japanese Karoshi (Death from Overwork),' Paper presented to the International Political Science Association, Berlin, August, 1994.

KATŌ, TETSURŌ and STEVEN, ROB (eds) (1993) *Is Japanese Capitalism Post-Fordism?* (Tokyo: Mado-sha, 1993).

LEAVER, RICHARD and RICHARDSON, JAMES (eds) (1993) *The Post-Cold War Order: Diagnoses and Prognoses* (Sydney: Allen and Unwin, 1993).

LENIN, V.I. (1975) *Imperialism: The Highest Stage of Capitalism* (Peking: Foreign Languages Press, 1975).

LINCOLN, EDWARD J. (1993) *Japan's New Global Role* (Washington, D.C.: The Brookings Institution, 1993).

MILES, ROBERT (1982) *Racism and Migrant Labour* (London: Routledge & Kegan Paul, 1982).

MORRIS-SUZUKI, TESSA (1992) 'Japanese Technology and the New International Division of Knowledge in Asia', in Tokunaga (ed) (1992a).

O'CONNOR, JAMES (1973) *The Fiscal Crisis of the State* (New York: St. Martin's Press, 1973).

ONO, SHUICHI (1992) 'Sino-Japanese Economic Relationships: Trade, Direct Investment and Future Strategy,' *World Bank Discussion Papers*, No. 146, 1992.

ORR, ROBERT M. JR. (1991) 'Japanese Foreign Aid in a New Global Era,' *SAIS Review: A Journal of International Affairs*, Vol. 11 (Summer–Fall 1991).

ROTHACHER, ALBRECHT (1993) *The Japanese Power Elite* (London: Macmillan, 1993).

SHAIKH, ANWAR (1979) 'Foreign Trade and the Law of Value,' Parts 1 and 2, *Science and Society*, Fall 1979 and Spring 1980.

STEVEN, ROB (1983) *Classes in Contemporary Japan* (London: Cambridge University Press).

STEVEN, ROB (1990) *Japan's New Imperialism* (London: Macmillan, 1990).

STEVEN, ROB (1994) 'The New World Order: A New Imperialism,' *Journal of Contemporary Asia*, Vol. 24, No. 3 (July 1994).

TANAKA, HIROSHI (1993) 'Investment by Japanese Consumer Electrical Appliance Industries in ASEAN and the Import of Such Products into Japan,' *Exim Review*, Vol. 13, No. 1 (1993).

TEECE, DAVID J. (1992) 'Foreign Investment and Technological Development in Silicon Valley,' *California Management Review*, Winter 1992.

TEJIMA, SHIGEKI (1993) 'Future Prospects of Japanese Foreign Direct Investment (FDI) in the 1990s, Based on the Trend and the Features of Japanese FDI in the 1980s,' *Exim Review*, Vol. 13, No. 1 (1993).

TOKUNAGA, SHOJIRO (ed) (1992a) *Japan's Foreign Investment and Asian Economic Interdependence: Production, Trade, and Financial Systems* (Tokyo: University of Tokyo Press, 1992).

TOKUNAGA, SHOJIRO (1992b) 'Moneyless Direct Investment and Development of Asian Financial Markets: Financial Linkages Between Local Markets and Offshore Centres,' in Tokunaga (ed) (1992a).

VAN WOLFEREN, KAREL (1989) *The Enigma of Japanese Power* (London: Macmillan, 1989).

WADA, HAJIME (1994) 'Recent Trends in Japan's Foreign Accounts,' Japan
    Development Bank Research Report, No. 39, April, 1994.
WILLIAMS, DAVID (1994) *Japan: Beyond the End of History* (London and New
    York: Routledge, 1994).
WILLIAMSON, HUGH (1994)   *Coping with the Miracle: Japan's Unions
    Explore New International Relations* (London: Pluto Press, 1994).
YOSHIHARA, KUNIO (1988) *The Rise of Ersatz Capitalism in South-East Asia*
    (Singapore: Oxford University Press, 1988).

Index